Chinese Business Etiquette and Culture

Kevin Bucknall

Boson Books
Raleigh, NC

Published by **Boson Books**
www.bosonbooks.com
Raleigh, NC

ISBN 0-917990-43-9

An imprint of **C & M Online Media, Inc.**
Cover Painting by **Joel Barr**: www.joelbarr.com

Design by Once Removed

C & M Online Media, Inc.
www.cmonline.com

Preface

This book is intended to make you and your organization, whether it is a business company or a government department, do a better job when dealing with Chinese institutions and people. Most of us learn about basic good manners and standard acceptable behavior when very young and are taught by our parents, especially our mother. Other good manners are picked up by observation and, for a few, by reading magazine articles or books on approved etiquette. The problem is that the good manners and business etiquette we learn rarely apply in other countries.

When you commit a social gaffe abroad, virtually everyone is too embarrassed to tell you about it, so you cannot improve your behavior. Left to yourself, if observant you may detect a few polite ways of behaving - but there is no way that you can notice the things that people *avoid* doing. Consequently, it is easy to visit a foreign country, or even spend many years living there, and unknowingly give offense. Your normal polite behavior can lose you a sale, or prevent the signing of an agreement, and you may never understand why. There are many possible ways of offending someone or making them feel uneasy: even the color of the clothing you wear or how you stand and sit can adversely affect your prospects.

You might question why it is necessary to bother to learn about another nation's customs and manners, and feel that your normal business manners are sufficient. This sounds reasonable, but the proposition can cost you time and money. If you agree with any of the following statements, then you might be undermining your abilities and endangering your success rate. It would be a good idea to rethink your position.

> "It is unnecessary to bother to learn about another nation's habits, customs and manners; they should behave as I do".

> "What worked successfully for me in the past in my country will also work well abroad".

> "My good manners at home will take me anywhere".

> "Why should I alter a winning formula and change my ways?"

Bear in mind that you do not reject your own culture by learning about someone else's. Nor is it obsequious to learn about someone else's values and avoid violating them. True, it would be easier for you if foreigners learned your values and followed them. But it's not going to happen!

Globalization helps to raise living standards, but it involves more con-

tact between those of different cultures; rather than leading to more tolerance, this increases the opportunity for people to annoy each other. Some
individuals may already have a vague grievance against people of your
nationality for historical reasons. Their country might once have been at
war with yours or been invaded by it; or at the individual level, possibly
they or a friend of theirs was once insulted by one of your compatriots.
Others may hold a grudge simply because your country is richer than
theirs. Such attitudes make it easy for them to take offense at totally innocent actions or statements by you. Clearly, the more you behave in ways
that they deem appropriate, the less you annoy people, the better you fit
in, and the quicker you can do well.

By following the advice below you should be able to make friends
more easily, negotiate better, sell more goods or services, sign more
agreements, achieve higher profits, and generally achieve whatever you
want more quickly. At the very least, you will give yourself an edge over
your competitors. You need not memorize all the points of advice at once,
nor need you follow all of them scrupulously. You can learn some, then
add to them over time as you gain experience. Nonetheless, the more you
can use, the better you will be able to function.

How you can improve your behavior to achieve greater success is explained in the context of Chinese culture. The information is practical and
provided in a direct way under a variety of heading. Chapter One ex-
plains some of the basics of Chinese culture, and Chapter Two considers
how you might modify your behavior to do better in China. Chapter
Three deals with ways of initiating contact while Chapter Four introduces
the generalities of meetings. This is followed in Chapter Five by a discussion of common Chinese negotiating tactics. Chapter Six turns to your
behavior in meetings and looks at some responses you can make to their
tactics. The important issue of socializing in China is covered in Chapter
Seven and the rather neglected area of how to receive Chinese visitors to
your city and company is dealt with in Chapter Eight. The last two chap-
ters discuss practical problems of living and working in China. An appendix describes the history of China and recent changes in the political,
economic, and social scene. Although not providing advice, this background knowledge can prove valuable during your discussions.

I would like to make two cautionary points. First, you should beware
of treating all Chinese as stereotypes who will always behave as described below. People are individuals and should be seen as such, even
though they operate within the general confines of their culture. You
will find that not everyone you meet conforms to the prevailing culture,
just as not all people do in your hometown. Some people do not

know how to behave and others simply do not care. This can be particularly true of relatively young, self-made, wealthy entrepreneurs, and there are a lot of these in China. However, one tends to find relatively few successful people who regularly behave in ways considered to be grossly offensive in their own country. If you see behavior in China that appears to conflict with the cultural norms described here, you can flatter yourself that you are able to recognize this.

Second, being adept at cross-cultural communication is valuable but it is not a solution to all your problems. It is a supplement to other skills, not a replacement. You still need to be a skilful manager, used to negotiating and relating to people, seeing opportunities, making good decisions, putting together deals, and devising profitable alternatives.

While I believe that the information provided here is the best currently available, you should be aware that societies alter, although culture does this more slowly than some facets of a nation, such as which are the best restaurants in town. Social change may mean that a point of advice becomes less useful, especially when dealing with the younger generation. In recent years, China has undergone rapid economic growth which puts pressure on traditional values and practices and may also influence the government to alter its policies. I would be delighted to hear from you if you find any advice that may be slipping out of date, or your experience reveals new points that can be added. You can email me with suggestions at: subs@primrose.gioserve.com

Disclaimer: the information and advice in this book are believed to be accurate and reliable. However, the publisher and author cannot accept responsibility for any losses, problems, or undesirable results that may occur from following any or all of the suggestions or advice. In return, the publisher and author promise that they will not try to claim any share of the profits that you make!

Note: all dollars are in US currency.

Contents

Preface   5

Chapter One: Chinese behavior patterns   12

Chapter Two: Your behavior in China   41

Chapter Three: Starting the business process   62

Chapter Four: Meetings and negotiations: generalities   79

Chapter Five: Meetings and negotiations: their tactics   99

Chapter Six: Meetings and negotiations: your tactics   124

Chapter Seven: Socializing and proper behavior   153

Chapter Eight: How to treat visitors to one's own country   168

Chapter Nine: Living in China   174

Chapter Ten: Working in China   191

Appendix: China's history, politics, economics and society   223

Index: 249

Endnotes: 258

List of Tables

1.1 Some traditional beliefs about animal symbolism   20

3.1 Possible reasons why you cannot meet someone   76

6.1 Phrases and words that can indicate "no"   130

9.1 Apartment rents in various international cities   187

10.1 A survey into problems in Shanghai in 1997   213

10.2 Problems faced by twenty-one US firms, 1994   213

ABBREVIATIONS

CAAC	Civil Aviation Administration of China; originally the state airline, now the department in charge of civil aviation in China.
CCP	The Chinese Communist Party.
CCPIT	The Chinese Council for the Promotion of International Trade, a nongovernment organization that promotes foreign relations and trade.
CEO	Chief Executive Officer.
Chaebols	Large groupings of companies in Korea, similar to the Japanese *keiretsu* or the old *zaibatsu*.
COFTEC	The Commission of Foreign Trade and Economic Cooperation, which is the regional branch of MOFTEC.
FEC	Foreign Exchange Certificates.
FESCO	Foreign Enterprise Service Company.
Ganbei	"Bottoms up!", the signal to empty one's glass when drinking.
GATT	General Agreement on Tariffs and Trade, now replaced by the World Trade Organization (WTO).
Guanxi	The use of contacts and favors to achieve what one wants.
Hukou	The Chinese household registration system, introduced in 1958 to prevent migration to the cities; people had to stay where they were registered and could not move without permission.
Maotai	An extremely strong, not very pleasant tasting alcoholic drink, sold in white ceramic bottles and often used for toasting at dinners.
MOFTEC	The Ministry of Foreign Trade and Economic Cooperation.
NPC	National People's Congress.
OECD	The Organisation for Economic Cooperation and Development.
PLA	The People's Liberation Army.
ROI	Return on investment.
SEZ	Special Economic Zone.

SETC	The State Economic and Trade Commission.
Shaoxing	A sherry-like rice wine, usually served warm and less strong than Maotai.
SOE	State operated enterprise.
Suiyi	"Let's please ourselves"; used when drinking toasts.
WTO	The World Trade Organisation, the successor to GATT.
Yin yang	An old Chinese idea that there are two opposite elements to everything, such as male-female, or light-dark; additionally, a small element of one always occurs in the other. Y*in* is female, y*ang* is male,

Chapter One: CHINESE BEHAVIOR PATTERNS

The influence of tradition and Confucius

Confucius reigns

The ideas and values regarded as Confucian are still of paramount importance when trying to understand Chinese behavior. Confucius (sixth to fifth century BC) wanted a political system where the emphasis was on properly ordered social relationships in society. Society was seen as pyramid shaped, with a paramount ruler at the top (the Emperor), a variety of officials administering the country in the middle, and families at the bottom. If everyone behaved properly one to another, then government would be stable, society would be well run, general harmony would prevail, and the nation would be prosperous and at peace.

In this Confucian system, the family played a central role. The male head of the family was responsible for the behavior of the entire family and he, or in extreme cases the entire family, could be punished if a member of it committed a crime. Within the family, each person had a clearly defined relationship to the others and a person's identity was in part established by his or her role within the group. Members were addressed as "Elder Daughter", or "Younger Brother" rather than by name, reinforcing the relationships. Anyone totally alone and without a family was generally pitied, and the state regarded them with some suspicion, as did people in general.

Superiors really are superior - Confucius

This principle applied both outside the family and within it. Lower classes respected those above them. Listing from the top down, the classes were scholars, officials, farmers, artisans, and merchants. Scholars and officials made up the respected "gentry". Despite these values, there was, and still is, a tendency for urban Chinese to despise rural dwellers as yokels. At the very bottom of traditional society were the outcast groups, such as actors (!), prostitutes, boat people and slaves.

In the workplace, one's superiors merited automatic respect by virtue of rank. In China, people still automatically defer to those above them in the work place, as well as in society in general.

Respect your family elders - Confucius

Within the family, the rule was "filial piety", the household equivalent of having to respect those who are superior in society. The family head had to be obeyed by all; younger brothers had to respect and obey elder brothers; and younger sisters elder ones. Females generally deferred to males, although the chief wife of the head of the family had much power and in the worst cases could be a mean domestic tyrant. The widespread Chinese respect for age and seniority comes from Confucian values; an older person is often seen as more experienced, wiser, and in some not clearly defined way, superior to those younger.

The family comes first, but the group matters

It often helps if you think of a Chinese person as being part of his or her family and group, rather than as a single individual. The family has long been the basic building block of the state and the natural center of an individual's attention. Major personal decisions, such as a suitable career for an adolescent which in the West would often be made by the individual, are often done by the family. The group tradition was reinforced by their experience of communism, where people were forced to participate in communal discussions and any individual who stood out might later be punished. The group is seen as a source of strength and comfort, and business decisions may be made on a consensus basis. If so, it is discussed within the framework dictated by the top person, be it a highly placed politician or public servant, the owner of the firm, or the chief executive officer (CEO).

This submergence in family and work group means that many adult Chinese are reluctant to take decisions on their own. A seemingly one-person problem in a factory may eventually be solved only after extended discussion by the group; otherwise it might not be resolved at all. If you find that a Chinese person's attitude to a topic seems vague, it is often the result of the person knowing that the final decision must be made by a group or by some process higher up and it is logical not to commit oneself. The views of this particular individual must be in line with that eventual determination.

The work unit commands a strong loyalty for two main reasons. First, it was intrinsic to the job-for-life approach adopted by the communist government, as well as being the means of delivering limited social welfare, such as rudimentary health care or unemployment pay. This facet of the work unit is being rapidly eroded. Second, the loyalty is part of the Confucian deferential attitude towards authority which is embodied within the unit.

The importance of belonging to and identifying with a group has a strong impact on the tolerance of humor and criticism. The Chinese do not find jokes about their country's political leaders or policy in any way funny; indeed such irreverence shocks them. You should make a point of not making jokes about these things, or even about your own government or its policies. In Chinese eyes, such disrespect demeans you.

Until very recently, the group attitude dominated job allocation. Personal preferences counted for little and the needs of the country (i.e., the largest group of all) overrode individual wishes, so that people were simply told what they would study at college, what job they would do, and where in China they would be sent. This gradually changed in recent years, and many can now choose where to seek employment.

"Keep us in our proper stations"

In both Confucian China and Nineteenth century England, people were educated and trained to know their place and to be content with it, so that deviations, criticisms and rebellious behavior were not tolerated. One practical consequence is that in China you might find it hard to get someone to give you his or her personal opinion. The views of higher authority will automatically be followed and presented as not only correct but also the actual views of the speakers themselves.

Rank is beautiful

Chinese society is strongly hierarchical and a person's rank counts for much. Every individual is slotted into a complex system of superior and subordinate beings. The person's place is not fixed and he or she can rise or fall within the ranks, but the ranks themselves continue unchanged. For a foreign businessperson, this means that someone who provided valuable help a few years ago may by now be of little use - or possibly even more valuable! If they have gone up, it also means that you must treat them with more respect than previously, as befits their new position.

The movement of others up and down the hierarchy can easily cause resentment and hurt feelings, with the result that office politics loom large in China. Most enterprises contain a variety of fluid factions.

Because everyone lives within this rigid hierarchy and harmony must prevail in society, specific rules of conduct are laid down and strictly taught to all children to be followed for life.

In contrast with a person's position is society, within the *family* a person's place is immutably fixed, so that the elder brother is always the elder brother, and treated accordingly.

Bureaucracy is an ancient Chinese art form and, like Chinese society, is strictly hierarchical in rank. The privileges of every level, and person, are clearly defined or recognized. The Chinese approach foreign visitors and residents in the same vein. Your particular status will be determined after careful scrutiny of your company and its national or international standing, and then your position within the company. That is worked out by your ranking on any lists you may have sent them, your job title, and any letters appearing after your name on your business card. In China, like meets with like, consequently the higher your status, the higher the officials you can meet. When your company makes its first approach, it should send someone with strong credentials, in order to gain entry as high as possible, and thereby meet more important people. They can ensure that those lower will do more for you down.

Despite being a communist country with an ideology that supposedly should emphasize egalitarianism and the workers, the demands of Confucian hierarchy easily dominate. Members of a foreign aristocracy are revered and this was true even in the extreme days of the Maoist left-wing period. Ex-heads of state are particularly well respected and regaled because of their old position, irrespective of their current status, past behavior, or even criminal record. Ex-President Nixon was always treated royally on his visits to China.

Learn your lessons well - Confucius

"Memorize lessons" was an important value in traditional education and this still prevails in China as well as in the diaspora of Overseas Chinese families. A common criticism of the students produced by the education system, as well as in Taiwan, Japan and Korea, is that they merely learn by rote to the detriment of understanding and being able to apply the concepts to practical problems.

Practice makes perfect - Confucius

"Practice skills" was another old rule which is still current - indeed some believe that it is even more strictly observed these days than it was in older times.

Guanxi, the secret of being successful in China

The Chinese have a tendency to divide people into insiders and outsiders, the former can be helped but the latter are often ignored. This habit, together with the Marxist predisposition to control social institutions from the top down and prevent lateral contact, have always been a major barrier to communications. To get around this, people develop a network of contacts and personal relationships for whom they do favors and from whom they ask favors in return. This is called *guanxi* (pronounced "go-an-see" with stress on the "an") which means possessing influence, or "pull", that you can use with your contacts. Without *guanxi* it is difficult or even impossible to accomplish much, with it you can open doors and achieve a surprising number of things. You need to work on developing *guanxi* from the moment you arrive in China.

Guanxi is a powerful asset, something like a valuable bank account of favors owed and owing, and people with bigger networks tend to do better. However, the bank account is not unlimited so after receiving, say, two or three favors in a row, people must repay when approached, even if it might disadvantage them in some way.

An example of the power of *guanxi* is provided by Tang Jinsheng, who is the president of the Zhonghua Company that produces motor vehicles. *Asiaweek* pointed out that "the cars have an iffy reputation. Doors fly open, wheels go rolling off, and engines catch fire".[1] About ten cars a day are made by hand without modern technology, they are of low quality and "are widely detested". Despite these obvious drawbacks, the firm has not gone bankrupt as one might expect. Mr. Tang happens to be the 45-year-old son of a high-ranking officer in the People's Liberation Army! This gives him immense status and contacts that he is able to use to stay in business. At one stage, he even managed to persuade the official Taxi Management Office in Beijing to encourage taxi operators to buy his product to use as their fleet car.

It can pay to hire someone to work for you purely for the contacts they have. The person may in fact do little work but can add immense value to your company by the sheer amount of their *guanxi*. Powerful family members can provide *guanxi* possibilities. The Wall Street investment bank Credit Suisse First Boston Company took on Dennis Zhu, in the days when his father Zhu Rongji was a rising star in the economic area but before he became Premier.[2] The company gained from this at the time but it is understood that Dennis became an even more valuable asset as his father rose to the top.

Getting along with harmony

Harmony is an important part of the Confucian heritage. It is believed that if everyone in society plays his or her proper role, then overall harmony will be preserved. For this reason, self-discipline and moderation are essential components of human behavior, to avoid disorder. For most foreigners, harmony is best preserved by avoiding confrontations, maintaining temper, not raising the voice, and smiling rather than looking angry. Not causing anyone to lose face is an important part of preserving harmony.

The preference for harmony does not preclude the Chinese from suddenly becoming forthright and even turning downright rude in their dealings with you, but such a switch is almost always tactical and a part of their negotiating strategy. They may be searching for weakness to see if you can be easily dominated, or may already have decided you can be, and are now going for the jugular.

Superstitious - me?

Most Chinese are superstitious and even well educated, apparently totally Westernized people may cling to traditional beliefs. Many important decisions may be deferred until what is seen as the optimal time. This might be quietly determined by fortune-tellers or by an individual referring to traditional books that are readily available in China. Unexplained delays in negotiations may be due to such factors, as well as to the better-known bureaucratic ones.

Many superstitions exist, and they vary in different parts of China, so that it is not easy to know what a particular person might believe in. Homonyms abound in the Chinese language, which is essentially mono-syllabic, so that one sound may stand for many different things and even a simple beginner's Chinese-English dictionary will have perhaps fifty different meanings for the word "li". The large number of homonyms means that some words are regarded as lucky or unlucky simply because they happen to sound like a completely different word that possesses a good or bad meaning. Some people, for example, believe it is good to see a deer as one of its homonyms means "prosperous". With local variations in pronunciation and several different, if related, languages in China, there can be a huge number of words that have lucky or unlucky connotations to someone somewhere.

Some superstitious beliefs are geared to the old lunar calendar. The seventh lunar month is one that is particularly concerned with the dead. The Hungry Ghost Festival involves being kind to those spirits who lack descendants to make offerings to them, or who died a violent death. These ghosts are ill-natured and some people choose to leave out food, as well as to burn joss sticks and paper money, to propitiate them. It is regarded as a bad month for celebrations, so that weddings and birthday parties are best avoided. It might not be the most opportune time for you to try to conclude negotiations for a business deal and then hold the necessary celebration dinner. During this festival, trips to the countryside are best avoided, as many spirits are thought to lurk there.

The number superstitions

Numbers have a special significance to Chinese. Most Cantonese believe that numbers 4, 44, 444 and so on are very bad, as they are a homonym for death; they would not buy a motor car with such a license plate or stay in a hotel room with such a number. Eight is however seen as very good and the more eights the better. Yaohan, a Japanese department store that opened in Beijing in 1992, provides a good example. More or less as a joke, the person in charge of the pens labeled a rather splendid 14 carat gold pen for sale at 88,888 *yuan* (approximately $11,000). The lucky numbers worked – he not only got it, but that was the first pen sold in the store![2] In the eyes of some, eight is seen as lucky as it may be associated with business expansion and economic improvement.

In traditional China, the odd numbers were traditionally seen as masculine and the even ones as feminine, which meant in a society with a strong preference for boys, odd numbers were generally preferred. Three is a good lucky number as is five, which is probably connected with an old belief in five elements, five grains and five tastes as well as the old Imperial ranking system of officials. Seven is also often seen as a lucky number, as are multiples of it such as 14, 21, or 35. Nine was an extremely lucky number, and 81, the square of nine particularly so; on your travels you might notice that almost all ancient gates in China have eighty-one stud heads on them. At weddings in some parts of China, as part of social custom the groom was forced to pay sums of money to the bridesmaids in order to get to see his bride. He handed it over in multiples of nine.

The meaning of colors

Colors play an important part in superstitions and can influence what you decide to wear. White is the color of death and plain white, e.g., as a dress, a suit, or shirt and trousers, tends to give the appearance of traditional mourning garments and so is best avoided. Would you respond quickly and warmly to someone dressed in the somber garb of a traditional undertaker? It is quite acceptable to wear a white shirt or blouse, but it is best to team it with a suit or skirt of a different color. Red is considered a very "happy" color, so that a red tie with a white shirt, or red buttons on a white dress, easily offsets the death image.

Death might also be suggested in China by a mixture of blue and white or blue and yellow At a traditional funeral, the gift of money would often be placed in a yellow envelope with a blue stripe, so this combination of colors is best avoided. Blue trousers and white shirt should be fine, but you might choose to avoid a striped tie in heavy blue and white, or blue and yellow, for example.

Yellow on its own can be connected with death, although a darkish yellow was also associated with the emperors of history (only they were allowed to have yellow roofs on buildings) and also with some monks. Because of the different traditions, there is no real problem with wearing yellow, and it might give you a useful talking point.

A green hat should definitely be avoided, as in some parts of China it suggests a cuckolded person. There is a story that one senior foreign negotiator presented a green baseball cap with his company logo on it to each member of the team with which he had negotiated – and then wondered why no one was actually prepared to wear it!

Red is a particularly good or happy color in much of Asia, including Japan and Korea as well as China. In certain areas, such as in the city of Chengdu, white bread loaves always seem to have a splash of edible red dye on them to make them look more attractive. At first glance, it rather looks to a Westerner as if the baker must have cut himself! Wearing too much red can look a bit silly however. For foreign women, it might look excessive to wear a totally bright red dress with matching shoes and handbag. This is the sort of thing that little girls wear for very special celebrations, when they are adorned with heavy adult makeup.

Paintings and scrolls

Traditional scrolls and painting often featured a scene with mountains and streams with usually a tiny figure of a human, possibly fishing. This was a reflection of the Taoist (pronounced "dow-ist") world view of the importance and grandeur of nature, the insignificance of humans, and perhaps the Confucian idea of the importance of how people fit in.

Certain elements in a painting may represent specific things; for instance the dragon represents the Emperor, the phoenix the Empress. Particular animals had strong symbolism attached to them (see Table 1.1, p.20) and it is worth knowing about one or two.

The value of knowing about traditional beliefs

If you can comment on traditional views about the significance of numbers, colors, a painting, or an animal, it will impress the Chinese – it

Kevin Bucknall

demonstrates you have a genuine interest in their culture. It can be most useful when socializing and casting around for good and safe topics of conversation. Understanding traditions can be helpful. I once witnessed an Australian trained in classical Chinese reading aloud the inscription on a temple wall in Chengdu, Sichuan and it immediately attracted an impressed crowd of locals. In part it was the novelty of seeing an obvious foreigner reading Chinese aloud! More strikingly, most of them could not read it for themselves, because modern Chinese characters are different and most people are cut off from their literary past. They were interested to know what it meant.

You should be careful when demonstrating your knowledge not to sound arrogant. You should also avoid asking bluntly if someone understands a traditional issue: if they do not it will make them lose face. Many younger Chinese missed out on the traditional value training and know relatively little about China's past and the old beliefs, so that it is particularly easy to embarrass them. If you demonstrate a vast knowledge, it just might backfire on you - it is widely felt that foreigners should be interested in China but not actually know more than a Chinese! The classically trained Australian above had no problem as he benefited from the immense Chinese respect for education and scholarship.

If you really wish to impress someone and regularly do business in China, you might perhaps learn a line of poetry from one of the classic periods, like the Tang, and say it approvingly. That would be very well regarded.

Table 1.1 Some traditional beliefs about animal symbolism

Tortoise	Long life.
White cockerel	Good; it can ward off evil spirits.
Red cockerel	Good; it might ward off house fires.
Bats	Lucky; homonym with happiness.
Foxes	Really a sly spirit; it can change into human form, especially a seductive female one; it specializes in helping you to find lost documents.
Tiger	Male, fierce; the king of the land (in China

	it is not considered to be the lion).
Tortoise	Longevity.
Horse	Speed, endurance.
One wild goose	Masculinity; the spirit of *yang*.
Two geese	Symbol of the married state.
Fish	Symbol of wealth.
Deer	Longevity; wealth and prosperity.
Pair of Mandarin ducks	Happily married life
Crows	Unlucky
Dragon	The dragon king is generally seen as a benevolent creature with divine powers, intelligent, and able to end droughts. Might be hot tempered.

Change is constant and rapid

China is in a state of transition from poverty to riches, from centrally-planned Communism to the market mechanism, and from an old-fashioned to a modern economy. The changes that have occurred are great and they are continuing. As long ago as 1840, the traditional culture was placed under heavy pressure, from contact with Britain followed by war. The pressure continued through the Nineteenth Century with the partial colonization of China and the beginnings of industrialization. The Twentieth Century added to the pressures, with the collapse of the Imperial system in 1911, civil war (1928-37 and 1946-49), invasion and occupation by Japan (1931-45), decades of Marxist education, followed by contemporary Western-oriented market policies (1978+). Once cut off from contact with the outside, among ordinary people there is now an awareness of the world and its values.

Many traditional manners persist, and old superstitions including witchcraft have reappeared, particularly in rural areas, after decades of being attacked or banned by the Party. Nonetheless, values are changing, especially among the young city dwellers. Of the people with whom you are likely to deal, the older might tend to be more traditional, while the younger ones may have adopted more modern or Western standards. You will recognize some excellent modern Western management types but be on guard, as they are often closely imitated by the growing ranks of crooks and con artists.

Some Chinese who are actually still traditional have adopted modern "foreign" ways when dealing with Westerners (e.g., using one hand not two to pass things to another person), but remain traditional when dealing among themselves. Although they seem to you as modern or normal in a Western sense, they will immediately notice and appreciate your sensitivity if you follow a traditional practice.

Very strong values are still attached to:
- The Chinese family.
- Group loyalty.
- Respect for hierarchy.
- The preference for harmony.

Old ways persist in that:

- The traditional bureaucratic ways continue.
- Personal ties and obligations are still stressed.
- Manual workers are often held in low esteem, although not as much as peasants.

The values have weakened but are still present for:

- Female subordination.
- Kinship commitment (people sharing the same surname).
- A vague allegiance to individuals from the same city or province.

The traditional low esteem for soldiers has been raised by constant propaganda over the years. The devastating floods of 1998, the worst since 1954, were turned to good use by the government: the people were bombarded with constant stories of heroism by the People's Liberation Army (PLA) soldiers accompanied by television shots of them in action on the dikes and in the water.

Things are getting better

Facilities in China have improved immensely since trade and investment opened up in the 1980s and things continue to get better. Hotels are much more comfortable, telephones work better, direct dialing is now possible, and a night life now exists, including Western style discotheques, karaoke bars and night clubs. The variety and quality of consumer goods have signally improved since the early 1980s. Computers are becoming a relatively normal consumer good in urban areas with 9 million users at the end of 1999 and 13 million with access to the Internet.[3] Wireless application protocol (WAP) technology for mobile phones appeared in May 2000, there are 60 million mobile phones operating, and the number grows rapidly. Many urban Chinese are gadget conscious and wish to buy the latest technological consumer goods available.

Rapid change, high stress

The rapid improvements come at a cost. In communist China, changes have always come abruptly in unpredictable fashion. What was correct one day could be totally wrong the next; even this new state of affairs could suddenly be reversed again if there were changes in the power structure. Many people were tense whenever forced to discuss social, political or economic issues in compulsory meetings; in private they would either refused to do so or else would rigidly parrot the Party line. The recent high speed of change has increased the stress level of many urban Chinese and the flood of migrants from rural areas suffer great tension.

The introduction of market mechanisms has encouraged the emergence of a new breed of young, entrepreneurial Chinese who have little memory of the past and no interest in communism or its ethics. The middle aged and elderly find it hard to cope with the new policies and values, and suffer spiritually. This is particularly true of those people who still believe in communism or traditional Buddhism, Taoism and Confucianism. People on fixed incomes have suffered materially owing to inflation, and feel irked as they watch income distributions widen and the nouveau riche flaunt their newly gained wealth in gauche and rather offensive ways.

Chinese attitudes to themselves and to others

Patriotism looms large

Dr. Johnson referred scathingly to patriotism as the last refuge of a scoundrel; this is not the case in China where people are intensely nationalistic. There is a deep and unquestioned belief in China's historical and cultural greatness and the name for the country, "Middle Kingdom", indicates that the world revolves around the country. All Chinese are proud of their nation and race, and regard others as definite unfortunates if not absolute barbarians. Minority peoples within China tend to be despised and not accepted as proper Chinese by the dominant Han group.

A schizophrenic attitude towards foreigners

Many Chinese are a little ambivalent about foreigners. On the one hand, they admire and respect foreigners for their achievements and particularly for their advanced technology, which they believe, can be of great assistance to China. On the other hand, they feel that foreigners are inferior, lack culture and manners, and are often nationals of some country that treated China badly in the past. You can encounter individuals who are fascinated by foreigners and others who may be repelled.

The things about foreigners that most upset many Chinese are greed and profit seeking, overly sharp business practices, rowdy unseemly behavior, loud foreign pop music, and anything connected with sex and drugs. The up-and-coming young entrepreneurs tend to be less critical of these things and often engage in them themselves but it is best not to demonstrate you are like that.

It is common for a Chinese person to feel that he or she can learn much from foreign technology but little or nothing from foreign social or philosophical teachings, which are often regarded as trite or barbarically incorrect. Even the sort of communism that emerged in China was very "Chinese", and until Liberation in 1949, many top ranking communist leaders knew surprisingly little of world Marxist thought. I recall that back in 1967 I raised names like Rosa Luxemburg, Karl Kautsky, and Herbert Marcuse, with a specialist Marxist philosophy professor at a Chinese university, only to discover he had never heard of any of them! Indeed, he seemed to know only about Marx, Engels, Lenin, Stalin and Mao Zedong.

You might find that small town Chinese expect more Chinese-style manners and behavior from you than the big city ones, as the latter are both more tolerant and used to dealing with "big noses", an old and vulgar slang word for "foreign barbarians".

How the Chinese see various nationalities

The Chinese have a view of other nationalities that is often based on an unpleasant historical relationship. The lessons and experience of history are most important to educated Chinese who are well versed in their own history and often refer to it for relevant examples and analogies for the present circumstances. They have been taught about the actions of a few foreign nations that have hurt China, especially by invasions, colonization, and forced unfair treaties. Rather like the Irish, the Chinese are very aware of their history and much bitterness persists. Consequently, the natural suspicion of foreigners, common it seems to all nations and races, is reinforced in China. Please do not feel insulted by the portrait of any of the nationalities that follow – these are common Chinese attitudes, not held by all, and certainly are not intended as my views or a description of reality.

The Japanese tend to be seen as hard working, efficient, successful, and extremely loyal to their firm and to Japan. Japanese success at coping with Western impact during and after the nineteenth century is admired. On the negative side they are often seen as cruel (the legacy of occupation and Japanese behavior during the 1930s and 1940s); too dominating and hegemonic; and essentially untrustworthy. The lack of trust is reinforced by the Japanese culture of excessively refined politeness, which causes them to be easily seen as two-faced, i.e., they are extremely polite to your face, but are still planning to take unfair advantage. They are frequently believed to be self-serving and not truly interested in helping China, which many Chinese think they should. Japan is seen as owing a debt because of its past behavior, as well as being wealthy in its own right and able to do more. The Japanese are seen as being willing to take advantage of Chinese weakness or ignorance and not behaving as friends should. Privately, some Chinese still refer to Japanese as "poisonous dwarves" or "Japanese monsters", common terms of abuse during the Maoist era.

Americans are often seen as open, warm, friendly and trusting. Some Chinese see them as possibly a little childlike and naive as a result. American society is considered essentially shallow, with little history and culture of which to boast. As a consequence of cultural differences, Americans all too often come across as tending to be brash, arrogant, boastful and pushy, as well as being impatient and lacking in proper self-discipline. A few are seen as uncouth loudmouthed bullies. The attitude of some old New England families towards newly oil-rich Texans is perhaps similar!

The Koreans are regarded as a stubborn people, and even harder working than the Chinese. These perceived traits mean that they are not particularly liked, but they are preferred to the Japanese. After all, China successfully invaded Korea on occasion, which kept them in their place; in contrast, Japan invaded China and occupied all the important coastal areas. This is keenly felt to be a failing of China and a downright insult by Japan into the bargain.

The British are reasonably well regarded, especially considering the rather sad history of their colonial occupation of China and often unfortunate treatment of Chinese individuals. The English are seen as clever and even reasonably sophisticated, especially considering they are foreigners. On the negative side, they are felt to be cold, hold themselves aloof, and never really become involved much. They are seen as deliberately holding others at arms' length and not a people with whom it is easy to develop a close personal relationship.

Australians are seen as acceptable, but often brash, slightly abrasive, and lacking in sophistication. They are known to be uncultured, appearing a little like strong but rather dumb farmhands. Australians tend however to be trusted, as the Chinese have discovered that they say what they mean and mean what they say. Consequently, individual Chinese can sometimes develop a closer relationship with an Australian, than is possible with the English. The boisterous, somewhat larrikin, Australian behavior when drinking is neither admired nor understood.

The Chinese are different from the Japanese

You might have experience of dealing with Japanese business people or officials. This can serve you in good stead, in that you have learned something about Asia's rich cultures. Although the Japanese culture shares some things in common with the Chinese - such as regarding the group as important, acting cautiously in the early stages, and looking for long term relationships - they are different in many other ways. This means you cannot replicate the behavior learned from your Japanese experience and expect it to work perfectly in China.

The Chinese tend to base their loyalties on family, but the Japanese on the nation. The Chinese never bow and find Japanese politeness ludicrous and misleadingly false. Many Chinese were taught as children to hate the Japanese for invading China and particularly for "the Rape of Nanjing" (1937), when Japanese troops ran amok, reportedly slaughtering hundreds of thousands in cruel ways. At an early age, most urban children will have been shown a movie that graphically and harshly depicts this incident. I have seen this and it is a truly horrifying sight for an adult, let alone a six year old child.

China itself is different from Japan: it is poor, lacks infrastructure, skilled labor, and modern technology, and still has relatively little awareness of the need for quality. The Japanese tend to be more formally behaved and dressed, more traditional in attitude, quite racist, and more group minded. These are just a few of the differences, and it is important not to blindly reproduce in China some things you may have learned from doing business with the Japanese, or indeed vice versa.

China is one country but all Chinese are not the same

Many countries have stereotype views of certain groups of foreigners e.g., French women are always chic and French men are sexy, being constantly involved in amorous pursuits. Such views of other nations are commonplace. Alongside these, attitudes towards *regional* differences exist in probably every nation. In China, many individuals have strong stereotype expectations about their compatriots from other parts of the country.

- Northerners from around Beijing are seen by Southerners as phlegmatic and stolid people, who are cold and hold themselves aloof. They have a tendency to be bookish, ivory-towered, or dilettantes. They do not really know how to enjoy themselves.
- Those coming from the province of Hunan and Sichuan are regarded elsewhere as being fiery, rebellious, and quick to lose their temper. They find it more difficult to preserve harmony. This view is probably based on the local preference for hot, spicy foods.
- Those coming from Shanghai are thought of as devious city slickers, the kind of people who enter a revolving door behind you and come out in front. They are seen as being ultra stylish, caring much about their appearance, and prone to spend money easily on fine clothes and good living. Hairdressers and tailors from Shanghai are well regarded in the rest of China.
- Southerners, especially the Cantonese from Guangdong province, are felt by Northerners to be noisy, boisterous, and a bit earthy. They are seen as a definite distraction when gathered in numbers in restaurants chattering loudly and in groups are definitely best avoided. Some Northerners see the Cantonese as not being fully Chinese or totally civilized and only a cut above barbarians, especially as they tend to eat dogs and snakes for medicinal purposes. They are considered in much the same way some Northern Europeans regard the inhabitants of rural southern Italy.
- The Cantonese themselves tend to pride themselves, probably correctly, as being the descendants of the "true" Chinese who were pushed south by northern invaders. In turn, they often feel that Northerners are not quite "proper Chinese" but the mixed blood descendants of barbaric hordes.

Naturally, each group does not normally subscribe to the stereotype of itself! Individuals might easily be hurt if they were pigeonholed in this way. Should you get talking about regional differences, be careful first to ascertain the person's native province as well as where he or she has lived the longest. If in ignorance you point out the stereotype of their home-town, the individual could easily feel hurt and suffer a loss of face. This would not improve your business prospects!

Two broad types of Chinese you might meet

Most senior Chinese officials and business people are old-fashioned, conservative in manner, and traditional in approach. Because age and rank often go together, they are often powerful people. Most government officials are in this group and the interior of China is full of such types. The advice contained in this book is perfect for dealing with them.

The second sort you will meet is younger, more Westernized and has often thrown off traditions in an effort to be trendy and modern. They are largely confined to big cities in the coastal region - Hong Kong has a lot and Shanghai is striving to catch up. They recognize the traditional ways if you follow them, but are themselves dropping the old-fashioned, self-effacing, polite manners. A clear generational gap has emerged. If one of the young tearaways tells you that "no one does that anymore", he is wrong, but it is a strong signal that you can relax your efforts to fit in, and return to your more normal business approach when you are with him or her.

Foreigners' attitudes to regional differences

Experience in China has persuaded some foreigners that in contract negotiations, the Beijing people are straightforward and easy to deal with; the Shanghainese are cunning but are well-versed in Western business practice, which makes doing business easier; and the Cantonese are some-times devious or unscrupulous and more care must be taken when doing business with them. Whether these views are true is hard to say. As a rule of thumb, the south does seem to contain more crooks and con artists than the north, and the coastal areas more than the interior. The dyna-mism and opportunities attract all kinds. Things may change as more foreigners penetrate the less accessible areas which in turn may become more unrestrained. Shenzhen and Guangdong in particular have a repu-tation for lawlessness and being something of a "Wild West" area.

It is not difficult to be gypped or robbed in China, even for big Western firms. A company as large and well-known as Compaq Computers was ripped off. In 1995, several of their distributors did not pay for the com-puters they had already received; one of them, Cheflink Computers that had worked with Compaq for almost three years, owed $32 million and would not pay.[4] Compaq's total loss is unknown but industry rumors at the time suggested that perhaps $100 million might be close.

What should you be particularly wary about? A survey of credit ratings of enterprises in China done in 1997 reported the following were the main risks that foreign investors in China should guard against.[5]

- Firms using fraudulent business licenses.
- Companies that fail to implement a production plan or have no money to pay for equipment.
- Enterprises that produce unmarketable products and cannot pay for raw materials.
- Cooperative projects that are halted because of a change in government industrial policy or environmental protection measures.

The bossy, interfering, middle-aged woman

Do not be surprised if occasionally you encounter a noisy, inquisitive, rather assertive woman, who might approach you on the street or in a store. Such people were once important in the Street Committees and had great power over their neighbors. Maoism weakened after 1976 and they lost their influence and function, so that some are now bored busybodies with a strong sense of frustration. If they speak some English and bustle up to you, they can be helpful if you want to know something like the correct way back to your hotel, although their level of English is normally not high. In the late 1990s, there was some effort to rebuild street committees so their presence might increase.

About face

The concept of "face" is important in Chinese culture. It is important that you take care not to cause anyone a loss of face. Although face is a personal thing, it can spill over into the group. Each person has a place in the group with a particular role to play so that if you cause someone to lose face, it can mean that everyone in the group feels bad about it. Individual member would then find it harder to respond positively to you.

It is not always easy to determine what might cause a loss of face but the following will usually do it and should be avoided.

- Saying no to someone in public.
- Rejecting a proposal out of hand without at least appearing to consider it.
- Criticizing someone in public.
- Interrupting anyone.

- Addressing the interpreter rather than the leader.
- Ignoring the Chinese leader or greeting an underling first.
- Giving a gift to an organization that is too cheap or made in China.
- Paying someone less than others of similar ability or experience.
- Giving perks to expatriate managers but not to the Chinese side.
- Demoting someone – even if he or she is performing badly.
- Publicly threatening to fire someone.

If you seriously upset someone by causing them loss of face, you have made an enemy. Should you inadvertently do this to someone important, what can you do to rectify the situation? In most cases the best approach is to employ an intermediary, your liaison officer would be perfect, to go and apologize for what you did or said. He or she can explain that as a barbarian you could not be expected to behave properly and there was no deliberate intention to insult. Another way might be to ask your intermediary to talk to the person's immediate superior and ask if *he* will pass the apology down. Coming down through the hierarchy turns it into a more powerful apology.

Giving face to someone is the other side of the coin and is an excellent thing to do. It can be achieved by such things as:

- complimenting someone in public;
- obviously going out of your way to do something for someone;
- praising and giving public recognition to someone's achievement;
- using their title ("Chief Engineer Wang") rather than "Mr. Wang";
- inviting them to a banquet;
- giving someone the seat of honor, facing the door;
- presenting a person with a gift;
- generally, anything that you can think of that boosts a person's ego.

Note that dealing with a large well known international firm gives face to a Chinese firm, as well as to its managers, which is one reason they tend to prefer the big Western companies over small or little-known ones.

Insider-outsider: do you belong?

The Chinese have a cultural tendency to see people as essentially either "insiders", who are members of the group or organization, or "outsiders", who are strangers. They behave quite differently with each of these informal classifications. Outsiders are often treated with an indifference that can easily border on contempt and no one feels the slightest obligation to look after them or deal with a simple request. If you try to get assistance from another organization it might prove a hassle, as the people there feel no responsibility to assist you, the outsider, and some of them may feel a compulsion to frustrate you. If you are having trouble gaining cooperation from another organization, you might find you have to get a higher official to step in and instruct those lower down to help you. Even if you succeed in getting their help in this way, the other unit may resent it and might undertake some other action as an act of petty revenge.

Insiders on the other hand have to be cosseted and assisted. The definition or nature of the insider group is however fluid and varies with the context or the issue. Everyone within an organization is a member of several insider groups – the work team, the section, the department, the division and the business itself, as well as perhaps a table tennis team or similar social club. Cooperation between members of the same work group is high, but between different groups it may be competitive.

The strongest insider group in China is the family, but there are other powerful network groups to which a person can belong; within the group there is a feeling of special relationship and *guanxi* may develop between members. These network groups can include people who attended the same school or university (particularly in the same year), or worked for the same organization, served in the same military unit, or were members of a delegation to a different city or country. As a last resort, people coming from the same city or province may share some insider feelings and may help each other a little.

These insider groupings can be complex when there are different rival sets within an organization. Virtually all Chinese organizations are riven with factions, each with its own head person who leads and protects a set of people underneath. The use of *guanxi* is the way most Chinese try to get around both the outsider and the rival faction problems.

"Give me the latest!"

The Chinese tend to go for the best, which is identified as being the most prestigious product. This is partly the result of the Confucian heritage and the hierarchical view of the world: some product has to be at the top. It is much safer for a Chinese purchasing agent to buy the best known product, for a superior is unlikely to criticize him for this. The situation is not unlike that of many purchasing officers in Western firms in the 1980s who preferred to buy IBM personal computers at a high price rather than perfectly satisfactory and substantially cheaper clones. The Chinese also like to deal with the "best" firm where they can and may gain kudos from this. In part, it is because of lingering fears that foreigners may cheat them, and internationally known companies are felt to be safer.

In technology, the latest "cutting edge" method is usually preferred. Rarely will the most appropriate be chosen over the most prestigious, which means that sales pitches along the lines of being suitable for Chinese conditions may fall on deaf ears. It might even be seen as mildly insulting. If you are trying to sell, the Chinese will automatically compare your product or technology with what else can be bought internationally, to see if anything better is available. However, once they have made their minds up and bought the item, they are often brand loyal. They do not seem to like having to make new purchasing decisions among the variety of choices offered by the international market system. Eventually, when a product which is demonstrably superior to yours appears, despite the verbal emphasis on "old friends", they will often be willing to dump you, particularly if your company is small and the new product is from a major international player.

Laughter, a defense mechanism

You cannot assume that the laughter you hear always means happiness. It can be genuine, but the laugh may indicate embarrassment and uncertainty about how to react. If someone trips and falls over, or hurts himself or herself seriously, you might encounter laughter rather than obvious sympathy. In this case, the laughter suggests that the person is in a dilemma about what to do or feel. If someone seriously offends an important canon of behavior, maybe losing their temper and screaming abuse at an official, those around might laugh uneasily. The announcement of a personal tragedy may also cause laughter, apparently acting as a tension releasing device, and it does not imply callousness.

If you are unfortunate enough to trip and fall over, you might find that people will stand and watch but no one will help you. The Chinese often fear to take individual responsibility for anything, and as a foreigner you are something of an unknown quantity. Do not get angry at anyone who laughs at your predicament, it probably does not reflect amusement. If you lose your temper, it is likely to make things worse; others will probably join in the laughter out of acute embarrassment.

Chinese people often do not smile when introduced, but this does not mean they are unfriendly, they merely have different social customs. A smile is not always friendly and can indicate embarrassment, especially if it is rather fixed and occurs in response to a statement by you. Smiles may conceal anger, again usually in response to something that has just been said or done. They can also be just like Western ones, indicating friendship and enjoyment. It is a complex culture and can take a bit of understanding!

Look at me when you're talking to me!

You are probably used to making and seeking eye contact when negotiating in your own country. In China, frequent eye contact when addressing someone is similarly desirable. Many Chinese become worried if they are talking and the listener, although concentrating, persistently stares away. They begin to wonder what you are up to and what message you are signaling that they do not understand. However, many Chinese find *constant* eye contact to be aggressive or challenging, so that it is better to glance away regularly rather than hold their gaze.

You should be aware that traditionally it is bad manners to gaze into the eyes of a total stranger, so do not be alarmed if on introduction a person does not look straight at you. Guard against your instinct that might tell you the person you are meeting is shifty and untrustworthy; it is merely a different cultural body language. If you have a habit of pondering what is being said to you by gazing at the ceiling or out of the window, it is best not to do this in China. It might suggest that you are treating the person who is talking as a stranger, and this would interfere with building up mutual trust.

Smokers' paradise

You will observe a lot of smoking in China and notice cigarette burns in carpets or on furniture. Cigarettes are cheap and readily available. Most of us in the West are aware of the dangers of smoking, but until relatively recently the information was concealed from the people of China. The government had total control of the media, and news from the outside world was heavily censored. Many people developed the smoking habit in ignorance of the health dangers involved. The main problem was that the paramount leader, Mao Zedong, was both a dictator and a chain smoker. No publicity about the ill effects of smoking was allowed during his lifetime and he lived until 1976.

Because they have grown up surrounded by smokers, few Chinese realize that these days smoking is offensive to many foreigners. You are advised to ignore the smoke and try not to look concerned. Under no circumstances should you criticize people for smoking in your presence: not only will no one understand your concern, it will cause a severe loss of face to those who are smoking, or perhaps smoked earlier on. If on the other hand you are still an unreconstructed smoker, try the local brands for yourself. You will be surprised how cheap they are but will probably decide they taste unpleasantly coarse and strong.

Things to take in with you

Many visitors to China find it useful to buy any medicines they might need either before leaving home or else in Hong Kong. Even if you are in good health, you may fall ill, especially with minor ailments like colds and upper respiratory tract infections. Take with you what you might need. When you have a cold, it is amazing how a lemon flavored aspirin hot drink in your hotel room can improve the way you feel. A supply of your preferred painkillers, throat lozenges, antibiotics and antidiarrheal tablets is essential. In winter, you will probably need a lip salve and perhaps a good skin cream.

It is a good idea to take a portable shortwave radio with you to keep in touch with world events. China is different from most other countries, it is easy to feel cut off and isolated, and many visitors suffer from a mild version of culture shock, especially if traveling or living alone. A small radio-cassette player can make a lot of difference, especially if you are on a long train journey and have brought some of your favorite tapes with you. Chinese batteries can be inferior, so take lots in with you.

A Swiss army knife is useful, especially the corkscrew, bottle opener, and can opener attachments. If I am staying for more than a week or two, I find a cheap plastic juice squeezer that sits on a mug useful. It allows me to buy cheap fruit in the market and spoil myself with fresh juice of my choice. Most of these seem to mix well with duty-free gin, which can be useful.

Should your visit be in late December, remember to take lots of Christmas cards with you, preferably *not* ones with a Chinese motif. You should avoid any that contain jokes or innuendo and look for those that are serious, old-fashioned and look impressive. Send one to every important contact you make, for although few Chinese are Christians they enjoy receiving cards. It will help to develop your relationships further.

They don't "do lunch" but they take long breaks

It is common to find people take a long lunch break. In China, many people start work early in the morning and then stop for a lunch break of perhaps two or even two and a half hours. As noon approaches, if you find the meeting you are in is showing signs of being suddenly brought to a close or you are being hurried back to the hotel, this is probably the reason. After eating lunch, many Chinese take a siesta, then wake up refreshed for the afternoon work. One reason why state enterprise managers do not take you to their office to talk is that it is probably poorly furnished and decorated – and it might well have a bed in it! If you are tempted to indulge in a few beers before or with lunch, remember that they might make you sleepy and you will shortly be facing negotiators who have just had a refreshing nap and are in peak form. Proper wine is relatively expensive in China, so if you must indulge in alcohol, beer is often the preferred tipple.

It is mostly a waste of time trying to contact Chinese colleagues or your contact person or the members of their team between noon and two-thirty: they are often asleep and cannot be located. If your telephone call wakes them up, it will not endear you. As a result of not taking a siesta, as well as being kept on the go visiting museums and the like, Western visitors often get surprisingly tired in China.

Names and titles

Most Chinese have three names, with the surname coming first on their business card. A few Chinese have only two names, and a very few have as many as four. Traditionally, the surname came first on cards, so that Peng Lian is "Mr. Peng". If he or she has a title such as Director of an Institute it is polite to address him or her by the title, and you should certainly do so. Their title pins them down in the hierarchy and using it gives them definite face, since it points out that they are senior people. You should always say "Director Peng" or "Vice-Chairman Wang" rather than plain Mr. or Madame. "Madame" is often used for women rather than "Mrs.", as it sounds more imposing. A second reason is that for many years in Mao's China, "Mrs." had a derogatory feel about it and usually referred to a woman who was wealthy, but empty, selfish and uncaring. Such people were regarded with antipathy by the Party and the majority of the people at the time.

You should avoid addressing someone as "comrade" or referring to one of your colleagues as a comrade, as it suggests political activity and the Communist Party. This could detract from the point you wish to make or inadvertently pass a message that you did not intend.

Noisy laughter

China can be a noisy place and you might encounter shouting or rowdy behavior. In part it is inherent in the society and language: two Cantonese friends who are getting along famously and really enjoying themselves often sound as if they are arguing and about to come to blows. With groups it is often sheer exuberant high spirits. In noisy restaurants, it is usually the result of the large number of people, each trying to be heard above the crowd.

Some not so nice things

The local environment and housing might not impress you

Apart from the obviously new building work, many Chinese cities look old, worn down, poverty-stricken, and often downright ugly. You should not be surprised at this. China is poor, and for decades the housing stock was allowed to deteriorate, largely because rents were set at levels much too low to allow for maintenance. Housing upkeep was always a low priority for the planners and if more money became available to the government, housing was not the sort of area that received help. The state now wants to get out of the business of supplying cheap housing. On July 1 1998, the State tried to stop doing this, and hoped to transfer the provision of accommodation over to the private sector. The attempt had to be postponed because the task was too difficult to implement quickly.

In the north especially, the predominant appearance is a dusty grey, with usually a blanket of smoke or smog. Air pollution, severe under the earlier communist policy of industrialization at all costs, worsened dramatically during the 1990s with economic growth and the advent of private motor vehicles. Most cities suffer from mile after mile of grey concrete buildings that look as if they might stretch forever and look particularly uninspiring. These edifices have been thrown up since the Revolution of 1949 and cheapness, not aesthetics, has been the preference. Socialist architecture seems particularly boring the world over.

Benevolent dictatorship - mostly

The government is autocratic and unpredictable and although generally benign, it can be ruthless if it feels that the interests of the Party or China are seriously threatened. The Tiananmen massacre of June 1989 is an example of the extent to which the government will go if pressed.

The Party controls the government and currently is divided into four loose factions. The ruling group is a reformist promarket moderate one, currently led by Jiang Zemin, President of China (the heir of Deng Xiaoping who was the midwife of the reformist policies in 1978), and Zhu Rongji, the Premier. This faction is opposed by three others: a somewhat old fashioned Stalinist central planning faction who merely want to put the clock back to central planning; another group which is happy to use some market mechanism (but less than now exists) and keep some central planning; and a small rump of extreme Maoist leftists. There is no sign that any of these opposing factions have the numbers to seize power. The stance of the People's Liberation Army is crucial; so far, the generals have supported the ruling promarket faction.

Do you want to know a secret?

China is a secretive society. The Chinese have long seen information about their country and society as a matter for themselves alone. If you notice a scuffle in the street or see criminals being paraded around town on lorries with placards hanging around their necks and ask what it is about, you may be told "this is not a matter for foreigners". The tendency to secrecy is so endemic that even at universities one can find that economics books are only made available to economics students, law books to law students, and so on! Wide ranging investigation and creative thinking is actively discouraged. The problem goes back to the cultural habit of making the distinction between insiders and outsiders, which permeates the Chinese way of thinking together with a portion of control freakery. Unlike in most developed countries, the Chinese are quite used to not getting information from institutions or their government and are equally accustomed to refusing to pass information to others.

The pursuit of secrecy can be taken to extremes. One ethnic Chinese employee of a multinational oil company was arrested in 1996 for the crime of "obtaining state secrets". His company had merely asked him to find out the stage reached in the approval process for their intended project, and if there was any way of speeding up the approval![6] His efforts to do so proved too much for the Chinese authorities and he was imprisoned.

Hawking and spitting

You will encounter noisy throat clearing, often followed by enthusiastic spitting. Some locals believe that the flatter Chinese nasal system encourages sinus problems, others that the dust blowing in from the inland deserts in the north of China, and the bad air pollution of most Chinese cities, are responsible. Certainly spitting in China has a long history and spittoons are often provided (and well-used!) in many institutions, and also along some streets. Spitting is regarded as a natural body function, even if some are starting to consider it a trifle unrefined.

When you encounter it, try not to let it bother you, do not look disgusted, and never complain. Should you encounter someone breaking wind, he is probably of low class, as this is definitely considered impolite in company. The common term for it (pronounced "fang pee") is a minor swear word (fart) that street urchins might use.

Racist attitudes

It is best not to express surprise if you encounter racist attitudes; political correctness has not yet made deep inroads in China. Traditionally, the people simply saw themselves as the best and this applied to skin color too. A well known folk tale refers to God baking the first people in the oven of life: the first batch were underdone and turned out white and pasty (Occidental), the next batch were overdone and burnt black (Negro) but the third time God got it right and they came out a perfect golden brown - the Chinese.

Between white and black, white is preferred. Women from Suzhou are often regarded as the prettiest in China, in part because they are traditionally very pale skinned. You will probably observe people, women especially, holding up an umbrella or newspaper when crossing a sunny street, even for a few short yards, in order to stay as pale as possible. Sunbathing is generally not popular because it darkens the skin. Many years of Marxist propaganda against racism fell on thoroughly deaf ears.

The lure of the huge market

It is best not to expect you will be able to sell in an enormous market that will instantly earn you substantial profits. The enticement of the vast China market has been around since the middle of the Nineteenth Century when a British industrialist pondered how much more cloth could be profitably sold if each Chinese man could be persuaded to add one inch to his shirttail. The optimism resurfaced when China began to open up during the 1970s but so far it has been something of an illusion for many foreign companies. This does not only apply to Western ones: even the Japanese, who are regarded in the West as being able to understand China and adept at dealing there, have had their problems. The electronic giant Matsushita set up a joint venture to produce videocassette recorders and initially planned to sell eighty percent of them within the Chinese market, which it erroneously believed was large. Matsushita found itself unable to meet its target.[7]

It is in China's interests to promote the idea of a huge market that can quickly make you rich because it strengthens their negotiating position. As one example of many, towards the end of 1997, a Deputy Division

Chief of the People's Bank of China published an article about foreign insurance companies and their prospects in China. This was entitled "Massive market lures insurers"[8] and said "Foreign insurance companies are banging on the door of the Chinese market, lured by the huge potential for insurance business...". Shades of the Nineteenth Century shirttail beliefs....!

During the early negotiations, you might find the team opposite dangling the bait of a huge market in an attempt to make you bite. In reality, China provides a good and steadily expanding market, rather than a gigantic one. Economic growth peaked in 1992 at 14.2 percent, then drifted slowly down until the Asian financial crash of 1997 when growth fell to a decent 8.8 percent. For the near future, expansion in the range 7-10 percent seems more likely than a return to the low teens. In mid 2000, the population was estimated to be 1.262 billion and it is expected to increase to 1.6 billion by the year 2030. Despite the large numbers, the majority of the people are poor and one has to bear in mind that it needs a high disposable income to make a good market. Making money in China requires hard work and patience, as it does in most areas of the world.

Crime generally is on the increase

Embezzlement and misappropriation are frequently reported crimes. In 1998, Vice-premier Wu Bangguo told provincial officials in charge of the nation's employment and welfare system that some $987 million (8.2 billion *yuan*) had been misappropriated from pension funds for those forced into retirement from state operated enterprises (SOEs). The loss had delayed payments to over one million workers.[9]

The mammoth Three Gorges dam project has reportedly suffered from the embezzlement of $60 million from the resettlement fund of $2.1 billion although the construction fund has been spared.[10]

It must be admitted that compatriots from Hong Kong and Taiwan are often not widely liked: they have too much money, they flaunt it, and some behave in ways that insult the locals. Many Overseas Chinese have reported that antagonism towards them has increased since the mid 1990s. Local criminal gangs and robbers usually target them (as well as other locals) rather than Westerners.[11] A number of Overseas Chinese have been kidnapped and held for ransom. Where Westerners are targeted, the crime usually takes place in upmarket four and five star hotels, and robbery is usually the motive.

The increase in crime is particularly noticeable in coastal regions, especially in the south of China, but the problem can easily be overstated.

The crime rate used to be exceedingly low, the result of ruthlessly tight social control, and the recent increase still leaves China as one of the safest places in the world to visit or live.

Crime can even present opportunities for legitimate profit. Safe Car, a small Texas based company specializing in bulletproof armored vehicles, spent three years trying hard in China before receiving orders for 4,000 vehicles for the year 1997 alone. These are shipped to China in completely knocked down form and assembled locally. Richard Medlin, the President of Safe Car, anticipated that sales of up to 10,000 a year were possible: crime, it seems, does pay – especially if your business is selling things to prevent it.[12]

Human rights and the death penalty

The government has little interest in promoting human rights and regularly puts forward the view that they are a luxury that wealthier nations can afford - but not the less developed ones. China argues that it has too many immediate problems, such as housing, clothing and feeding the people, to deal with and only after the country becomes richer can human rights be moved up the agenda.

In China, unfair trials, arbitrary arrests, police brutality and torture are regularly reported by organizations such as Amnesty International. China routinely uses the death penalty for crimes, such as petty theft, smuggling, or embezzlement, that would elsewhere be regarded as minor. Amnesty's annual report for 1998 revealed that a minimum of 1,876 people were reported executed in 1997, a figure that exceeded the rest of the world combined - and felt that the true figure could well be higher.[13]

Many American companies regret these events but relatively few have taken action. The normal response is to adopt the view of former American President Coolidge that "the business of America is business",[14] not politics; most also point out that if they were to take action, it would disadvantage them against companies from Europe and elsewhere. However, a few have done something: the companies Timberland and Levi-Strauss have withdrawn from China until the human rights' situation improves. In addition, Reebok International Ltd. has made determined efforts not to buy goods produced with prison labor and has also introduced various human rights practices in its factories, including fair wages and a safe, healthy work environment. The company maintains a special interest in avoiding the exploitation of child labor.

Chapter Two: YOUR BEHAVIOR IN CHINA

The generalities

The first day

It is never a good idea to start trying to negotiate the day you arrive. You will be tired, probably jet lagged, and not fit to make serious decisions. Remember that when you are suffering from jet lag, it is easy to feel you have recovered when actually you are not yet functioning normally. In my experience a journey half way round the world needs at least four days before normality starts to return. Everyone differs in their recovery time, so you may need a bit more or a bit less. In order to succeed in China you may need to adjust some of your habitual patterns of behavior, including your negotiation tactics. If you are tired, this will be more difficult to do. Remember that if you are there with a large project to discuss, you might be negotiating for a long time, maybe up to two years (for some substantial projects it has been ten!) so that an initial short period to relax and recover costs you little and might result in net gains.

Avoid drinking the water

All tap water must be boiled before drinking. Centuries of seeing people fall sick or die after drinking unboiled water has taught the Chinese how risky the habit can be. In your hotel, water from the refrigerator or thermos flask is perfectly safe to drink; as for teeth cleaning, it is safer to use the water in the carafe in your room. I usually use tap water, but then I have lived around Asia for a long time and no doubt have a good collection of antibodies! Bottled drinking water is inexpensive and easily available, with the Laoshan brand a popular one.

You might be pestered by those wishing to practice English

Do not be surprised if strangers come up to talk to you. Many Chinese study English and want to practice with foreigners. It can be a nuisance being buttonholed in hotel lobbies by complete strangers, claiming to be teachers of English or language students, who wish to converse with you. If you have the time and patience it can be fun at first, but eventually it tends to get wearing. When it becomes too much to bear, you can politely say you have an appointment and must go. If you have a smattering of some exotic language you could try replying in that, but they will probably not believe that you do not have minimal English.

Changing money

Renminbi,[15] the local currency, can be obtained from all banks and Western hotels. The exchange rate is fixed by the state and so far does not vary, so it does not matter where you change money. Whenever the *yuan* has been overvalued, in the past a common situation, an illegal black market for foreign exchange sprang up and people on the street suggested you change money. If you are asked, it is unwise to take up the offer. It is illegal to do so, and although the rate may look attractive, it is rarely worth the risk of ruining your business prospects by being caught and arrested for petty currency fraud.

Hong Kong dollars and American dollars circulate in China, although this is not strictly legal. Credit cards have become widely accepted in Western hotels and shops in all major cities. They have not yet reached much of the interior, although this can be expected to change. If heading inland, it is wise to carry plenty of cash with you. Automatic Teller Machines have started to appear in larger cities, but you cannot yet rely on finding one.

Other requests from strangers

If a stranger asks you to do a favor, you should think very careful before agreeing. It may involve doing something that is dangerous or illegal, such as smuggling out a letter. If you do this, you might be arrested, and the issue could possibly blow up into an international incident with you at the center. If this occurs, your chances of future business must be reckoned as nonexistent.

Guard your tongue

It is a mistake to assume the people around you do not speak English and you should be careful not to engage in criticism or make jocular remarks at the expense of China. A simple joke in doubtful taste can later prove extremely embarrassing. The person next to you might suddenly address you in decent English and clearly understood what you said some time earlier. If he or she is someone with whom you might be negotiating, it could prove hard to overcome the probable hostility that you thoughtlessly created.

Better not ask about Party membership

It is not a good idea to ask if someone is a Party member; this would embarrass anyone who is not a member but would like to be, while those present who actually are members might start to wonder why you want to know such things. Could you be a member of your country's intelligence service? They will certainly report the incident and it could lead to you being carefully watched. Worse, instructions may be issued to delay the negotiations while investigations are made. The secrecy endemic to China precludes such questions, at least until you know the person well.

Bragging that you broke a rule gives offense

It is reasonably common in Western societies to socialize with business people and hear someone impishly pointing out ways they have managed to avoid or work round some rule or law. You should not boast about such things in China as it always irritates people. Rather than endearing yourself by showing you are human and possess the ability to circumnavigate restrictions, you are inadvertently destroying your own reputation. To many Chinese, it seems a dreadful thing to do and certainly something to be carefully concealed. Be particularly careful when you are out in the evening drinking and socializing when the alcohol and general ambience may cause you to drop your guard.

Kissing and cuddling

Displaying affection publicly, like kissing or cuddling, is offensive to older Chinese. Many younger ones now do such things, in part because they have no privacy at home and have to seize whatever chance they can get, but it is still a cause of scandal to the mature and elderly. If your partner is with you, it is better wait to get back to the hotel before kissing or caressing.

It would be most unwise for expatriate husbands or wives to allow themselves to become emotionally involved with a Chinese citizen. The immediate response of the authorities would be to worry about lax morals and treat it as a threat to state security. They are likely to put you the foreigner on the next flight out of China and declare you *persona non grata* into the bargain. It could prove hard to explain to your CEO exactly why you are back early and unable to return!

Photographing people

You should not try to photograph anyone without first seeking his or her permission. Northern Chinese in particular may object to being photographed, as there is a superstition that to be photographed brings sorrow in its wake. In the south it is different, and many Cantonese and boat people not only do not object to be photographed, some actually want their picture taken, especially at certain festivals when it is thought to bring good luck. Others, especially Hakkas standing around scenic spots in their picturesque wide brimmed straw hats that look like plates, may demand a small amount of money for the right to take their picture.

Buying antiques

You are advised to be careful purchasing antiques in China unless you are an expert. If an item in a state store is marked as antique it will certainly be genuine but it can be remarkably expensive. Legally you can buy only from antique shops designated for foreigners, and the antiques that you are allowed to export from China date back only to the Qing dynasty, i.e. are of relatively recent origin. In order for an antique to be exported, it must have a red sealing wax blob with its chop (a seal or signature) underneath. You can often buy the same or better items in Hong Kong or Taipei for a lower price. Again a multi-price system operates, and in ordinary shops the price of an antique might be only five or ten percent of the price set in the shops restricted to foreigners - but it lacks the sealing wax export permit. Smuggling is unwise.

Blowing your nose

Try not to blow your nose in public. The flamboyant use of a handkerchief is particularly offensive. You should never blow your nose when dining: if you must deal with the problem, you should leave the table, go to the rest room, and blow your nose quietly in private.

The doorway behavior

When arriving at a door, it is polite not to simply enter in front of someone, but hang back and let him or her go first, as you would with your CEO at home. In China, everyone does this to everyone, the idea being to allow the other person to gain face by demonstrating he or she is above you in the hierarchy. You might find you have to put up with a certain amount of jockeying for position. The Chinese are not too bad though - I have seen a group of Japanese (who take this even more seriously) standing in a group bowing to each other in front of an open elevator door until the Chinese attendant got bored and whisked the lift up empty, leaving the Japanese visitors staring at each other in baffled surprise!

Jokes are a bad idea

It is rarely a good idea to tell jokes, especially political ones. Humor does not easily cross cultural boundaries and what you find amusing will often seem totally unfunny to the Chinese. You may remember the Doonesbury cartoon where the Chinese interpreter listens to the joke the American ambassador is telling, then as a translation announces "The foreigner just told a joke, everybody laugh!" She had a lot of sense. In particular you must avoid trying to joke about China, Chinese leaders, or their government policies. Even jokey name-calling or banter among your team when no outsiders are involved is rarely seen as amusing and merely looks rude to a Chinese individual .

Never use their given ("Christian") name

It is tempting, especially if American or Australian, to start to use the Christian or given name as in these societies it suggests friendliness and informality, which can help to cement a business relationship more quickly. Never do this in China, as it would be extremely rude and actually drive a powerful wedge into the relationship. Eventually, if you get to know a Chinese person well, rather than you continuing to address him by his family name, he might ask you to use the initial letters of his two given names (as in "please after all this time you may call me 'CN'"). This is a common mode of address among close friends, but you must never use his initials until asked to do so.

Avoid "I hope you are well"

The Chinese listen carefully to what others say and analyze it, looking for subtle hidden meanings. If you say you hope they are well some of them are likely to start to wonder why you hope this and may then suspect you hope they are not well or why would you bother to mention it? If you are living in China, this use of indirect phrases and hidden meanings is similar to being engaged in permanent office politics at home. A traditional greeting that you might still hear was "have you eaten yet", reflecting the poverty of Old China, but it will rarely if ever be said to a foreigner.

Better not ask someone if they think it will rain

In rural areas of north China, to ask someone if they think it might rain could just be taken as an insult! There is an old belief that the tortoise had the gift of knowing when it was going to rain, and asking someone their opinion might make them feel akin to a tortoise. The problem is that if you call someone a tortoise, or even worse a turtle's egg, you seriously insult them (roughly "you bastard!"). It sounds far fetched, but speculating about the weather is not always a good idea!

Good manners mean being modest and unassuming

Demonstrating good manners in China often means being self-deprecating. If flattered, one must deny what was just said about you. In the West when complimented we might perhaps say "thank you", "how kind", or something of the sort when complimented and perhaps look slightly embarrassed. In China, such statements would appear extremely arrogant. The attribute must be denied. Good responses include "I do not deserve it", "Oh no, no" "You are much too kind", "I am really only a beginner", "I still have a lot to learn" and "You are very polite, but I must deny it".

Whenever someone says to you they are not good enough at doing something in their job, it is merely a polite formula and not to be believed. You should reply that they clearly are very good in that area or that their abilities are well known. This pretence is not regarded as two-faced or deceitful, the way it might be seen in some Western countries, for in Chinese culture, emotions have to be well concealed. What is said is not automatically taken to reflect reality. Good manners are distinctly separated from true feelings, and normally take precedence.

This attitude to good manners and behavior can make your job more difficult. If you are in China to sell, you face a problem that the culture demands you appear humble and not boast. At the same time, they mostly wish to buy the very best (so you have to demonstrate your product or technology is exactly that) but it is bad form to trumpet that it *is* the best! One way round this is to produce a glowing review by some third party, or perhaps display sales figures and graphs that demonstrate very good growth rates or a high ranking in the companies in your industry. If you then use deprecating words, like "some consider we are not too bad" or "we find other firms often imitate our product (or method etc.)" the Chinese will immediately understand that your product is good and yet you have avoided unseemly boasting.

May I ask you a personal question?

Be prepared to be constantly asked questions. Common questions include where you are from, how many times have you been to China, have you been to Beijing or their home city or province, can you speak any Chinese, do you like Chinese food, and can you buy it in your country? Many questions might seem extremely personal and impertinent to foreigners, for example how old are you, have you been divorced, how much did your suit cost, was your watch expensive, or what salary do you now earn? Such questions are not considered rude in China. If you are asked about salary and choose to answer, the sum will sound astronomical to most Chinese. You should point out that everything in your country costs much more than in China and it does not mean that you and people like you are incredibly rich. You could even say how lucky they are having to pay so little for things, in a polite sort of way, but do not push it hard. They know their country is a lot poorer than yours.

In simple question and answer sessions, Chinese comments may sound banal to the western ear. Statements such as "yours is a big country", or "you have come a long way", are so obviously true that they may leave you with little obvious to say. If they have asked if you are married and have children, you can return the question. If they have a son, remember to compliment them on this, as male children are preferred, but do not of course commiserate if they have a girl. The "one child" policy of the government means that many people will probably never have a son, and deep inside they may resent it keenly.

The reason for all these personal questions is that in Chinese culture they indicate a genuine interest in the other person. Asking them is an attempt to start building a friendly relationship, without which it is difficult to do business. In Western culture, it may sound intrusive and impertinent, but a Chinese person means no harm by it.

Good manners, posture and body language

Boasting, giving orders, or being condescending are all bad

Do not boast about anything, as this offends the basic tenet of good manners, to be self-deprecating. Neither should you state in a dictatorial way what must be done or has to be avoided. Instead, you can try suggesting that "we found this way to be quite useful" or "what about if we try…" as these sit much better in the culture. When passing on information or instructions it is important not to sound condescending. It is surprisingly easy to offend, when one has more knowledge and experience of an issue and has to inform someone who may be ignorant but who is certainly not stupid. Condescension is particularly offensive in China, as they may see it as smacking of racist attitudes, colonialism, or superior wealth which, given their history, patriotism and relative poverty, can upset them greatly.

Loud behavior is not a good idea

Loud extravagant behavior is considered bad manners. All noisy, flashy and unruly conduct, such as punching playfully on the arm, or boisterous, mischievous, roughhousing, is offensive. In Chinese culture, they are simply not ways of enjoying oneself. Even touching a Chinese person should be avoided, other than making a handshake.

When visiting or living in China, try to avoid holding noisy parties. If you feel you have to let off steam, do it as quietly as you can and away from the people with whom you are holding discussions. If you must drink too much, it is better to do it in the privacy of your hotel bedroom rather than in public.

If in Chinese eyes you behave badly, they are often surprisingly understanding. They are used to foreigners conducting themselves in ways that are considered bad manners, e.g., noisy drunken parties, and they will often make generous allowances for you. The cultural arrogance of believing that they are innately superior helps you here, for the Chinese simply do not expect inferior beings, such as all foreigners, to understand or be able to live up to Chinese values. As a corollary, they are usually very impressed if you do.

You should note that it is often not easy to know when you have insulted someone, as people have been trained since birth to conceal their true feelings. If a Chinese person was behaving normally and in friendly fashion but suddenly looks inscrutable and blank, you have probably hurt his or her feelings in some way.

If you manage to develop a real friendship with a Chinese man, remember to avoid what seems to you friendly banter or touching. It may seem a mark of true friendship to you but it is more likely to hurt the recipient. A deep friendship between two Chinese individuals might seem rather austere to you. The Cantonese are probably the ones who respond best to lively behavior and northerners the worst. If your friend is of the opposite sex it is even more important not to touch or pat, as it may be taken as a sexual advance.

Posture is important

The way you sit and stand is meaningful. It transmits a message about you and your attitudes that the Chinese automatically read. Particularly when talking business, think about your posture and try to sit upright in your chair. If you lounge or slump in your seat it is thought rude and uncaring and might be taken as an insult to those present. To an older traditional Chinese person, something as simple as you crossing your legs might be seen as indicating a lack of respect or true concern for what is going on. It is a good idea to watch the way the Chinese sit at meetings and copy them. Generally, they sit upright, keeping both feet together on the floor.

Putting your feet up on a low table is considered by many as rather disgusting, even if done in the privacy of your hotel room while drinking with friends.

Hands off your hips!

Do not stand with your hands on your hips. As you are usually the taller, it has the effect of making you look down your nose, so that the stance looks arrogant and condescending. Recall that it is important to avoid giving any hint of superciliousness, especially if explaining something like modern technology or how things are done in your country. On the whole, it is usually best not to try to explain how things are done elsewhere unless you are directly asked or you are deliberately using it as an indirect way of politely suggesting that something be done.

Pointing: It's thataway!

Pointing with the index finger is not felt to be a good thing in China. In olden days there was a superstitious belief that it was particularly bad to point at a rainbow because it could result in the finger being broken later. The ingrained dislike of pointing may stem from this. If you do point at someone, it will be taken as a hostile gesture, at the least a criticism and most probably as a warning.

It is important not to indicate directions with a jerk of the head, the way you might casually do at home, because this will often be perceived as a sign of scorn. Any person vaguely in line with the direction indicated could take offense, and those around will consider you ill-mannered.

Few Chinese gesture much or use their hands when speaking, unlike the Italians, so you should try to keep you hand gestures to a minimum. It is particularly important not to put your fingers in your mouth, which is a vulgar form of behavior. If you have a hangnail, tear your fingernail, or have something stuck in your teeth, you must do your best to ignore it until you are alone.

Use of the foot

Using the foot to do something that is normally done with the hand is considered bad manners. It is easy to forget this and, for example, when waiting in a line at an airport Westerners are likely to nudge their bags forward with their foot. This looks unpleasant to a well brought up Chinese. In like fashion, we might drop a pencil in the office and then use our foot to hook it within easy reach. Such careless use of the foot, instead of stooping and employing the hand, is frowned upon in China as indicating laziness or behavior more suited to an animal.

Beckoning and waving

Like many Asians, the Chinese do not beckon with the palm uppermost and finger crooked upwards, in the Western fashion. If you have to beckon, you should hold the palm down and wave the fingers towards you. The normal Western gesture is unlikely to be understood.

If you ever have to wave goodbye to someone, you should try to wave your hand side-to-side, rather than waggling the fingers up and down, in the way you probably do normally. In China, the standard western wave looks as if you are beckoning them. If you wave goodbye in the way you normally do, the person might just come back and ask you what you want!

People stand close: "Stop breathing on me!"

You might become uncomfortably aware that the Chinese tend to stand closer to you than you are accustomed to or like and you might see it as infringing your personal space. Try not to let it grate on you and when it occurs, as eventually it must, endeavour to avoid moving backward a step. If you do this, the person will usually advance to fill the gap because he or she unconsciously feels slightly remote, and then you will be forced to step back again. To anyone watching, it will look as if you are both engaged in a slow, stately dance. If you are lucky, your terpsichorean partner will not have been eating garlic or curry!

Lord, I'm tired!

Do not be surprised if you feel tired. You will experience much that is new and culture shock can be exhausting. In addition, you are often working long hours and may get sent off sightseeing between meetings, particularly if you are negotiating with government officials who may have a lot of checking back to do. Should you be unlucky enough to develop a minor infection, like the ubiquitous sore throat, your energy level will further decrease.

Some Chinese tend to think of foreigners as rather effete and physically incapable, so that it is better not to admit to being tired unless you are exhausted. It merely reinforces their prejudices and they may then start to try to use it as a weapon in negotiations, tiring you out deliberately.

Clap back if applauded

The Chinese often show appreciation of a person or group by clapping hands when they encounter them. In the culture, this gives face to the person or group. You may be welcomed to an institute such as a school, or to a meeting, in this way. When some group applauds you by clapping, do not just put on a rueful grin and nod appreciatively, as this would look arrogant. Chinese good manners dictate that you must clap back, although you do this less vigorously in a token way, and preferably with a small smile and nod of the head as an acknowledgement.

The tipping issue

Tipping is still illegal in China but in major cities it has crept into Western hotels and restaurants. A small gift that can be slipped into a pocket is often more acceptable than money, as small imported items are often unavailable and hence prized. What seems a cheap plastic or glass "novelty" item in New York, London or Sydney can still be highly esteemed in China. If present trends continue, there is little doubt that tipping will become the norm. Note that in more remote areas and inland China generally, which lags lag well behind the coastal cities, you might actually embarrass the recipient if you attempt to tip.

Safe topics of conversation

At your first meeting you will probably be asked about your trip to China and a few personal questions; in turn you can ask if they have ever been to your country and if so where, or have they always lived in Beijing or wherever you happen to be at the time. Safe topics of conversation include the weather, the size and diversity of China, Chinese scenery, China's historic landmarks, and Chinese cooking. It is also fine to discuss language and the difficulties of learning both Chinese and your own language, and compliment them upon their ability if they have spoken any of it at all.

Other safe topics are Chinese history, art and culture; the importance of the family unit; and the splendid progress that China has made towards modernization and development. You can mention all the building activity or dynamic traffic flow you noticed as you drove in from the airport (make no complaints!). Chinese medicine is also a reliable and interesting topic. It might lead you closer to developing the relationship, if for example you both have a relative suffering from rheumatism and you can compare treatments and results.

It is best not to say much about your own country, even if asked. Few Chinese seem genuinely interested in a foreign country unless they have been there or hope one day to visit. If they really want to know, they will ask you again.

At some stage you might be gently asked if you could send an English magazine to read as either the person or some relative of theirs is study-ing English. If you have any magazines with you (it is a good idea to take some), you should immediately offer to supply one at the next meeting - and remember to do so. If you do not have one with you, agree at once to organize a magazine to be sent to them. Make a note, follow it up at the first opportunity by faxing your HQ, and arranging for them to send not one but several current magazines to you by air. It is better if you hand them over personally and this small favor will go in the bank account of *guanxi* memories. This can help your negotiations, as the person involved will feel some obligation to you.

Unsafe topics of conversation

Certain topics should *not* be raised by you. These include sex or any-thing to do with it, such as prostitution or AIDS; political issues, like Tai-wan, Tibet, human rights, or the Cultural Revolution; and economic com-parisons, such as the relative wealth of your country and theirs, or any poor Chinese facilities you have encountered. You should also avoid rais-ing issues about current or recent Chinese leaders. Mao Zedong and Zhou Enlai are respected, but it is wise to avoid talking about them as you might inadvertently say the wrong thing and put everyone off. Most Chinese would prefer not to discuss a dangerous topic such as a living or recently deceased leader. Even international politics are best avoided, as again you could inadvertently cause offense here and probably never even know it.

Criticism of Chinese food, even mentioning one bad meal you have had, will be taken badly because, as in France, eating is a central part of the culture. Should you have been offered something to eat which you find totally repellent, perhaps sea slugs, snakes, pigeon heads or bears' paws, keep quiet - and do not even think of trying to make a joke about it!

The acceptance and reverence for hierarchy mean that even criticizing you own government and its policies is a bad idea. Most people will find it hard to understand that in your country you are allowed to do this or that you would even want to. In like manner, you should not criticize your own firm or colleagues, even if attempting to explain why something has gone wrong. Such criticism might shock the people opposite and rather than helping your explanation, it could cause them to wonder if they should be doing business with someone so unreliable.

The differences in the way things are done in China and West are not particularly interesting to many Chinese, are hardly worth mentioning, and may be taken as an oblique criticism, so the topic is best avoided. The one exception is modern technology and production methods, in which they often take a keen interest because you might be able to help China do better. It is information about the different social and political approaches that tends to bore them – after all, they already know their way is better!

Dangerous words and phrases

You must never refer to Taiwan as a country or say "the Republic of China", nor unthinkingly include Taiwan in a list of countries. If it must be on a list, you can perhaps call the list "countries and regions" or add it at the bottom as "and the Chinese Province of Taiwan". Likewise avoid the phrase "Communist China", "Mainland China" and "Red China", all of which will result in consternation and possibly a walkout by the Chinese side. You should avoid using the phrase "you Chinese" which sounds patronizing or even aggressive. Describing them or some group of Overseas Chinese as "Oriental", rather than "Asian", is also best avoided because some people find the word offensive. It is quite wrong to use the old-fashioned word "Chinaman" these days.

Some possible problem areas

You also serve who only stand and wait

When negotiating with government bodies, you can expect to be forced to spend much time waiting in the hotel or be sent on numerous sightseeing trips. This can be both boring and tiring.

There are many possible reasons for this, including:

- They wish you to be happy and to understand something of their past.
- Another organization has yet to contact them with a response, without which they cannot proceed to the next stage.
- You have asked for something they did not anticipate and they have to discuss it themselves and clear it with other groups.
- An essential *guanxi* contact of theirs is away and they cannot proceed

until his or her return.

- Someone above them in their organization has not yet decided what should be done, possibly because they are on holiday or out of the country and traveling in a delegation.
- They are checking abroad to see if something you told them was true.
- They are engaged in parallel negotiations with other foreign companies and those other negotiations are lagging behind yours.
- They have decided that you are impatient and they think you are likely to make more concessions if they spin things out.
- They have got wind of a possible change in government policy and are stalling until the situation is clarified.

All the possible reasons for delay mean that what in the early flush of enthusiasm might look like a straightforward proposition can take a long time to complete. Xerox Corporation spent about four years negotiating a joint venture in Shanghai to make copiers. It could have taken them even longer, but Xerox had sensibly set up a representative office in China the year before, which gained them experience and developed contacts which must have speeded things up.[16] This time span pales into insignificance when compared with Shell, which took all of ten years to gain permission to construct a petrochemical complex in Guangdong Province.[17]

Transport problems and getting about

Transport problems and bad traffic conditions abound. Most large Chinese cities have traffic difficulties, with Shanghai being the worst. Beijing is rapidly catching up and serious traffic jams are now common. Until recently, the massed ranks of bicycles were the main problem, and although there was the constant hazard of cyclists wobbling about in the road, or falling off in front of your motorcar, the situation was tolerable. The reason that people fall off at low speeds is that many people ride bicycles that are too large for them and some cannot actually reach the road with their feet, even when sitting on the cross bar. This is the penalty of having a one-size-fits-all bicycle in a family.

Since 1995, when private purchasers replaced state government and work units as the chief market for motorcars,[18] the traffic jams have become more serious. In Beijing, the authority's response has apparently been to target bicycles for extinction. Removing the painted lines that once attempted to separate bicycles from motorized traffic suggests that the authorities may be pinning their hopes on cyclists' fear, injury, or death, as a means of eradicating the problem! The hope is probably forlorn. The thought of curbing motor vehicles as a solution to the traffic jams may have crossed a few minds but if so, it has so far failed to lodge.

Taxis, relatively inexpensive and plentiful in all major cities, are often your best means of transport. Most drivers are honest, but it is wise to negotiate a price before you set off. This involves obtaining the help of a speaker of Chinese or getting the address written down by a hotel clerk, asking a probably price, and then negotiating with the cab driver probably in mime. Beijing has an excellent cab service with around 70,000 vehicles in 1998 and also possesses a good fleet of mini buses.

If traveling by bus, which is cheap but often extremely crowded, you can expect a savage scramble to board; you may have to use your superior weight and height to avoid being left behind. Once on board, you may find that attitudes abruptly change. At the bus stop, everyone was an outsider and in competition; now everyone on board is part of a clearly defined group and you are a temporary insider. You may be embarrassed to be offered a seat by some little old man or woman who looks as if they need it a lot more than you! If no one voluntarily offers you a seat, some activist type might start a small mass movement to bully someone into offering you theirs - which is even more embarrassing. Should this happen to you, it is easier to give in and take the seat, as the person who offered will lose face should you refuse. Remember that the offer of a seat came as a result of a public argument, so that a refusal by you would mean than everyone who previously argued in your favor would also lose face. Smile, nod your head all round, say thank you if you can (*xiexie*) and sit down! This is pronounced "see-hay, see-hay" and you should stress the first half, letting the second one die away.

Motorcycles, once a dangerous scourge ridden with macho bravado by young males, have become less of a problem in Beijing, as a result of a strictly enforced law of 1985 that restricted the issuance of new licenses.

Buying train tickets can be difficult, as far more people wish to travel than there are seats available. You must book in advance, and you might find that seats will not be sold until three days before your intended date of travel. When you get to the station, the line of people waiting to book can easily be several hours long. Many foreigners are seized by some official and walked to the front of the line where they are forced to jump the queue. This may seem unjust and embarrass you, but it does save you many hours' lining up. It is difficult to refuse and if you did it would cause a severe loss of face to the official concerned in full view of those waiting. In most cases, whichever host unit is responsible for you will send someone to the station do all this for you, and with any luck you will remain unaware of the difficulties involved.

There are three classes of seats: Soft Sleeper with four berth compartments and some service attached (the best and definitely the one to go for); Hard Sleeper, which is a sort of dormitory accommodation with thin padding and barely acceptable quality; and Hard Seat (the pits!) which is overcrowded, full of crates and boxes, and is strictly for backpackers on limited budgets.

With the airlines, you should be aware that flights are often canceled without warning. In some parts of China, the `plane will not fly if the weather looks bad and particularly if it starts to rain. The rumor that `planes dissolve in moisture is probably untrue but some airports behave in ways that help perpetuate it. The problem seems to have reduced in the last few years but has not yet disappeared.

You can often find that a seat previously booked by you, and later confirmed, is suddenly no longer available, so it is wise to keep checking that you still have one. Chinese airlines have at last put in a computerized system but some booking is still done by hand; if a person starts in the south to fly to somewhere in the north, the people located at an airport midway may not know how many are already on board and therefore overbook locally.

You might be able to get your reservation back if you can immediately produce documents from some important organization or person to show you have an appointment and must get there that particular day. The Confucian deference to those higher up can work for you. A rudimentary knowledge of Chinese helps here, especially if you can ingratiate yourself. Someone may well have just had you bumped off the flight because of "pull" and you should not be ashamed to try to bump someone else off in turn. I once managed to reinstate a vanished but previously confirmed seat by looking mildly exasperated and then calling the person at the desk "rice barrel" in Chinese, an insult that would normally be delivered by a four–year old to a fatter child, but adults do not normally use. The desk clerk was so delighted with this he burst out laughing, and instantly rubbed out someone's name and wrote mine in! I glanced at the list and saw that every single booking was made in pencil in order to make rubbing out easy - and there were a large number of erasers lying around....

Chinese `planes are improving but too many are still old and deteriorating and it must be admitted that the safety record is appalling. Once aboard, Western standards of service are largely unknown. Some expatriates prefer to travel by train where possible, on safety grounds, but the distances in China are great and journeys can be long and tedious.

Your clothing

A man will need a suit and tie, as the Chinese are aware that this is normal smart wear for foreigners, even if they do not always subscribe to it themselves. It will also enhance your status in this class-conscious society and can get you better or speedier treatment. If you are at a social function there may also be other foreigners present, who might well look askance if you dress in casual garb. You can take sports coats and trousers for relaxing in the evening. You will never need full evening dress, at least not yet. For a woman, trouser suits are quite acceptable, as are jumpers and skirts, but it is still better not to wear anything too revealing, sexy or ostentatious, such as furs or a lot of jewelry.

Particularly in Shanghai, you will see rich locals dressing up in such clothes, but it does not present a good image if you do it. When engaged in negotiating, it could really irritate any unreconstructed Marxists in the group, and this would certainly work to your disadvantage. This said, times have changed and many urban Chinese are very fashion conscious, so that foreigners can now wear better and more fashionable clothing although it is wise to eschew the more bizarre and extreme fashions. It will not be long, in my view, before foreigners in impressive clothing start to do better in China than those who are merely tidily dressed.

Spring and autumn visits are often the most comfortable

The best times to visit China, when you are less likely suffer from either freezing cold or excessive heat, are autumn and spring. Most of China is then at a reasonable temperature and the damper southern areas are not too wet. This is of course the time of the year when hotels are likely to be fully booked and charging the highest rates. Like so much in life, a trade-off is necessary.

But winter can be bad

China enjoys a winter monsoon, when icy cold air sweeping out of East Europe and Central Asia reduces the temperature all the way down to Hong Kong. The major cities for doing business in the northern parts include Beijing, Tianjin, Harbin, Shenyang and Jilin, and more minor ones include Xian, and Zhengzhou. In winter, they are all bitterly cold, and it is unlikely that the temperature will rise more than a few degrees above freezing from mid December to early March, although the actual starting and finishing time varies from year to year. The temperature in the nation's capital, Beijing, often lies between minus 10 degrees and plus 4 degrees Centigrade in that period, but I have been in Beijing when it was minus 22 C. The more northerly Manchurian area can get down to minus 40 degrees C, which I recall was the temperature in the permanent deep-freeze in the ice-cream factory I once worked in as a student! The wind-chill factor can make it seem even colder.

It is very dry in the north and visitors often find that their lips get sore and crack easily. In winter you will need lip salve. Around Beijing, in the late winter and spring, dust storms are common and unpleasant, as the wind picks up sand from the desert. Many people wear masks to avoid breathing in the dust, although some of the mask wearers you see may simply have a cold, or are hoping to avoid contracting one from someone else.

Winter further south is often damp and unpleasant but not really cold; rainproof outer clothing is a good idea. In the really deep south, winter can be very pleasant, as the normal, disagreeably sticky weather disappears for a time. On rare occasions it can get surprisingly cold, with over-coats needed in parts of the province of Guangdong, where it has even been known to snow.

In winter you will need to take warm clothing

You will need to take warm woolen clothing for winter, including "long johns" and warm vests. Pantsuits are totally acceptable for Western women, which allows you to wear long johns, as Chinese women do. In the center and north, it is certainly cold outside - but it can be far worse inside. Your hotel will be warm, maybe too warm, but the heating in houses and work places is often totally inadequate or even nonexistent. Surprisingly, you can actually be colder inside buildings in the middle of China than in the north, as regulations restrict the heating of buildings south of the Yangtze River. With magnificent disregard of climate, on April 15 all furnaces for heating public buildings are turned off and not turned back on until November 15, whatever the weather! If the far north is your destination, you are advised not go at all in winter if possible because of the bitter cold.

Summer ills

In summer, the north is hot and dry, and the temperature may reach 40 degrees C. As a consequence of having a continental climate, the hottest part of China is not, as might be expected in the Deep South, but about half way up, and inland from Shanghai. Wuhan, in the middle Yangtze River region, has a summer temperature higher than Guangdong in the south and is sometimes referred to as a furnace.

The south is hot and humid because of the summer monsoon. This sweeps hot humid air from the tropics up the coastal provinces, and it can penetrate a good distance inland. At this time of the year, the south is generally hot, sticky, and unpleasant, and those unused to it will find it exhausting. Temperatures of 38 degrees with high humidity take their toll. At this time of the year, it frequently rains steadily. Along the southeast coast, typhoons can be a problem in summer; on average there are around five a year, and airline flights cease when a typhoon is approaching. Even the Star Ferry in Hong Kong closes when a typhoon gets close enough.

Wherever you intend to visit in summer, you need to wear lightweight cotton garments that breathe easily and you should take enough with you to change your clothes frequently.

The clothing you can buy will probably not fit

Although larger sizes have begun to appear, unless you are a small person, it is unlikely that you will be able to find much suitable clothing you can buy. Chinese people on average are smaller than occidentals, local production is geared to them, and not many large sizes are available. If you are larger than average Western size, you can spend a lot of time looking and still fail. Buying shoes can be particularly difficult; save time and start by asking if they have *anything* at all that would fit your feet.

If you find clothes in China that will fit, you will probably still be disappointed despite them being inexpensive. What you can buy is frequently of poor design and often ugly, the colors are limited, the designs are relatively basic, and garments tend to fall apart quickly. With the influx of a few quality Western luxury suppliers in recent years, the situation has improved, but much locally made produce is still well below Western standards.

Lengths of material are a much better buy: silk in particular is worth purchasing. If living in China, you can get such material made up cheaply, but you should take a garment for them to copy or at least a good picture so that they can see what you want made. As they measure you, it is wise to indicate that you would like the waist tighter, or the trouser legs narrower or flared, as the case may be, to avoid a dreary result. Their natural instinct it to make the garment to look like the unexciting clothing of the masses you see around you.

You will see badly dressed people

You should not be surprised if some of the Chinese you see are badly dressed. There are reasons for this. First, China is a poor country and many, especially the peasants and the itinerant workers, have little money to spend on clothing. Secondly, until the end of Maoism in the mid 1970s, it was dangerous for an individual to stand out. Indulging in different or high quality clothing could be seen as indicating capitalist tendencies, for which one could be severely punished, or perhaps even killed. Thirdly, cut off as China was for so many years from the world and the idea of fashion, many Chinese were simply unaware of and uninterested in clothing fashions or styles, and some still dress in ways that look crude or unkempt to foreign business people. Their clothes may be ill fitting and display a complete disregard for color matching.

Among the younger and more yuppie-like Chinese, especially those making large sums of money in the new market sector, smart is highly desirable. Conspicuous consumption is the norm and there is a need to wear the latest Western styles. The younger people can be very brand conscious in clothing, accessories and household goods. They will often ask for a product by brand name, for example specifying a *Carrier* air conditioner. Designer labels are often flaunted; you might see someone wearing imported sunglasses with the brand name still stuck on the lens, partially obscuring vision.

Try to forget your Western experience that says important people dress well - the scruffy individual in the corner can easily be the most powerful present, while the best dressed person in the room may be a young trainee with stylish pretensions and no power at all.

Hey, they're staring at me!

Do not be surprised if someone stares or points at you. Many people who live in the big cities such as Beijing, Shanghai, Tianjin and Guangzhou are used to seeing foreigners. Even there, those living in outlying suburbs where foreigners do not often penetrate, or any recent arrivals from rural China (where foreigners are either a rarity or unknown), may find you a fascinating sight. If you wander away from the central areas of a city, you might find a crowd gathers or children follow you. Do not be disconcerted for there is no malevolence involved and Chinese cities are generally safe places.

Do not be tempted to smuggle

Despite the high tariffs on many imported goods, it would be foolhardy in the extreme to attempt to smuggle things into China. Generally, the authorities take a dim view of drugs, pornography and weapons, but can be heavy handed in their response to any smuggling offense. In extreme cases, the death penalty is meted out for serious offenses, and not only for drugs. Foreigners have been warned that this penalty will also apply to them and in 1998 a Hong Kong businessman was executed.[19]

Do not be afraid of making mistakes

If you get business or social etiquette wrong, it is often less important than you might think. The Chinese rather expect you as a barbarian to do peculiar things and can easily forgive you for being a foreigner and not knowing better. If you are constantly worried about behaving properly it will impact adversely on your negotiating power, so try to relax.

Chapter Three: STARTING THE BUSINESS PROCESS

What do you want to do there?

You need to be clear in your mind what it is you wish to do in China. The main forms of business dealing consist of:

- Straight buying or selling.
- Licensing technology or equipment.
- Compensation trade, where you accept goods, often from the machinery you sell, instead of money.
- Equity joint venture (profits distributed according to capital contributed).
- Cooperative or contract joint venture (profits distributed according to the terms of the contract).
- Wholly owned foreign enterprise (buy out an existing firm or set up from scratch).
- A representative office - this is the most common form of foreign business in China.

Representative offices are simply liaison offices and technically are not allowed to undertake business in their own right. Many in fact do so. In 1998, Shanghai ordered the closure of 194 such offices for behaving illegally. In most cases, the crime would not seem serious to international business people: many had simply forgotten to renew their permits to operate. Others had been involved in negotiating and signing contracts, which is technically illegal but often done. The US chemical giant Dupont was one of the companies at fault but strongly denied any wrongdoing, claiming a mistake had been made.[20]

Approaching China

Starting off

It is best to make the initial contact by mail. The China Council for Promotion of International Trade (CCPIT) is a good starting place and they can ensure you get off on the right track. The Chinese Embassy in your country is another useful place and you can ask them to introduce you to a suitable Foreign Trade Corporation or Ministry, or recommend a reliable private company. You should also approach your embassy in Beijing as it has, or should have, experience, contacts and *guanxi*. The staff can call on their special personal relationships to gain you access to better levels or individuals than you could manage on your own.

The proposal itself should include more than you would normally send in the West. You might send a complete description of your firm, including its history, share of the market, a recent profit and loss statement or annual report, the ownership profile, and the director list. You should also include a detailed description of the product and much technical information to indicate its high quality and performance. It is better to send a mass of information on a few main products that you have to sell, or wish to buy, rather than skimpy information on many products. If you send information about many products, some will probably come under the auspices of different Chinese institutions. Consequently, it will not be clear to the initial recipient where exactly to send the information and it is tempting simply to bin it and ignore.

In your initial approach, you are trying to convince the Chinese that you are worth dealing with and are not someone who will let them down or try to rob them. There is still suspicion about Western firms in China that you have to overcome. It is a good idea to send references and, if you can, a copy of a magazine or newspaper article about your firm. You should specify exactly what you wish to do, e.g., sell a good, license some technology, or buy a particular item; you should also clearly state the sort of business arrangement you are interested in discussing, as well as make a suggestion as to where and when you might like to meet in China.

Generally, you should try to put forward the strongest credentials you can, because the higher they assess your ranking as a company, the more that will be done for you, and the more important people you can see. These VIPs can then pass the word down the line that you should be helped.

The letter itself must be translated into Chinese as well as being sent in English, but the rest of the material can be in English if you cannot get a translation done, although a translation is highly desirable. This must be in modern Chinese, using simplified characters, and avoiding archaic expressions or any vocabulary or expressions associated specifically with Taiwan or Southeast Asia. It is far easier to jump the first hurdle and get someone interested in you and your product if the first people you approach can read about you immediately in their own language. It also shows you are taking the proposal seriously and working hard at it. Do send multiple copies of your initial proposal package, twenty or so is not too many, so that it can be considered quickly by several people at once and not be unnecessarily delayed. Copying machines can be scarce in Chinese institutions.

If you can find a suitable agent or intermediary then it is best to go through them. The use of intermediaries as opposed to a direct approach has a long history in China, including the very personal area of finding a suitable marriage partner, and if you come recommended by someone known to the firm, you will be taken more seriously.

Your delegation list

Once you have a visit agreed, you should chose your delegation carefully (see "Your team", p.66) and send a list of their names to the Chinese side. Ensure that the leader's name comes first and if you can manage a rough "pecking order" of importance rather than an alphabetical listing it can speed up the negotiations. Alongside each name should appear their title, any honors or degrees they have been awarded, and possibly a short job description. Not only do you need to impress the Chinese side with the quality of your team, they will spend a lot of time evaluating your delegation for relative power, and the easier you make it for them, the faster they can get through that stage and get down to business. This saves you time and money.

If you ask for and get a detailed list from the Chinese side, it may give you clues about how serious they are. If they have a leader who looks less significant than yours, it might indicate they are not terribly serious, but if s/he looks powerful, it can be a healthy sign.

The letter black hole

It is useful to ask for an acknowledgement of your letter whenever you write to anyone for the first time. It is common for Chinese not to respond to letters, particularly from someone they do not personally know. Many Chinese feel no obligation towards strangers who are not considered to be "insiders" or part of their network. This lack of response does not have the feeling of rudeness that would accompany such action in the West. You should be aware, however, that a lack of reply often means "no". If you go through a respected intermediary it normally means you can be guaranteed a reply.

Send your material early

If you send your material well in advance, it gives the Chinese time to decide which institutions should be represented at the meetings you will have. Time is needed for each of the different organizations to make the most suitable people available. The team you will meet usually prepares the questions and position in advance, clearing them with others in the bureaucracy, which again can be a lengthy process. If you do not allow them enough time to do all this, they will either not bother with you (because they are aware that they could not possibly meet your suggested deadline) or else make you wait.

Preparatory homework can help you a lot and save you time

Before you visit China for the first time, you would benefit greatly from reading and learning something about Chinese history and culture. It can pay off handsomely in building trust and friendship. During the negotiations, you might hear mention of a certain dynasty or individual from history, and it impresses the other side if you can demonstrate knowledge of when this was, who they were, and what the allusion means. If you wait until you get to China to start learning about it, you are likely to find the lessons you learn there are the hard ones of experience, and the fruit of getting it wrong can be sour.

It would be a good idea for another person in your home office to go through this preliminary learning and training process with you. If you are the only one in the company that understands the culture and business practices, then once you are in China you are likely to find that the people in HQ will not understand what is happening and why there seem to be constant delays. They might eventually start to wonder if you have gone native and are starting to represent the views of the Chinese more that that of your company. Friction with HQ is to be avoided while you are involved in detailed negotiations; things are hard enough in China without that!

Take masses of technical information with you

If selling or looking to establish a joint venture, you should take a great deal of detailed information with you about your product, for example, how it is actually made, what are the tolerances, what is the breaking strain, what is its expected life, or whatever data best fits your particular product. If you have previously sold to or invested in another country, a detailed history of what happened, what problems you faced, how you tackled them, and what were the results can impress and make your task easier. You need lots of statistics, tables, graphs and overhead transparencies, to be really effective. At some point in the negotiations, you should be able to offer them an example of how it could work in China. Although computer technology allows for color printing and impressive slides, the materials may be better done in black and white. There are so many superstitions connected with different colors, that it is easy to give unwanted messages and unintentionally amuse the audience by the inappropriate use of a certain color in a certain place, or mix two colors in a way that may have unpleasant connotations.

Your team

It is always a team game

It is a bad idea to send a lone person to negotiate however good he or she may be. The individual will forfeit respect, since traditionally a leader does not engage in nuts-and-bolts negotiating, and needs a coterie of flunkies and advisors. One person would also be heavily outnumbered which can be very tiring. He or she is unlikely to be able to cope fully with all the questions that will be asked, and some of them will be highly technical. Eventually the person could easily become exhausted, especially as they have no one with whom to relax in the evening.

If yours is a small company then a team of two would be the absolute minimum; a large international company might send up to a dozen people; around five or six might be suitable for other companies (see "The composition of your team", p.68 for the various functional areas that might be covered).

A good leader is essential

Your group needs a strong, identifiable leader. On all documents you send that include a list of your team members, do put the leader's name first and bracket "Leader" after it; even better, you can make the first heading "Team Leader" with his or her name, then have a heading "Team Members" with their names. The Chinese will probably understand the order of names as representing their actual power positions, rather than being random or alphabetical.

Your leader should preferably be an experienced, older person with expertise, and a friendly and sensitive type but possessing dignity. Such a leader fits in with the hierarchical nature of the society and your choice of a suitable person reassures them, shows you are serious in intent, and are probably committed to a long-term presence.

Women as leaders

You can safely send a woman to lead the team, as the Chinese regard your foreign-ness as much more significant than your gender. This is a distinct contrast to Japan and many Middle Eastern countries.

Bad attitudes

It would be unwise to send anyone who is likely to be heavy-handed, arrogant, impatient, rigid, tense, racist, aloof, or simply loud. These are not desirable traits for business success in many countries but they are the complete antithesis of what works well in China. What you need are sensitive people, who get along with foreigners; they should be warm and outgoing but in a quiet way. Flexibility in approach and good reserves of energy are desirable.

Youth is not an asset

Age is revered in China. Confucius felt that under the age of thirty, a man was not properly mature. This view is still accepted by many in China and any one younger than that is not really taken seriously in business or politics. Status in China is also connected with age and possessing grey hair is a definite plus. A middle-aged foreigner who is active and who has a grey beard will be esteemed both for age (the beard color means the Chinese will assume he is ancient) and the energy he displays. Some years ago, I traveled round China with the Australian Ambassador of the day who fitted that description quite well. As soon as he had boarded the train and departed for Hong Kong, the interpreter told me how impressed she was that such an old man could work so hard without flagging. I asked how old she thought he was and was told probably around sixty-five. He was actually forty-three but his beard *was* very grey!

Physical appearance can harm your cause

In Chinese theater and film, there is a traditional way of representing an insincere foreign villain. In an old American B grade cowboy movie, he is the mustachioed evil banker in a black hat – the one who menaces the heroine by threatening to foreclose on the farm but gets his comeuppance in the final reel. In China, the stereotype foreign villains have long wavy hair and a mustache; as soon as he appears we all know who he is without having to be told. Beijing Opera operates on similar principles, with many of its stock characters using makeup and accessories such as fans to symbolize the character and denote their personality. If at all possible, avoid sending someone with wavy hair and a mustache on the team, and definitely he should not be the leader. If your best person happens to look like that, try to talk them into shaving their lip for the trip - it will grow back faster than lost business will!

Another stock character that can put the Chinese off, is anyone with a hawk like nose and thin eyebrows. Their appearance immediately suggests they are cunning liars with a treacherous disposition. Trust can be hard to build up, especially if the other side sees you as the spitting image of a diabolical pirate! There is little you can do except not send them; a nose job is clearly out of the question.

The composition of your team

The choice of whom you take depends both on the size of your company and what you want to do in China. In addition to the leader you will probably need on the team:

- One or more engineers or high grade technicians.
- One or more sales representatives.
- A financial person.
- Maybe a lawyer (especially if planning to invest).
- Someone to take detailed notes.
- An interpreter (can be hired locally).

If selling machinery or technology, the engineers and technicians are crucial, as you will face many detailed questions, far beyond the ability of nonspecialists to answer fully. For example, Rolligon Corporation, a Houston company specializing in rough terrain vehicles, rapidly discovered that their negotiator had underestimated the interest in detailed questions and had brought far too little technical information with him.[21]

If buying machinery you need someone on your team who is familiar with the manufacturing process and not just the market in your country. One small importer of equipment for the sand and gravel industry failed to do this and paid a heavy price. Without technical expertise, the team purchased apparently attractive but actually poorly made equipment, which quickly broke down when used in America. After putting in all the effort of purchasing and importing, the company eventually decided to compensate its customers for the poor machines, which offset all the advantages of buying more cheaply from China.[22]

The skills needed on your team vary with what you hope to do but you are likely to find the following crucial:

- In first place come technical business knowledge and skills. Without these, you are wasting your time and money from the start.
- The second need is a strong awareness of Chinese history and culture. This means both sensitivity and the background to develop the rela-

tionship quickly.

- Finally, fluent language ability. At least one person on the team should be fluent in Chinese, in order to check on the interpreter and monitor what their team are saying. This ensures your side understands exactly what it going on. After every session, this person can explain to the whole team what just happened, what they might have missed, why the Chinese reacted as they did, or the reason they raised an issue in a certain way. This helps to close the cultural gap.

These three points are "best practice"; if for reasons of finance you have to drop one of them, the language factor is perhaps the most dispensable.

Keep your team together

It might seem an efficient way of proceeding to separate your group and let individuals do different things, e.g., the engineers can look at machinery while the financial wizard talks to the accountants. Such a suggestion would confuse and alarm the Chinese, who always view a group as a unit having a common interest and a single voice that is expressed through the leader.

The group should not only keep together, it should also avoid openly arguing. If you wish to discuss what should be done next, it is best to ask for an adjournment and retire to do it in private. If you are going to argue, it must be done outside the negotiating chamber; publicly you should aim to present a united front.

Try to keep the same team

When revisiting China, try not to change members of your team. The Chinese wish to see you as "old friends" and a new member of the team conflicts with this need of theirs. In practical terms, it might slow down negotiations should the Chinese elect to delay things in order to get to know the new person, whom they will not automatically trust. Similarly, in long drawn out negotiations, it is best not to withdraw someone and replace them. The other side will certainly wonder what you are up to, discuss it in private, report it up, and generally worry about what is going on. Their customary tactic is then to delay things and watch carefully to see what you are up to.

The Overseas Chinese issue

It is often desirable to have an Overseas Chinese as part of your team,

Kevin Bucknall

as he or she will be more culturally aware, help to avoid mistakes for your side, and can understand what is being said. Check first that they are fluent in the Mandarin dialect. It is vital that you do not rely upon them to translate, as translators are not regarded as a part of the team by the Chinese, and it would sharply reduce the status of the Overseas Chinese member. Both the individual concerned and the Chinese team will be aware of this.

A major advantage of having an Overseas Chinese on the team is that the Chinese will often approach him or her outside the meetings, and explain what they really wanted or meant in the earlier session, or sound him or her out about issues and "fly kites" about new proposals. This can be extremely useful and speed up negotiations. It is part of the preferred indirect approach and seeking of harmony rather than confrontation. They are unlikely to approach non-Chinese members of your delegation in the same way. An Overseas Chinese can also check on reactions and feelings by watching their body language. Chinese body language is different from Western, so that *you* are unlikely to be able to judge what it means. Almost nothing you learned on courses or from books about selling and body language in your society applies outside the Western cultural framework, so that it is easy to misunderstand and make mistakes.

You should note, however, that Overseas Chinese carry a particular burden. Although able to speak the language and being familiar with the culture, they may know little or nothing about the Chinese economy and structural or institutional networks. As a consequence, it can be dangerous to assume automatically that their views are inevitably correct. It is also common to find that in the beginning, you and your team place great reliance on their every utterance; later, when the other team members have learned more, the opinions of the Overseas Chinese person may be regarded with less admiration. This causes a loss of face to the Overseas Chinese and places stress on them. Another problem is that if he or she has family in China, as is common, they will expect him or her to help them. This usually involves going to see them and taking gifts. If at a later stage you place the Overseas Chinese permanently in China, for instance as a manager in a joint venture, the expectations of the family will grow and the demands widen, e.g., they will ask for jobs. It can place the Overseas Chinese in a difficult or impossible position.

Things you need to know

Are these the right people?

Shortly after you arrive, it is worth checking that you are dealing with the appropriate organization. China is a large country and is in the process of altering from a centrally-planned to a market system. Change is the order of the day and it is not always clear what suitable organizations exist and which is the most advantageous unit to which one should talk. Once there was a handful of Foreign Trade Corporations and that was all. Now there is a plethora of organizations at provincial and municipal level, and a variety of private bodies, as well as geographical areas like Special Economic Zones (SEZs) and Free Trade Areas. This is where the CCPIT, embassy and your liaison officer should be of assistance. Do not ignore the opinions and advice of expatriate business people in the area who have both experience and local knowledge that could help you avoid a major mistake.

If some apparently suitable factory approaches you to do business, it just might be under the control of the wrong Ministry or be unable to obtain essential materials when required. You need to check carefully. If you choose to go with the wrong partner, you can get badly burned.

The sheer speed of change can also complicate things. What might have seemed a good potential partner last year may suddenly have become totally undesirable. A new piece of legislation may have changed the economic scene or some new and better company may have come into existence. Even if you decide that the original one is still better, you need to think about the newcomer. Will he be a strong rival? Has he perhaps filled the niche market you spotted and there is now little or no room for you? Might it be better to move the project to another geographical part of the country?

Telephones are getting better

In the remoter parts of China, using the telephone is often difficult: lines are usually of poor quality and operators unhelpful. In the larger cities, things have improved substantially, and direct dialing is now possible in the modern hotels.

When you want to call a Chinese colleague or contact, it is a big help if you have the person's direct desk number. If you have to go through a switchboard, you might find that the person at the other end has a tendency to shout rather than speak in a normal voice, so that a truly private telephone call is not always possible. The person answering the telephone may seem less than helpful, almost like a gatekeeper with instructions to keep out undesirables. You may be interrogated as to why you wish to speak to a particular person; clearly there is little intention of putting you through unless satisfactory answers are received. If you are able to leave a message, and many gate keepers will simply refuse to take one, it might eventually get to the right person but in too many cases it simply seems to languish around a desk or even be thrown out. You are a victim of being an "outsider" trying to get inside, and the person answering the telephone may feel no obligation to help you in any way, even by passing on a message.

In some parts of China, and in some hotels, you might find yourself cut off in mid call. You are advised to fax if possible, as this method gets around the gate keeper mentality. All offices now seem to have a fax machine.

If you meet someone whom you think you might wish to contact in the future, you should take down their telephone and fax numbers. If you do not do this, you may find it next to impossible to work your way through the bureaucracy and find them. There is a general attitude of secrecy about information including telephone numbers, so switchboards are often unhelpful when you are trying to reach someone. You might also find the person answering merely says hello, ("wei") and refuses to state the name of the organization even when you ask! The "gate keeper" might reluctantly reveal the firm's name if you ask (correctly) if it is the so-and-so company, but might not be willing identify the unit otherwise. You should state the name of your company, rather than your personal name, as this often gets more respect. Be prepared to explain why you are calling, and what you want to discuss, rather than expect merely to be put through. If you keep hearing the word "wei", do not worry. It is repeated often during telephone calls, as a way of ensuring you are still there (not unreasonably in view of the dropped connections caused by poor equipment), but it is also used simply to fill any gaps in the conversation.

Choosing a good name

It is important to select a good Chinese name for yourself and product. Names are very symbolic to the Chinese, and company names such as "Happy something", "Delightful something" or "Prosperity something" are quite common. You cannot change the name of your company to suit Chinese culture, but you can ensure that the actual Chinese characters you choose mean something nice and attractive, rather than neutral or even actively repellent. Imagine the amusement in your country if you found a foreign company called "Fly-by-Night Removals" or "Sewage Ice Cream" and you will appreciate how things can go wrong. Prudential insurance cleverly selected *Pu Tian Shou* or "Long life for everyone under the sky" for its Chinese name.[23] Coca Cola is probably the best known of the extremely well chosen names: in Chinese, it loosely means "Tastes nice and makes you happy".

Some companies manage well by using their initials and not worrying about a translation. ITT kept its initials as its Chinese name; IBM on the other hand first tried out a cumbersome Chinese name, found it messy, quietly dropped it, and successfully went with "IBM".[24]

In similar fashion, your personal name should be attractive when put into Chinese characters. For a man, something that sounds bold and successful is good; for a woman something that sounds beautiful and perhaps flowery fits well. My name, chosen for me by a Chinese colleague, translates as "Mr. White who overcomes majestic power"; so far, this has failed to have prophetic value! When offered what seems to be good choice for a name in Chinese, it is a good idea to check that there are no really unpleasant or downright dirty homonym phrases for the particular characters selected. If the sound of your name can also mean something like "Goes to the lavatory often" or "Big belly", it can be guaranteed to make you the butt of jokes behind your back. Being a tonal language with relatively few different sounds in it, searching for homonyms with funny meanings provides a traditional form of amusement.

You need a liaison officer!

You will find it really useful to have a liaison officer or helpmate resident in China, who should preferably be Chinese not a foreigner. The person must be someone who knows the ropes and has many contacts in positions of authority. This individual can help you see the right people, choose the most appropriate company to deal with, check up on the interpreter's ability, keep you informed about any private discussions in Chinese within the opposite team and perhaps spot body language signals that you would not understand. Your liaison officer can read over documents before you sign them to ensure they are satisfactory. As a local resident, the liaison officer can also look out for your interests after you have left China. There are firms that specialize in such work and for an up to date list contact your embassy and the CCPIT.

When first looking for a liaison officer, it is important not to accept at face value any claims by a person to be a representative of the government, related to important local officials, or possessing fantastic contacts. Always check up on anyone who approaches you. They might turn out to be genuine, but they may simply be individuals with little to offer who are touting for business; some could be con artists intent on ripping you off.

Once negotiations are well advanced, you might feel you could dispense with your liaison officer. This is not the case; if you drop him, the people with whom you are still negotiating will immediately see you as essentially disloyal and therefore probably not to be trusted. If you have on-going business, keep him! Your liaison officer can also be useful to act as an intermediary if anything goes wrong and you have to communicate some painful information to your counterpart. The Chinese prefer the indirectness of an intermediary, as it avoids a confrontation and probable loss of face for someone.

There will be someone on their team who acts as the contact point for you. You should establish early who this will be and get his or her work address and telephone number, a mobile telephone number if possible, and the office fax number.

Business cards

It is most important to have your business card in both English and Chinese; you should ensure that it contains all your job titles within the company, any awards you may have earned such as academic degrees, or any honors you may have been granted. The business associations of which you are a member can also usefully appear. The greater the string of letters after your name, the more impressive you will appear and the more help you can expect. The cards can be printed in Hong Kong quickly and inexpensively, but you should take an example with you, in modern simplified characters, which can quickly be copied. In many Western countries you can get such cards printed but they will usually be more expensive.

If your company is particularly important in some way, for instance it is the oldest or the largest in that industry, appears in some listing of major companies, or perhaps won some local, national or international award, this could usefully go on the business card. This sort of thing impresses all that read it – and everyone studies business cards carefully, searching for just such information. If the name of your company appears in gold, this is particularly impressive, for gold represents prosperity. This might be overkill for ordinary business contacts of course.

It is useful to write your hotel name and room number on your card before you present it, so that the person can easily contact you later. Prepare your cards in advance, in your hotel room, and do not underestimate the number you will need. Each individual in the Chinese team should receive one. If you find yourself running low during the day, at the very least make sure that the leader of the group gets a card, smile and apologize to the lower ranking members, and make sure you stock up well for the morrow.

Nice guys finish first

Those in the delegation should preferably be warm, friendly, flexible, tactful, and sensitive types. This is of course desirable whatever foreign country you are visiting, but Asian societies with their different social rules and special sensitivity to what is *not* said, require particularly delicate treatment for success. Sincere friendliness is needed and you cannot fake it; the Chinese are adept at recognizing false emotions as they have a lifetime of experience of deciphering concealed ones. Flexible attitudes, patience, not becoming irritated or losing one's temper, and the energy to cope with a long working week while under stress, are desirable.

You should try to send someone who can either hold their liquor well, which can be most useful at Chinese banquets when the toasting begins, or at the other extreme a teetotaler. The latter is acceptable, as many Chinese do not drink and others may turn bright red with even a small amount of alcohol inside them. This embarrasses them and they feel a loss of face, so they prefer to avoid alcohol completely. The Chinese usually understand if you plead an allergy and ask for a soft drink.

Learn a few words of Chinese

If you can manage to learn a few greeting phrases, such as *ni hao* (pronounced "knee how?" meaning "how do you do? or "how are you?"); *zenme yang* (pronounced "zummer yang" meaning "how's it going?") may come in useful. This latter should only to be used when you are definitely friends rather than merely colleagues, as it is a bit slangy. If the person you are greeting is really exalted "*nin hao*" is more polite than *nihao*. Saying "thank you" is also a good idea: *xiexie* ("see-hay, see-hay").

If you are a visitor, the Chinese do not yet expect you to speak the language, but they will appreciate your attempt at a few words. A relationship develops more quickly if you demonstrate you are making an effort to learn even a small amount about their culture and language. If you intend to live in China then you *have* to learn to speak some of the language, partly to survive on the street, but also because of the respect you will earn.

Listen to how they pronounce the phrase, as Chinese is a tonal language and to be understood you need to imitate the correct sound, not just learn syllables from a list. In my early days, I once tried to order an omelette in Cantonese and realized something was wrong when the waiter, stifling a smile muttered "excuse me" and raced off into the kitchen. A few seconds later, guffaws of laughter spilled out through the batwing door. When he returned and I asked him what my mangled pronunciation had meant, he was reluctant to say, but finally admitted that I had ordered "an omelette made from, er, umm, a lady's undergarments"! Those tones will get you into trouble sooner or later!!

Business is a personal matter

Remember that face-to-face negotiations are essential. Little or nothing can be accomplished by mail or fax. A letter may not be answered and the telephone is often a source of irritation rather than a convenience. As rumors persist of telephones being bugged or operators listening to calls, you might feel that private information is better transmitted face-to-face in any case. It must be admitted however that it can sometimes be difficult to arrange to meet a particular person (see Table 3.1, p.76, for various possible reasons and suggested solutions).

Be calm and poised at all times

Try to be poised, self-controlled, and use "soft sell" tactics. The Chinese feel that venting frustrations in public, or displaying extreme emotion, is childish and thoroughly bad mannered. They tend to have little confidence in anyone doing this and may not wish to work with him or her. Self-discipline, reserve and calmness reap rewards. The Chinese often use the analogy of the bamboo bending in a gale and surviving unscathed, but a rigid powerful tree like an oak snapping and falling. To succeed, you should bend with the wind not fight it furiously.

Table 3.1 Possible reasons why you cannot get to meet someone

POSSIBLE PROBLEMS	POSSIBLE SOLUTIONS
They do not know you and feel no obligation to see you.	Use a go-between or letter of introduction.
They have an extremely busy schedule.	Ask earlier. Ask someone above them to pass the word down to see you.
The person, or an important individual involved, is ill.	You will have to wait.

The person, or an important individual involved, is out of town or abroad	You will have to wait.
Some meeting has to be arranged and a decision made before you can be seen.	You will have to wait.
You have not supplied enough information about your company or product.	Send masses of detailed information early on.

Foreign service trades must manufacture in China

The law currently insists that if you are engaged in a service trade such as repair and maintenance, it can only be done if you produce the goods in China. The reason is that the authorities wish to attract manufacturing facilities that export some or all of their product, and not service firms. This keeps foreign companies out of the distribution system, although a few have been allowed into retailing under a special dispensation. Impatient local governments have acted to approve retail stores, and although technically illegal, this is by far the easiest route to entry if this is your interest. Buying into an existing Chinese firm is another way of getting in.

Other avenues to retailing include the indirect routes of factory outlet stores, TV and mail order sales, management contracts, counter rentals, consignment sales and direct sales.[25] In 1998, direct selling was suddenly prohibited, but after some confusion, it transpired that banning pyramid selling was the real aim of the sloppily written new rule. Yet respectable direct sellers suffered from the ban. Avon, a traditional direct seller of cosmetics, was forced to cancel its normal door-to-door business using agents, and establish a retail chain. According to John Gregory, Vice-President of Marketing with Avon Products (Guangzhou) Company Ltd., the lack of experience in this area meant that the switch over was both slow and difficult so that total sales fell off. Other direct sellers hurt by the sudden change in rules were the American companies Amway Corp., Sarah Lee Corp., and Mary Kay Cosmetics.[26]

The first steps have been taken to allow foreign insurance and banking companies, but only under heavy restrictions. Twenty-three cities and Hainan Island have allowed foreign banks to set up branches, but only the Pudong area of Shanghai has allowed *renminbi* business and there it is on a trial basis. Foreign insurance companies have so far been approved in Shanghai and Guangzhou only.[27] Things will probably gradually relax and it is expected that foreigners will be allowed into the tourist agency business and internet service providers before long.

They meet you in and send you off

You can expect to be met at the airport and at any organization you visit. This is normal behavior for the Chinese, and after being met, you will be escorted to where you are supposed to go. The host need not be on the steps to meet you in person, but a representative must be there. As the Chinese are status and hierarchical conscious, you can often judge how well your visit went by the rank of the person involved. The level of the person meeting you shows how they rate you; the level of the person seeing you off is an indication of how well the visit went. If the one who met you in later sees you off, or even better if someone of higher rank does so, then you have done well; if someone more junior sees you off, then your mission might have to be rated as not very successful.

July is the cruelest month

For ancient superstitious reasons, some Chinese believe that no important decisions should be taken in the month of July. This means of course that if possible you should avoid going to negotiate at that time. It is extremely hot and humid in large parts of coastal China then anyway, and there is a danger of typhoons along the southeast coast including Hong Kong.

Chapter Four: MEETINGS AND NEGOTIATIONS: GENERALITIES

The meeting room

At a Ministry or factory, you can expect to be shown to a special room that is kept solely for meetings. In the occasional new building it might be different but typically it is rather warm, furnished with soft old-fashioned sofas and chairs, and has a meeting table with hard chairs around it. It strongly resembles a period piece from a film set and is far superior to the rooms in which the Chinese actually work. These are so Spartan and poorly equipped that it is essential to have the special meeting rooms for entertaining visitors, especially foreigners. It is possible that further down the track, when you have developed a good relationship, you will find that you are led to a different and probably not quite so nice room. If this happens, relax! It shows they have begun to feel easy with you and trust is beginning to develop. Decent rooms are at premium and many people wish to meet their visitors in the best one.

If they suggest that you could all assemble in your hotel, go for this. It is easier for you as it involves less traveling; you have access to your files and notebook computer; the conditions are more comfortable; and the Chinese will enjoy the luxury, including having access to things like Coca Cola. This helps to put them in a happier state of mind. Make an effort to get sufficient chairs moved into the room as many people would feel uncomfortable if asked to sit on the bed. Try to get all such drinks or food items put on your bill - insist on this while smiling courteously. This gains you an edge, and a little leverage, because they will feel they owe you something and might feel obliged to repay in some way that might be useful to you. Traditionally, it is the job of the host to look after guests and if they demur you can point this out with a gracious smile.

The introduction ritual and early meetings

Identify their leader!

Protocol demands that you look first at their leader and greet him or her before turning to the others. If you have been led to an empty room, then he or she will be the first to come through the door. If the Chinese are waiting for you in the room, then their leader will at once acknowledge you and will probably be standing closest to the door, or by the main seat in the room. As the leader of your team, you walk in ahead of the others. You will be introduced to their leader, then to the team members in their pecking order. You shake hands all round, unless the number is clearly excessive, but it is polite for you to wait for them to extend their hand first. If someone is not introduced to you, ignore it. They might be trainee observers and too lowly to be dignified by an introduction so you should not insist on being introduced or asking who they are. Sometimes they are Party representatives; if they look old, tough, or exceptionally competent, you might suspect this to be the case.

Do not expect a firm vigorous handshake. In China a handshake is often loose and limp. If you insist on using a hard macho grip, they will not be impressed, quite the reverse in fact. You might find that the person gives you a much longer clasp than you are used to in the West. If you know someone well, have already enjoyed a few social gatherings with them, and are meeting up again after a long absence, perhaps on a third visit to China, you might find he gives you a two-handed shake; this is a mark of close friendship. Be careful not to initiate this yourself as it would be too presumptuous.

If you ever see anyone make a fist with the left hand and spread the right hand over it, then pump his or her arms up and down, this is an outdated traditional form of respect that borders on reverence. Elderly beggars might do this in return for a generous donation from you as there is a strong feeling of "thank you" about it, but few others will. You must never do this, as it would look strange in the extreme for a foreigner to behave in this way.

The seating ritual

You will be shown where to sit and there is a clear protocol on this. You should never just sit down without being shown your seat. The principal guest is usually escorted by the main host to the seat of honor, facing the entry door. Other important guests are then shown where to sit; if your team is large, down at the bottom end there may be a slight tendency to let people choose among the last few seats. The interpreters usually sit next to the host and main guest for convenience. Only after the host and guests sit down will the rest of the Chinese sit. Good manners require them to recognize and defer to the hierarchy, and you as a foreign guest must be given face.

Memorize those names!

Try to learn the Chinese names before the meeting. The list of team members will normally have been sent to you earlier with the documentation. If the list is long, you should be sure you at least know the names of those people high on the list. If you falter over names and misidentify people, it does not endear you. Imagine how you would feel if people kept forgetting your name! It is hard at first to remember Chinese names, but it gets easier with practice. They can have trouble with Western names in turn!

Introductions and business cards

There is a ritual to introductions: first you shake hands, next you nod slightly, then you carefully exchange business cards. A typical scenario is:

- Take your card in both hands to pass it over, pronouncing your name clearly so they know how to say it.
- Release one hand and accept their card.
- Examine their card slowly and carefully, repeating their name aloud.
- Do not put their card in your pocket.
- Smile and nod, then lay their card on the table in front of you or if you are in an armchair, on its arm.
- If you lay the cards you receive on the table in the order the Chinese are sitting, you will be able to address them by name more easily and it is a start in putting faces to names.

When exchanging cards, it is polite to hold your card in both hands as you present it. This is an old-fashioned courtesy that many Westernized Chinese no longer bother to do with foreigners, as they have discovered it does not matter to us. They will notice at once, and appreciate it, if you use both hands. They might make a remark that you are familiar with the traditional culture or something of that kind, which is a start in the process of developing the personal relationship.

You should read their business card slowly and carefully because in China a person is primarily identified by the company for which they work and after that by their position within it. You might even hear a Chinese individual say something like "I am IBM" by which they mean of course that they work for IBM. This specifies that they are in a major foreign firm and hence someone of importance. Really, the card is seen as an extension of themselves.

To glance at a card and put it immediately in your pocket is discourteous in China, signifying that you consider they are not worth bothering about. It is particularly bad to place a card in your back trouser pocket where it will be sat upon, as the symbolism is not lost on the Chinese, if unintended by you. Even if the card you receive is in Chinese you can study it – if asked if you can read it, you can say no, but were admiring the appearance and care that had been taken with the design. This gives face, even in your ignorance of the language.

I hope you like tea?

During meetings, you can expect to drink lots of tea without milk and sugar, poured by service personnel (never "servants") from thermos flasks. Be careful not to overdo it and strain your bladder as there seem to be few "comfort breaks". The reason is probably that the host would probably prefer you not to see the state of the lavatories in institutions that were not designed for foreigners. Chinese plumbing is often deficient and Asian-style toilets are common, i.e., there is no pedestal, just a hole in the floor. Where there is a pedestal, it is often forbidden to place used toilet paper in it because in some buildings it can be guaranteed to block the pipes! In such cases, a bucket is provided at the side for the paper. It would embarrass the host to have to explain this somewhat personal fact of life to you, and he would probably feel that it reflects badly on both China and the institution. In any case, the Chinese are adept at sipping tea for hours without apparent discomfort.

The ritual of the meeting

You will find that most meetings follow a set protocol. You will relax more if you know what to expect - and it is a waste of your time to try to change the format. Meetings generally begin with small talk. You can expect to listen to bland introductions, often full of happy platitudes. Be prepared to deliver similar speeches that sound mundane to you but mean a lot in the context of Chinese culture.

The first meeting is not a business meeting

The first meeting is to start the process of getting to know you, which means you should take it easy, be very sociable and friendly, go slowly, and smile regularly but not grin all the time. They are only happy doing business with someone they know and trust, and this takes time. At this first meeting they will probably not start to talk business or negotiate and neither should you. If you try, it would frighten and alienate them and they will think you are merely a crass barbarian, totally lacking in an appreciation of proper behavior.

During the early exchanges of small talk, be careful not to look impatient, glance at your watch, or look bored. You are being closely scrutinized by those present, to see if you are worthy and proper, and therefore someone that they might be able to trust. The early talk will almost always be about your trip, with questions such as how long did it take, are you feeling tired as a result, is this your first visit, if not, how many times have you been and which cities have you visited, or have you been to such and such a place? (see the list of "Safe topics of conversation", p.51).

The second and subsequent meetings

You just might find the Chinese ready to start talking business at the second meeting but it will more likely be later; it depends on several things, including simply how they feel. Once they initiate the business discussions, a set pattern follows. The leader on each side speaks in a rather formal way, and the rest listen. The Chinese are likely to invite you start first.

Your introductory speech – start off in the approved fashion

Both sides make their opening speech as an icebreaker to start the process of getting to know each other. Your aim is to persuade them that you and your company are reliable, important, able to deliver, and well regarded in your country and, if relevant, internationally. Keeping your introduction short will not impress those opposite and rather than seeming businesslike and efficient, you will be perceived as not trying hard enough. Spend as much time as you can on making this a long and strong presentation. This could be the start of a beautiful friendship!

You should read your speech from prepared text. In it you should refer to your country and to China, and to the host organization (the company or Ministry people opposite), as well as to your firm. It is desirable to pepper your talk with sweeping fine phrases. You can use glowing terms, sound optimistic and stress friendship, cooperation and mutual benefit. It can pay you handsomely to spend a lot of time writing this speech as it might be useful later to refer back to the words you used, if negotiations get sticky.

When you have dealt with the sweeping generalities, you need to explain clearly such things as:

- Who is on your team and what are their roles and functions in the company; you can refer to any honours they have earned or any achievements for which they are known.
- The background history of your company, including anything notable

it has achieved anywhere in the world.
- How your company is organized and why this works well.
- What products you make, where you sell them, and to which internationally known companies or maybe government organizations.
- How you see your company's future in its relationship with China.
- What your company can do to assist China in its modernization.
- What gains the side opposite can obtain by working with your company, always stressing that the benefits are mutual (you had better not mention profits at this stage).
- You might chose to conclude by asking them to explain their hopes for China and their organization, and how they see this particular project fitting in. This leads them nicely into their first speech.

In this first major speech, you should not turn to specifics, mention any figures, or suggest anything about control or shares in the board of management (if you are there to discuss a joint venture) and in particular exclude any mention of prices. At this stage, keep it general. In later meetings, you will get down to more specific and detailed discussion.

If this is a first meeting on a *return* visit, your opening speech can usefully go over the history of the relationship including nonbusiness elements. Remember to include lots of bland statements about the relationship, your past experiences with them, your hopes for the future, and so on. It would be a bad move to jump straight in with the latest proposal etc. that you have worked on back at HQ without softening them up first and reestablishing the relationship you developed earlier.

The behavior of your team

Remember that each side takes turns, with the onus on the leaders to make most of the running. The less senior team members of the Chinese team will often not speak until their leader invites them to comment, especially in the early meetings. In the Chinese context, it would be nice if you could get your team to act like this, but knowing Western individualism, it might be difficult to get them to comply! Furthermore, since it is probably alien to your team members, they might not work well like this. As the Chinese gain experience of talking with Westerners, they understand that a more freewheeling approach is normal with Westerners; although they might feel privately shocked at one of your team interrupting you, their leader, they will not be particularly surprised. Be careful not to interrupt *them* of course, as this would be most rude and cause the individual a loss of face.

It is equally important not to press anyone for information they seem unwilling to give you, such as who is really responsible for the decision or what the shipping tonnage available actually is. If you need to know and they are being coy, you can try asking them if they could take it up after the meeting and see if they can find the answer to tell you later. That allows them to agree to your suggestion and lets them off the hook. They might indeed deliver the information later, once this has been approved by a higher level.

Pay attention during the probably boring speeches

Try to listen carefully in the early meetings, even when being assaulted by waves of platitudes. You might get hints and ideas about what the Chinese really want, in case they have trouble coming out into the open to tell you.

Honestly! They live to meet!

Three-hour meetings are common in China. They often start at 9 a.m., with perhaps a two or two-and-a-half hour lunch break, then reconvene if necessary around 2 or 2.30 p.m. for a further three hours. It can be tiring for foreigners who may not be used to this. Business meetings in the West are often kept as short as possible. In China, time is not particularly regarded as money, nor as something that must be carefully used, which means that meetings can drag on in an interminable way. Decades of sitting through political meetings that could literally last for days, with breaks for sleep, have trained many Chinese to endure sessions that resemble filibusters.

What if someone suddenly walks out?

Assuming that you have not done something really awful and they are staging a mass walk out in protest, you might find that someone opposite might suddenly mutter something in Chinese, get up and walk out. Just ignore it! As they get to know you and relax, they might move about the room, talk among themselves or leave and return without explanation. This is not considered impolite in China and you should not take offense, or even show you have noticed their behavior. They are not likely to do this in the early meetings because they do not know you well enough and this more casual behavior is normally reserved for when both sides are feeling more relaxed.

More things you need to know

The host organization determines your status

Your invitation to visit China will be from some organization, which is your host. This institution is responsible for looking after you, including making hotel and travel bookings, and, in effect, vouches for you and your behavior. A powerful host can achieve just about anything it wants and you might get to places and see people that are otherwise inaccessible. A weak one means you can face many minor problems that irritate and waste both time and money. The once strict insistence on you having a host organization has been relaxed but it still makes a lot of sense for you to have one, as it makes your stay easier and many mundane matters will be undertaken on your behalf.

Ask your host organization if you want anything

You should approach your host organization for all requests. It is the function of your host to do everything for you, even to arrange things like sightseeing trips. Naturally, the host organizes your appointments with the appropriate government departments or pertinent private organizations.

The bureaucracy does not get along well

You might discover that your host is finding it difficult to make proper arrangements with other units. The "insider-outsider" problem exists throughout society, and few organizations in China will do much to help another one; many will refuse to cooperate or even go out of their way to be obstructive.

There is little lateral communication in China: reports and instructions constantly go up and down, but few units ever seem to communicate sideways with others at their own level. Unknown to you, your host may be constantly negotiating on your behalf with other units and the amount of power and *guanxi* (personal relationship) your host enjoys determines how successful it can be.

If your host makes a mistake in the complex web that is China and fails to talk to some essential organization located at the periphery, you might find that when negotiations are well under way, things suddenly grind to a halt. Your host may be forced to go back several steps in order to propitiate some organization that should have been consulted earlier. Once it is sorted out, your talks can recommence.

You will probably discover that the central government lacks control over local affairs and day-to-day events. There is much decentralization, local authorities often ignore the laws or instructions coming down, and rapid economic change has caused more than a degree of chaos. Remember, however, that in the end, the central government has absolute power and if and when it decides to act, it can be rather ruthless.

Underneath, they really worry

Many Chinese negotiators have a permanent worry that they will make a mistake, as a result of which China will be exploited by foreigners. They are less nervous now than during the 1980s just after China moved out into the international arena and still had much to learn, but it is still a factor. Some foreign firms go to China looking for a quick profit, on an in-and-out basis; the Chinese have learned to fear them and are watching to make sure you are there on a more permanent and trustworthy basis.

Some of the delays you will encounter can be attributed to these fears. They are based in part upon the long historical record, for after 1840 many powerful foreign countries used their strength to exploit China and set up colonial areas. When China began to open up in the 1970s, they encountered various dubious foreign business people, which reinforced their prejudices.

The love of detail

Observe that the Chinese are patient and attentive to detail. They often enjoy hearing a mass of points, then being shown how they relate to some major element or process. This seems to satisfy their need to see how things will fit together, allows them to consider who else will be involved, and what actions this might mean for them. There is a tendency to love details to a greater extent than in most Western societies, and once the introductory "big picture" meetings are over, they do not respond well to a broad-brush approach unless it is backed up by frequent reference to particulars.

They will probably expect you to be a master of detail about your industry and product and will direct complex questions to you. It is best if you can answer off the top of your head, but if you cannot remember an obscure fact, it is acceptable if you immediately look it up in your file. Now is the payoff time for all the effort you put in preparing the detailed kit before you left home! When you simply do not know the answer, promptly assure them that you will find out as quickly as possible. Then fax your HQ, marking your request Priority One.

If you have anything important to communicate about your company, its business history, your product, or the technology you are trying to sell, it would be an excellent idea to prepare a detailed document in advance, and hand it over at the meeting. Make sure you have a copy for each member of both teams. You can then talk to it, taking them through systematically. They will appreciate what you have done. It can be a valuable method of speeding up the negotiations: not only does it assist them in reaching speedier decisions, they will find it helpful to use when keeping their higher level sweet. If you hand over a copy of your introductory speech, it may assist you later should minor disputes arise. It is much easier to defend your present position if you can relate the issue back to the words used and accepted earlier.

What do you mean, "Why do I answer a question with a question?"

Appreciate that if you ask a question you may get another question in reply. This is common in Chinese culture, as part of the general preference for an indirect approach and a cautious sounding out of others without revealing much of one's own position. It is a preferred negotiating tactic in circumstances where a definite answer might be wrong or perhaps offend you, whereas a vague answer maintains harmony and keeps them safe.

Really senior people have no place in the early meetings

It is a common situation for a foreign CEO to go China, decide to invest there, and then send a team to do the detailed negotiations. If yours is a large company, there is no place for a really senior person at the actual negotiating table. Traditionally, all details are discussed by underlings and the seniors only come in at the end to sign. It would be a mistake to try to get your CEO back during the substantive negotiations, for both you and he would lose face and the Chinese would not know what to do with him. However, if you are the head of a relatively small firm, there may be no one else suitable to send as team leader. Still, if you are the boss, at least you will have the power to make instant decisions.

Those informal suggestions

You might find the team opposite floats an idea at you in a social gathering to see how you respond. If you seem enthusiastic, it will later be put to you formally, probably at the next meeting. The idea is to save face in public and to ensure in principle you are not likely to oppose the suggestion when it is properly presented. If you do not like what they suggest, say something like "it might be a bit difficult" or use some other unenthusiastic phrase but do not just say "no", "impossible" or "out of the question", which is far too blunt (see Table 6.1, p.130, for alternative ways of indicating no)

If your company is not number one in your field

Symbolism is important in the culture. Usually the Chinese prefer to have the most prestigious brand or technology, without much regard for whether it is the most suitable. If yours is not the leading product, you must be careful *not* to stress it is cheaper, which they can all too easily associate with inferior. Instead, you should try to demonstrate that it is actually better in some way. When about to enthusiastically promote your product, prepare carefully and go back to examine your maiden speech in case you managed to get in a broad principle to which you can now appeal. If you can openly link to that principle, they can appreciate the relevance and will often find it harder to reject. You can see it is worth spending a deal of time drafting your introductory speech!

If buying machinery, a field test is a good idea

China is capable of making high quality machines – it has ICBMs that put up satellites, its updated cruise missile is claimed partially to outperform the American Tomahawk,[28] and its Silkworm missile is generally well regarded. Yet not every factory is up to that standard and if you are buying machinery or equipment, you cannot get by with a short inspection of the plant and a quick glance over the product. It is wise to have the equipment examined by one of your technical experts and then to run a field test: the quality is not necessarily all that it seems.

One American importer of machinery fell into this trap and failed to examine carefully what he was buying or conduct field tests. He subsequently discovered that the firm was incapable of making to the required standards and serious defects were concealed by the simple and totally unsuitable method of filling in holes and concealing this by painting them over before delivering the low-quality products![29]

Remember to order enough spare parts

When placing his order, the same machinery importer was remiss about spare parts that would later be needed. For most of the machines he failed to ask for any spare parts and then ordered inadequate quantities for the remainder. When the inferior machines rapidly broke down, there were considerable delays getting the necessary parts. The defective machine had then to be taken out of service until the part finally arrived.

The company sometimes managed to buy an American equivalent for the broken component but it was always more expensive than the Chinese one.

Feasibility studies can be overly optimistic

It is generally in the interests of Chinese officials and your potential Chinese partner to present an optimistic picture of the market potential for whatever you are considering. Even if an "independent study" is produced, it might have been done by a local firm with much to be gained from a positive result, or possibly by an organization run by a relative of your partner-to-be, or someone who owes a debt to him.

With hindsight, the Xerox Corporation confessed that the feasibility study upon which they relied had been much too optimistic, although admittedly some of the problems that arose could not have been foreseen. These included devaluation of the *yuan* and new government regulations that severely restricted the market.[30]

Why on earth do they want me to separate the project into smaller pieces?

You might find that late in the negotiations, when it is clear to all that they will sign, you are suddenly asked to repackage your investment project into several smaller ones. Even if you are still unsure whether they will sign or not, should they ask for a split up, it is a strong signal that they intend to reach agreement with you. What they are almost certainly doing is asking for the repackaging in order to evade central scrutiny and need for approval. They do this by getting each individual element of the deal below the figure specified for mandatory central authorization by the Ministry of Foreign Trade and Economic Cooperation (MOFTEC). The relevant figure is usually $30 million in coastal areas and $10 million in the interior. Breaking up projects in this way is technically illegal but many authorities do seem to get away with it.

Local officials might wish to bypass MOFTEC because it is a remote organization; it can be slow and may legally take up to three months before having to make a decision; and they may have little or no *guanxi* possibilities with it. They often prefer to try to gain approval from the local COFTEC (Commission of Foreign Trade and Economic Cooperation, which is the regional branch of MOFTEC). The officials normally have developed a strong relationship with members of their local COFTEC and this means that things happen faster.

Similarly, it may be possible, if probably illegal, to use salami tactics and put in a figure of, say, $25 million, followed by a later extension of the project of $15 million, thereby bringing it in well over the $30 million total limit! One company in Shanghai reportedly had an initial intended investment of over $150 million, but gained approval by the local Shanghai Foreign Investment Commission using *five* almost simultaneous approvals, each just below the limit.[31] Many local authorities are likely to be sympathetic to such a suggestion, as it helps them to obtain an expensive project with less hassle.

In late 1998, China announced that it intended to change the approval system for foreign enterprises, end the need for approval by MOFTEC and SETC, replacing it by a simpler registration process.

Some tips on what to do in meetings

Get there on time

It is important to be punctual and to arrive on time for appointments, even for something as mundane as a sightseeing trip. Aim to be a few minutes early if you can. Being unpunctual is considered strongly insulting, far worse than in the West, where it is merely impolite. If you keep someone waiting in China, they suffer a loss of face. Timing your arrival is important: if you arrive earlier than about ten minutes it tends to give the impression of ultra deference which should be avoided, and if your contact person has not yet arrived, he or she might feel guilty that you were not met in as well as suffering a loss of face.

If an escort is picking you up at the hotel, it is important to ensure you are down in the lobby a minute or two early and not keep him or her waiting beyond the appointed time. If for some unavoidable reason you are late, you should apologize profusely. However, you should not be twenty minutes early and arrive first, or it will embarrass the escort. It is a question of relative status – an escort is inferior to a foreign guest and should be the one to wait!

Where to sit

Generally, someone will indicate where you are to sit. You should avoid the " seat of honor" unless asked to sit there; this chair faces the door, with its back to a wall. It is regarded as the best seat, probably because in earlier and more violent times sitting there prevented someone sneaking in to attack you from behind. To be seated there was a guarantee that the host would not attack and kill you, or at least was not making it easy for himself!

Seating an Overseas Chinese

It would be a mistake to sit an Overseas Chinese immediately next to your leader, as this is where the interpreter usually sits. If you accidentally do this, their team will see the person as merely an interpreter, generally considered to have lowly status, rather than a full member of your team. Your Overseas Chinese colleague would lose face and the Chinese themselves would not listen to what he or she has to suggest. Although Overseas Chinese make good interpreters, and there is a clear cost saving by using, say, one of your engineers in this role, it can be dangerous to do so. The Overseas Chinese can help with technical phrases of course, making it clear that this is merely to help everyone present understand clearly what is involved and that he is not really an interpreter. (See "The Overseas Chinese issue", p.69, for more details).

Avoid Western acronyms and explain management jargon

Be careful not to throw out acronyms like IRR (internal rate of return), DCF (discounted cash flow), or even CEO (chief executive officer). Many such abbreviations are familiarly in Western business circles but the Chinese system has been different for so long that they will probably not understand, nor will the interpreter. They are usually loath to admit this, because not understanding something involves a loss of face. If they conceal their lack of understanding, they may subsequently have to meet privately to try to sort out what you meant, which can slow down the pace of negotiations.

When you use a technical term, make sure you carefully explain what it involves. It is a good idea to explain the meaning of the words, then tell them what the concept is used for, and finally give an example or two of its use in a specific business context. For instance, you could take the internal rate of return, and say it is a way of working out what an investment will be worth over time; then you could point out this is useful; next you could explain how it is actually calculated, with an example; finally you could demonstrate how comparisons between projects can be made and the value of this when there is a fixed amount of money to invest. You might have to get into discounted cash flow also!

Remember that the people sitting opposite are intelligent and experienced beings but they were not brought up in a Western business environment so that they are often ignorant of many things you probably take for granted. A straight translation of the term will often mean nothing to them. Once they have not understood an important term you have used, the points you go on to make will probably not be followed, and the rest of your talk could well be a total waste of time.

Keep careful notes or live to regret it

It is vital that you take careful notes of what is discussed as well as determined. It is possible that misunderstandings will later arise and one side thinks that X has been decided, but the other believes that the decision was Y. A more common problem is that one side thinks that X was agreed, the other side thinks it was merely discussed but left in the air. If in a later negotiating session you are told that you earlier agreed to something and this comes as surprise to you, it is valuable to be able to refer to your earlier notes. Producing your original notes is often enough to persuade the Chinese that you are correct and an extra benefit is that they will see you as a serious person with whom they can do business. Some Chinese negotiators might try it on, as a ruse to see if they can talk you into thinking you agreed to something earlier. They might also try to instil a feeling of guilt and attempt to embarrass you into agreeing to something they allege you accepted earlier (see p.103, "Are they laying a guilt trip on me? Shame!").

The interpreter problem

Taking your own interpreter is a good idea

You should take your own interpreter if possible. It is reasonably common for leading Chinese business people to speak some English but rare for them to negotiate in the language. Expect that all business will be transacted in Chinese. An interpreter is necessary and the Chinese will supply one, who will usually translate accurately enough. However there are several advantages of bringing your own interpreter with you. If you are negotiating a deal or agreement that contains complicated legal or business ideas, or has a mass of details, you can brief your own interpreter before you leave your own country. This ensures that he or she understands what you want and what the technical phrases in your industry actually mean. This can prevent a lot of misunderstanding once in China. Another reason is that your own interpreter can choose to soften your language, or select the best phrase to put a blunt point over, or correct the other person's name if you get it wrong. Their interpreter has nothing to gain from doing these things to help you. Finally, just like an Overseas

Chinese team member, your own interpreter can tell you what they are saying among themselves, watch their body language, check that they really do understand, and provide a valuable route for indirect communications.

By convention, if you take your own interpreter, he or she translates what *you* say, and the Chinese supplied one translates what *the other side* says.

If you cannot take an interpreter with you, then before going to China you should make a list of all the technical terms that you think might be used and get them properly translated. You could usefully send a copy of the list to the Chinese side before you leave, to allow their translators to brush up in these areas, which can reduce misunderstandings and speed up the negotiations.

Speak slowly and carefully

It is important to speak clearly and concisely when negotiating. It is easy for lack of communication to exist and for the Chinese side not really to understand what is being said. This is especially so if the interpreter is young or is not familiar with your sort of company or business. If you have your own interpreter or an Overseas Chinese on the team, warn them to listen to the translation and check it. When you are not getting your message across, the Chinese are unlikely to admit they do not understand (they would lose face), and in any case they may think they understand but really have an incorrect picture of what you are saying.

It is a good idea to repeat your points using different words, and hammer home the essence of what you want to say. Good teachers have been described as those who tell you what they will say, say it, then tell you what they said; the same approach can pay off for you. Only if your opposite number has excellent English should you not do this. Naturally if he lived in New York for fifteen years and is totally fluent, you would only annoy him - such people are however rare.

You should never feel embarrassed at repeating points made earlier by a colleague on your team - Chinese negotiators like repetition, and it helps them to see your team as being united and with a common message. This can lead them to trust your company more quickly. If different members of your team say different things, they might worry that you are unreliable and possibly are trying to treat them unfairly, or rob them in some devious foreign way.

Avoiding idiom or slang

Do not use slang while negotiating. When dealing with people from other countries, you should avoid colloquial expressions or words from a third language, such as "getting the show on the road", "looking at the bottom line", "deja vu" or "in extremis". Likewise avoid irony and sarcasm, as there is a better than even chance that the interpreter will translate the words directly into Chinese, with the result that the people opposite will incorrectly believe it to represent your view.

Using the interpreter well

When negotiating, do not turn to face the interpreter but look at the person you are really addressing, which is usually their leader. Stick to short sentences and pause often. Try to achieve a steady rhythm of saying perhaps two or three sentences, then stopping. The interpreter will quickly pick up your rhythm and work better, smoothly stepping in at the proper time, without interrupting you or losing track of what has been said. If the interpreter ever interrupts you, it means you are speaking in too big chunks, so take the hint. Naturally, you should not raise your voice if translations are apparently going badly; just keep saying the same thing but in different ways.

Checking on the interpreter

Checking on the standard of interpretation is not too difficult. If you are puzzled by what their interpreter says to you, or if you get an answer that does not fit the question you asked, then you have reason to be concerned about the interpretation. Similarly, if they look puzzled or keep discussing what the technical terms really mean, your interpreter may not be doing well. Be watchful for team members that are not interpreters suddenly interjecting a translation - it means that they understand that the interpreter is mistranslating and are correcting him or her. Considering this means a severe loss of face to the interpreter, they will usually only do this if the mistranslation is a serious one.

If you listen to five minutes in Chinese and get a simple statement of "it is not possible" then you know you are getting a poor translation. If you give any figures or statistics and the interpreter does not immediately seize a pencil and write the figures on a piece of paper, suspect he or she is not really good. As China has a different counting system over one thousand - it goes to units of ten thousands rather than to millions - it is hard to translate large numbers without writing them down first.

If you brought a poor interpreter then that is your fault and you must live with it. If the Chinese supplied a poor one, then it is hard, but not impossible, to ask for a different person. It is a difficult matter, for what you are doing is a serious criticism of the interpreter and will cause an extreme loss of face for him or her. Consider also the fact that you might get an even worse one as a replacement! Good English interpreters are in short supply in China, and there is a great demand for their services.

Start with the general, move to the particular

Observe that in negotiations, the Chinese prefer to start with general principles, and only move on to details later. The principles stated and agree at the beginning are more than ritual statements, so do not fall into the trap of thinking this stage is a waste of your time. You should think carefully about the principles the other side suggests before accepting them, for when you agree to a general principle, you accept it for all time. You should observe that the approach is the exact opposite of that in the West, where it is thought that an agreement is best obtained by focusing on specific details within a known and accepted legal framework.

Note that a "letter of intent", a "memorandum of understanding" or a "protocol" are not a contract in the Western sense, and are not legally binding or have any real force. It is quite common for foreigners to regard an agreement as having been signed, when the agreed memorandum is merely the start of the Chinese process of negotiation. You will probably be pressured to sign one of these. Unless there is something obviously wrong with it, you should always agree to sign, even though little may happen for some time after.

The American Motors Corporation signed a memorandum in January 1979 but for two years no significant progress was made, apparently because the Chinese were using the discussions with American Motors as a lever in their negotiations with Japanese Toyota! Ultimately the memorandum with American Motors led to the establishment of Beijing Jeep.[32]

You should examine the wording of the memorandum, letter, or protocol carefully because the other side might interpret it differently from you. What appears to be an acceptable bland statement, perhaps along the line of "proper concern will be paid to treating both sides equally", might later be argued by them as implying a 50-50 division of the proposed board of management, which was almost certainly not the intention of the foreign side.

You should be careful always to sound positive in these early stages and not make negative noises, even if you know something cannot be done - this is a matter to be raised later when details are discussed.

Why do the Chinese place so much emphasis on general principles? It is partly a matter of cultural tradition, but there are some practical advantages for China. The Chinese are adept at using the principles to increase the pressure when negotiating and they may choose words that might allow them to wring later concessions. They are engaged in assessing if you are reliable and sincere, as well as the proper person and firm with which to do business. They are also weighing up your vulnerability and degree of persistence. Be aware that some of the general principles being promoted might be on orders from above and hence cannot be dropped or altered without higher approval.

Because this is the stage of general principle setting, if you are asked to reveal detailed information, perhaps something that appears to you to have commercial value and which you do not want to give away, you might be able to defer the issue by pointing out that such matters are best considered later, when the details will be discussed.

They might take a different view from you

It is possible that the team opposite will see problems differently from you. Many Western business people have two main corporate goals: to make (increase) profit and to maintain (increase) market share. The Chinese may have these but can also have several additional aims. They are more aware of the nation and its efforts, and may wish to gain some technology so that China can modernize and become strong. This just might override thoughts of profit. They may wish to secure some particular investment for their province rather than let it go to a disliked rival province. They may be ultra cautious and have as a main desire the wish to avoid making a mistake. In their normal business life, they have to cope with more fear and intrigue than many Westerners. They have been trained to be cautious in order to survive, as in the past failure might have meant being forcibly sent to do manual work, moved to remote country areas, or perhaps even tortured and imprisoned during a brutal political movement. Alternatively, they may really be engaged in damage containment and trying to make up for some mistake they made elsewhere, and need a successful contract with you by way of atonement.

Many Western business people see business as a sort of sport, where they try to win both for their own pleasure and benefit, and for their organization. This is done by playing against opponents under more or less set rules. When the contract is signed, the first half is over; when the goods are delivered or project complete, the whole game is finished and a new one has to start. For the Chinese, business negotiations are more

Kevin Bucknall

complex and while the sport analogy has relevance, the process is also like a marriage, perhaps an arranged one, where the relationship starts off in ignorance of the other, but steadily grows and develops if the choice of partner was initially correct.

Chapter Five: MEETINGS AND NEGOTIATIONS: THEIR TACTICS

Early days

Why do I always have to go to them?

The Chinese prefer to negotiate in China rather than abroad. They gain several advantages from this, for as host they set the agenda and pace of negotiations, and can adjust these if they can see something to be gained. They can easily send large numbers of people to learn from you at low cost if, during the negotiations, they can persuade you to give a free demonstration or training seminar. They also have backup staff easily available and can check with higher levels more conveniently. As every decision made in China must normally be approved by someone higher up, this is a matter of great importance to them. Conversely, you are at a disadvantage, cut off as you are from your own society and firm, probably suffering from culture shock as well as being tired, and lacking backup staff. No wonder they do not want to come to you!

When they go abroad, Chinese delegations are often window-shopping and gaining information on different rival products and locations, rather than having a serious intention to negotiate. Such trips abroad are commonly used as payoffs for favors done, and little or no business may eventuate from some excursions. Even where the visit is a serious one with a strong intention of doing business, some people are probably there as a payback and doubtless they were not the best who could have been sent. "Buggin's turn" also operates in many Chinese institutions and some are sent who have nothing to contribute, but who have not been abroad yet. Irrespective of whether the trip is a genuine one or not, whatever is discussed, no decisions will be made in China until reports have been delivered to higher levels. Despite such problems, it is customary to invite your Chinese host to come to your country - you will of course pay.

Man, their team is huge!

The Chinese have a habit of fielding a large team. You are unlikely to know the area of responsibility of each member or even to which organization he or she reports. To an extent, the number on their team depends on why you are in China and what you wish to do. Who are they all? If you are trying to sell technology through an official Chinese foreign trade organization, there are likely to be representatives from that organization, as well as from the manufacturer of the equipment which will later embody the technology, and from the end users of the new machinery, so the numbers rapidly swell. Although it varies much, for a small deal, you might face a team of four to seven people but with a major deal, you could possibly find ten to sixteen people.

In buying or selling deals to the non-private sector, apart from their team leader, there will probably be some representative of the Communist Party who may also double as the trade union representative, possibly a few engineers and technicians, one or two sales or purchasing people, a finance person, and an interpreter. Others present may not have any obvious function at all. Some of these may well be trainees in the areas of business or interpreting, one or more may have an intelligence function, there may be a lawyer, and perhaps one or two local officials to keep an eye on things. Also present may be someone visiting the area from higher up the administrative or political ladder who has expressed an interest in seeing what goes on in meetings with foreigners. One person will be there simply to take notes and there may be another as a general gofer.

The Chinese team will rarely be united in view, as the main negotiator wants the lowest price, the engineers the best product or technology to solve a problem, different end users might want different things such as speed, quality, or low fuel consumption, while any financial representative will probably wish to minimize total expenditure, either in money terms or perhaps foreign exchange. Further, different members of the team will be reporting to different authorities, which complicates matters. Despite this, the Chinese team functions as a single unit and maintains total accord in public, almost never disagreeing among themselves. All signs of the different interests will be carefully concealed from you.

Discounting their enthusiasm

You should discount enthusiastic statements from the team leader opposite about the prospects for the product, project or relationship, as well as their own power and their ability to influence outcomes. Potential liaison people who are hoping to work with you are also likely to exaggerate their connections and closeness to the central authorities. In the early stages of negotiation, the Chinese tend to such overstatements and try to talk up the size of China's market. Whilst China has grown rapidly for some years, it remains a difficult, if eventually profitable, market for many foreign companies. As negotiations progress, you might find that the team with which you have been negotiating does not really have the power they indicated earlier. You might notice, for example, that now and then they are forced to ask for a meeting to be closed early, so that they can obtain instructions from higher levels.

You lay your cards on the table first

After the preliminary statements are over, you, the visitor, will be expected to reveal your position first. This can be difficult, as at this stage it is not always clear what the Chinese really want or even what are the problems for which they seek a solution. Their priorities are generally even more closely concealed. Do not be surprised to find that to a great extent you begin by groping in the dark. In this jockeying for early positions, take care that you do not inadvertently reveal more than you might wish.

After you have made your first pitch, the Chinese react to your presentation. It is common at this stage for them to try to get you to promise more than you can deliver, by trapping you into exaggerating your capabilities. Be watchful! They take copious notes and mostly have good memories, and if you agree to something it will be remembered. Further, they may be prepared to twist things slightly so that any concession you signal *might* be possible could reemerge later as something you actually promised! The solution is to make sure that someone on your team is taking careful notes that indicate what was discussed, what was agreed and what was merely floated as a possibility.

Tactical approaches

They might promise you the moon

It is unwise to believe any statements to the effect that you have the best chance of winning a competitive contract, as it is not unknown for *every* firm with which they are talking to be told the same. It has proved an effective tactic for gaining concessions and you should not be surprised if an open attempt is made to play you off against a competitor.

It is not only business people who may make empty promises. Local government officials might enter into commitments that are illegal and which they are unable to deliver. This happened in 1992, when the Vice-Mayor of Jinxi in Liaoning Province promised low 10-15 percent tax rates for investment projects which would be located in a special zone within the city. This was illegal, a fact subsequently picked up by the State Tax Bureau, and his pledges were overruled by higher authority.[33]

Big brother is watching you

An important reason for putting up calmly with the early meetings and lack of progress is that the Chinese start to assess you at once. As you know, the early meetings are designed to get to know you, start the relationship, and to gauge what you are like. They will examine you for weaknesses such as whether you are impatient, lack self-control, remember details or forget them, drink a lot at lunchtime and become less efficient, or are unable to cope well in long sessions. This scrutiny is continuous, including the occasions when you are off on excursions, visiting the theater, and going out to dinner.

Your body language will be scrutinized closely for signs of impatience, anger, relaxation, things that please you, and so forth. Some signals will be misinterpreted across the cultures, but they have gained much experience of dealing with Westerners and they pool their opinions. The information obtained in these ways will be used in deciding what approaches are likely to be the most advantageous to maximize the concessions that can be wrung from you.

Naturally, you should be doing the same and probing for weakness, but on their playing field and with their rules, you are at a distinct disadvantage.

The sound of silence

The Chinese are happier with silence than many Westerners and do not feel the need to break it. You might find that in one of the early meetings they sit in silence and observe how you react, watching to see if it puts pressure on you and if it could later be used as a weapon.

You might be given the silent treatment if you ask a question that they find awkward. Whether they are embarrassed by something you have suggested, or the way in which you did it, the silence could be an indirect way of saying "no". If you are assaulted by this weapon of silence, do not feel you have to say something to break it; it is better to sit quietly and wait them out. They will respect you for this – you just might be the first foreigner they have met that did not succumb! If you find this impossible to do, after a long pause, you might veer sideways and raise a totally different topic. The other team will usually be quite happy if you break the impasse by returning to something that has already been settled; they typically feel comfortable rehashing matters, so this can be a sensible choice for you.

They like to win

As negotiators, the Chinese stress mutual interests, rather than compromise, usually in the context of flowery rhetoric. It is received wisdom that harmony is always sought and aggressiveness is thought to be a weakness. Nonetheless, deep down inside they feel that all negotiations must involve winners and losers - and they try very hard to win! Everyone knows that a loser is someone who necessarily suffers a loss of face. Expect to find that if you negotiate a hard bargain and appear to win a point, they will not feel good about it. A common response is for the Chinese side to try to regain something, possibly by reopening one or more issues previously agreed in order to extract something new, and in this way improve their overall position.

"We deserve special help"

Traditionally the Chinese have seen their country as special, and one that merits particularly favorable treatment. They still do. Surprisingly, some otherwise hardheaded Western business people have fallen for this attitude. It is normal to be asked for special treatment for China, which is poor and trying to catch up, and yours is a wealthy developed country. You might be told that China was treated badly by certain Western countries in the past and the world owes China something. You should of course avoid feeling a sense of personal shame or guilt if your country once acted in this way or is fortunate enough to be wealthy.

The Chinese genuinely believe that once a mutual interest has been established, the richer party should do more for the poorer. As part of this, some have a tendency to expect that Westerners should take nonmonetary rewards, such as accepting the output produced from the machines we sell them, rather than China having to pay money to obtain the machine.

Are they laying a guilt trip on me? Shame!

Do not be surprised if you are made to feel guilty or called "unfriendly". It is common practice to try to make you feel shame or guilt for a variety of things, such as your behavior, your country's domestic or international political actions, or your company's refusal to help them more. Your best response is to be polite and dignified. You can point out that a nation's politics are not your business; that the friendship between your two companies is genuine; that the behavior of a President half a world away should not be allowed to interfere with this relationship; or that neither you nor they was born when the atrocities of some historical event have been thrown at you and it is the *future* that matters for both sides and you have a genuine concern to build a solid and reliable relationship. If something in China is criticized by you (and this is not a good thing to do!), the Chinese are quick to point out that internal politics are not a matter for foreigners. You could consider using this argument yourself, but you should be aware that it is moving towards the aggressive end of negotiating style.

Traditionally, causing an opponent to feel shame was a reliable and effective tactic to get what was wanted, because of the importance of "face" in the society. The Chinese are clever at trying to shame their opponents into agreeing; you too can adopt the tactic if you strongly need to achieve some end.

Playing you off against competitors

Chinese negotiators play hard ball and have few scruples about revealing information gained in negotiations with one company to pressure another to make concessions. Clearly if a round of competing offers can be established, this can be highly profitable for China. Sometimes they are openly talking to your competitors and make sure you know about it. When Combustion Engineering, a US company, were negotiating to license power generation to China, other foreign companies were competing for the same contract. The other companies were not only meeting in the same building at the same time, one of them (Babcock & Wilcox) could not be missed: they had been placed in very the next room![34]

You may be told that a competing Western firm has given them the information about something, so you should do the same, or perhaps the competitor has already offered a better deal than the one you propose. This may be true - but if they do not produce documentary evidence, consider carefully whether their negotiator could simply be using a tactical lie to gain an advantage over you.

Why are they angry?

Do not be surprised to meet anger from the Chinese. If during negotiations you find one member of their team suddenly gets angry, you should assume it is feigned and part of their tactics, perhaps to see how you respond. If anyone stridently lectures you on your behavior, or that of country, or even slams angrily out of the room, ask yourself why they are doing this at that particular point of the negotiations. Be careful not to become angered in turn or even look impatient, but explain calmly and politely why whatever they are demanding is extremely difficult. You can be persistent, even relentless, but this must be done in a context of calm rationality. Some foreign advisors advocate that a calculated occasional loss of temper by you, using their tactic, can be helpful. On the whole, this seems to me a dangerous form of negotiating. Unless you enjoy the occasional bullying session *and* like taking risks, it is better avoided.

That man is really rude!

You might meet rather insensitive Chinese behavior on occasion. Some individual Chinese have an immense capacity for single-minded behavior. They will press and continue to press for something and seemingly not get embarrassed or bored. They will return to a subject previously decided and start all over again. The degree of this self-centeredness can come as a surprise and to such people, your "face" is of no importance in the effort to achieve what they wish.

If you have been offered an unattractive proposition and wish to refuse, try to avoid saying "no". You can respond that you will think about it and let them know. When you do not get back to them, it will be seen as a refusal. This is a common Chinese method of turning something down. Alternatively, you could use one of the acceptable phrases from Table 6.1 (see p.130). Should you find that the subject still keeps being raised, you may eventually have to make a polite but firm rejection. If they do not drop it then, you may have to get tougher. Consider displaying a slight degree of irritation or perhaps even hint that you could go over their head to their boss. Most officials live in fear of complaints and being investigated, as it allows their enemies in the bureaucracy an opening to get them, so what may appear to be a gentle threat is actually severe and should tame them. It is only to be used as a last resort for something you really care about, because after such a threat they may adopt genuinely dislike you and adopt an all-round tougher stance, causing you to concede more elsewhere.

In China, the truth can be a flexible commodity

Traditionally, the Chinese have not found the truth to be an overwhelmingly important concept. It was widely accepted that in important areas like business, politics or the courts, if it was in one's interest to tell the truth, then it was sensible to do so, otherwise it was not felt to be an obligation.

In contemporary times, this traditional attitude has made it easier for many respectable Chinese officials to parrot the official Communist Party line in apparently sincere fashion, when they themselves did not believe a word of it. This was particularly the case in the hard-line Maoist period, when the official line was delivered as gospel by ex-capitalists and others with little reason to love the regime.

Another powerful reason for a Chinese person to dissemble is to save either his face or yours; a lie is generally felt to be more acceptable than causing a loss of face. People may try to avoid telling you what they think you would not wish to hear; some take this further and act in a positive fashion and tell you a lie because they believe the answer is what you wish to hear.

If you ask to see a building and are informed that it is "closed", it may mean that there is some reason why you are not allowed to visit it. For example, many churches during the Maoist period were taken over for other use, such as warehousing, and the state did not want foreigners to know this, so churches were reported as "closed for repair" or the like. I ran across this once. On a morning back in 1966, I was in the exhibition center in Guangzhou, and asked if I could visit a church that was visible from one of the windows, but was told that it was "closed". I persisted, and asked what it was being used for if not for worship and my guide said they were storing furniture in it. Clearly, he reported this incident back to his office, because immediately after lunch he met me looking very serious and said that he had a "self-criticism" to make. Earlier in the day he had told me that the church was used for storage, but China had freedom of religion so this must be untrue, and he wished to apologize for having made a mistake and misinformed me!

Simple good manners may also require a person to say what is proper for the occasion, rather than what is correct. A further reason can be that, as is the case with some used car sales personnel in the West, a confident statement delivered in winning fashion is often preferred to the truth. A straightforward reason for dissembling is that people do not like to admit that they are wrong and they might continue to hide mistakes, even if it means lying to do so.

If you are told that something has gone wrong because of the action, or lack of action, of another unit, the story might well be true because it is a common cause of problems. However, it is a widely used fabrication in order to conceal inefficiency, or it might be put forward as a convenient excuse when the real reason for failure is not known. It is an acceptable story, because it is generally acknowledged that cooperation between units frequently breaks down. This placing of blame elsewhere is in sharp contrast with Japanese practice, where explaining the reason for something is not felt essential and blaming another is definitely frowned upon.

You can benefit by checking on what you are told

Because of the Chinese habit of treating the truth in a somewhat cavalier fashion, it is a good idea to check on what you are told about things such as tax laws, labor regulations, and financial requirements. If possible, you should establish another channel of communication, perhaps checking with your embassy in China or one of the many commercial consultants around. Independent confirmation that you are not being misled or hoodwinked can be reassuring.

Beware the possibility of two set of books

If you are contemplating a joint venture, or taking over an existing firm, bear in mind that some Chinese managers, without any scruples, have been known to keep two sets of books: one, the real set, that you will never see, and a false second set that indicates that the firm is doing better than reality. You might expect that the feasibility study would reveal this fact, as indeed it should. However, unless you organize one independently, the study may be supplied by the Chinese partner, or by someone he knows, so that it may not reveal the true situation. In addition, officials of the local government may place pressure on whoever conducts the study to show things in the best possible light by exaggerating profits and minimizing costs, in order to attract foreign investment and provide employment.[35]

What if they suddenly stop?

Do not be alarmed if the Chinese suddenly stop negotiating with you; there are many holdups in the system and reasons for delays so that it probably does not mean much. Sometimes, however, they will do this as a ploy to increase tension and uncertainty if they believe it would be an effective pressure on you, so try to relax and not worry.

An alternative tactic has been for them suddenly to announce that they are ready to sign a contract really early during the negotiations before all the details are thrashed out. This can again be a ploy to shake you up and thereby increase pressure on you; equally, it might reflect intensified pressure from higher levels to get a quick decision, or else be the result of a change in policy at higher levels, and therefore is a genuine offer. Your liaison officer might be able to do a little private investigation to see what he can uncover.

Negotiations may drag on and on

Time is not seen as money

Virtually everything you want to do takes longer to accomplish than in the West, so be prepared to devote what might seem an inordinate length of time to what look to you like relatively simple matters.

Time and money are considered to be quite separate concepts in China, unlike in the West where the opportunity cost of time is well understood. Do not forget that labor in China is cheap and always has been, so that if someone spends much time on a task, it actually does not cost much. If running a joint venture in China, you are likely to come across this attitude to matters temporal. You might, for example, find a Chinese manager undertaking tasks that in a Western country would unhesitatingly be bought in from outside. Before you step in and alter his or her approach, it would be wise to discuss it carefully; there might be good reason for the behavior. It may be, for instance, that the skill required for the task is possessed by your manager but is otherwise unavailable locally.

Labor may be more expensive than you might think, for you might have to pay them a higher wage than they actually receive. This can occur if the worker is supplied by an official state organization for then the government might take the difference, which in effect places a tax on labor. If you go to China because of the low wage level, this practice can reduce the benefit to you; if you happen to be an internationally footloose firm, other venues might be worth considering. In any case, low wages do not always equal low costs, it all depends on the productivity of labor. For many years Chinese labor did not enjoy notably high levels of productivity, although it has improved substantially over the last decade or so.

Negotiating is not necessarily sequential – the philosophy is different

Observe that the Chinese may not see negotiations the way that you do. Many Asians have a different attitude to life from those of us raised in a Western culture. Rather than focusing on cause and effect, as we do in most Western societies, they envisage the world as a complex pattern, like a web, with links sideways as well as backwards and forwards in both time and place. Life is like a stream, a flowing process that is constantly changing. If you ask them why something has happened, they are inclined to interpret the problem in those terms. It is a formidable task for them to explain something to Westerners, who seek a simple cause of a problem, because the flowing interrelated pattern that they see is hard for them to describe, as well as for you to understand. If they start to explain, we might wonder why such a complex and convoluted answer results from a simply "why" question. It is the result of dissimilar vision of the world.

When you are faced with a concrete problem, this different way of looking at the world can make it harder to find a solution. What the Chinese side suggests may not seem to you to attack the root cause, and instead it seems to deal with the symptoms rather than the origins. The corollary is that a solution proposed by you might seem totally unsatisfactory to your Chinese partner, as although they see that what you suggest will successfully attack the cause of the problem, the process of doing this may be troublesome. It might upset the established pattern, annoy important people that they wish to keep on side, damage *guanxi* relationships, and cause new problems to arise elsewhere. Therefore, they are inclined to reject your solution because of the new difficulties it would cause and they see that it might possibly be worse, looking at the net gains and losses involved.

Negotiating never stops

Western culture often separates business and leisure, except perhaps on the golf course. In America, you might hear young managers boast that they work hard and play hard, viewing these as different activities. Chinese culture tends to regard business and leisure as intertwined and part of life's rich and complex flow. The practical result is that you can expect substantive bargaining issues to be raised on social occasions. The Chinese never really stop negotiating; a laughing concession made by you in a spirit of friendly fun while drinking at a banquet is likely appear at the next meeting as a settled issue to which you have already given your agreement. The moral is always to be on your guard - and do not drink too much!

They keep returning to points we settled earlier!

When this happens, be patient and smile. Partly it is merely a fascination with detail: many Chinese can cope endlessly with it without seeming to get bored and tend to dislike carelessness about the finer points. Vast amounts of detail might be required to satisfy them, which is why a knowledgeable engineer or high level technician should be a valuable member of your team. Partly this habit of reopening points that you believed were settled is a business tactic, as in Chinese eyes details can always be renegotiated.

Other points

Their changing power position

You should not be surprised if the negotiating power of the Chinese side appears to alter. At the start, they often seem to have full negotiating power, and may stress this to you. Later you may realize that they have not the power that they earlier pretended. In part, it may be matter of face, and the chief negotiator was trying to impress you, by feigning access to central power that he did not have.

Another possibility is that you were told the truth as the other side saw it. In China, clout near the grass roots is often limited. Decisions taken properly at lower levels can easily be subsequently overturned by higher authority. Additionally, high level factional disputes and changes mean that national policy can alter without warning. Consequently, you may find that some point previously agreed and then ratified by higher levels may suddenly be disallowed. The only explanation you are likely to be given is that it now conflicts with policy or violates some unspecified regulation.

Give me cutting edge technology

You might find that despite China having a serious problem of unemployment, the people opposite want the latest technology and have little interest in seeking to preserve jobs. Where there is a problem of local employment, they have a tendency to still go for the latest technology and then hire more people than are strictly necessary to run it.

They do not always understand economics and can get annoyed if someone suggests that their quest for the best might be misplaced. A former head of the American United Autoworkers, Leonard Woodcock, toured a truck plant in Changchun, Manchuria, and indicated that it would be a blunder for them to put in the latest technology. Based on his experience, he felt that it would entail them finding new jobs for 30-40 percent of the work force. They were clearly annoyed at this and told him that he was a colonialist, treating the Chinese people as second-class citizens![36]

It is common to encounter a rather naive belief that modern technology will offer a solution for all the problems of China. This erroneous view has a long history, was very popular in the last half of the Nineteenth Century, and has emerged once more. Over time, many in China have looked at the Japanese achievement in taking Western technology and modernizing their nation successfully, yet without losing touch with their culture. They tend to assume that there is some simple trick involved, and that China can easily do the same, once it works out how.

Do not despair if you keep being asked if yours is the best product or technology, even though the Chinese will not reveal what the problem is that they are trying to solve, or what they really need the product or technology for. The questioning is a reflection of the Chinese wanting the best, but being hemmed in by a desire for secrecy, an unwillingness to expose internal matters to "outsiders" and a knowledge that there is always a degree of uncertainty about whether the orders from above will change.

A good example of this refusal to state what the problem is or what is being sought occurred with the Chinese dealings with Kaiser Engineers from California, a company that provides a wide range of engineering and consulting services. The first invitation from the Chinese was to discuss "iron ore", and it took three more months to ascertain that the focal area of interest was actually iron ore beneficiation and mining. After suddenly being requested to extend their stay in China from two weeks to four, in which time the delegation visited many mines on a whirlwind tour, the team finally began to understand what the Chinese actually wanted – and succeeded in getting a contract.[37]

The need for freebies

It is common for the other side to press for much free information. The Chinese frequently do not appreciate the costs of developing technology and might ask for, or even insist upon, a lot of free information, free training seminars and free trips. "Old friends" and business partners are supposed to be supportive and some Chinese are genuinely bewildered to be told they cannot have such free assistance. Others have learned that real costs are involved, but still ask anyway. They might try to use your hopes for future business as a lever to extract free consultancy services from you.

Intellectual property rights are not always respected and there is a widespread view that knowledge should be shared. It is not unknown for China to import an item, then reverse engineer and copy it. Even samples supplied from abroad, sent by a company hoping for sales, have been used in this way. A Japanese friend of mine working for a computer firm in Hong Kong had this experience. She once sent a small computer part to China, with a suggestion that they might be interested in buying it. She never received a reply, but eighteen months' later a perfect copy appeared on the shelves in Hong Kong, stamped "made in China". As another example, if you go in a book shop in China you might see a door bearing a sign in English that says "No admittance"; this could well be the entrance to a special room, closed to foreigners, where pirated copies of foreign books are for sale at low prices to locals. I once saw that underneath the English on the sign someone had written the Chinese characters for "Special foreign books", so I took a chance and entered. I found half a dozen student-looking types avidly perusing the shelves before the bookshop staff swooped down and frantically ushered me out!

The Chinese position on intellectual property has improved, but there is still a long way to go. Microsoft Corporation in particular has suffered from widespread copying of its software and the company complains regularly about the problem. Estimates suggest that at least 96 percent of all software in use in China in 1997 was pirated,[38] yet this was an improvement over the 98 percent reported the previous year! In Beijing in 1998, pirate software on CD-ROM could easily be bought for a few dollars in Zhongguancun, the flourishing computer center near the university area. The figure is thought to have fallen recently and in the year 2000 could be as low as 93 percent.

China is the largest exporter of pirated software in the world, despite government efforts to reduce the problem. Despite rhetoric, this attempt dates back only to March 1995, when China signed an intellectual property rights agreement with the USA. In the early 1990s, the chief culprits producing pirated software were state-owned companies, but the government crack down resulted in them switching to other lines or closing down. These days the private sector is the main villain of the piece, not the state. By the late 1990s, the efforts of the authorities to stamp out pirated software in China had begun to pressure this business, with the result that Hong Kong is becoming the maj[39]or production and distribution center for pirated CDs. In China proper, the software pirates turned from computer programs to the profitable area of video compact discs, on which they release illegal copies of foreign movies. The Motion Picture Association of America estimated that it lost $20 million in China in 1997,[40] demonstrating that the black market is alive and well! In Beijing, Silk Alley is a well-known area to buy fake copies of consumer items like CDs, video discs and Prada handbags.

Although it rarely happens, China recently won a minor triumph in the software appropriation game: a Chinese court found Microsoft guilty of stealing an idea provided by a local company for an advertisement and fined Microsoft Corporation 200,000 yuan.[41]

They just turned down a good offer!

Do not be surprised if the Chinese team refuses things of benefit to them. It usually means they are being ultra cautious and stalling: possibly they have not finished their assessment and do not yet trust you; or possibly there are confused signals and lack of clear instructions, coming down to them from above. Without higher approval, nothing can happen, and if someone above is suspicious of the offer, they may be instructed to reject it or temporize.

Contracts

Contracts have to include a great deal and consequently can be sizeable, even up to 80-130 pages. When negotiating a joint venture, you should pay particular attention to the valuation of assets that the other side will bring to the deal. Usually, they will try to place a high value on the land, buildings, and machinery that they supply as their contribution to the joint venture. They are likely to be firm on the figure, however much you try to whittle it down and however logically you argue your case. In many cases they do not actually have any power to alter it, for it has been set by some much higher level body. In the end, you might just have to accept their valuation, but it is still worth making the effort to get it lowered.

One US manufacturing company managed this when negotiating a joint venture with two Chinese partners. The US side set what was seen as a high price on the technology being transferred and in turn the Chinese demanded a high price for land use fees. The local authorities, above the level of the firm, refused to accept the high technology price, and the US team agreed to lower this, but only in exchange for reduced land prices – and they succeeded.[42]

Concerning detailed provisions, you might want to ensure that office furniture is specified in the contract, as is the provision of telephones, water and electricity. Do not forget that in the future you will need to get profits out of China; although this is becoming much easier to achieve, a statement of this principle and the mechanism involved should appear in the contract. You definitely need a clause that ensures you can obtain the foreign exchange to remit your profits. In the past firms have found this difficult, although the problem receded over the 1990s, as foreign exchange became more widely available. The issue might return however.

Materials and parts are often of low quality in China. It is helpful if you can get a clause that is either vague on sources of supply, or else specifically allows purchase elsewhere, including other provinces of China or abroad without penalty, in the event that local quality is deficient or unavailable at a competitive price. Fujian Oak Tree, a joint venture set up in

Fujian Province by the Oak Tree Packaging Corp, New Jersey, manufactures packaging cartons. In the early days, the joint venture found local materials, including such items as ink, coatings, and glue, so poor that they all had to be imported. Only later was Fujian Oak Tree able to source its needs within China.[43]

If negotiating a joint venture, try to get as long a life as possible written into the contract. Do not accept a maximum of ten years unless you are absolutely convinced that you will make profits fast *and* you enjoy risk taking with odds worse than trying to draw to an inside straight. You could start by asking for thirty years and reluctantly let them argue you down to twenty-five or twenty. Remember to look worried and uncertain when you agree at last to their figure. It reassures them that they have won something and gives them face. A beaming smile and a statement that you are pleased to get it settled at last might worry them that somehow they have been gypped.

Another useful clause would be what happens if either side wishes to terminate the joint venture before the stipulated date. It is more likely to be valuable to you than the Chinese side and so is worth considering carefully. Will there be a financial penalty? If so, what will it be? Who will value the assets and on what basis? Can you get some or all of your initial investment back? If so, what mechanism and time frame will be involved? What happens to any undistributed profits?

You should attempt to get a clause in the contract covering any adverse policy or price changes, although this may be resisted. Try to obtain a clause that says both the English and Chinese versions of the contract are valid, as English can be a more precise language than Chinese. You can often put in addenda any minor details about the various responsibilities of each side.

Daniel Martin, manager of the investment program at the US-China Business Council, has supplied a good checklist of what needs to go into the contract for a joint venture:[44]

- The names, countries of registration and legal addresses of the parties and their legal representatives.
- The name, address, purpose and scope of the proposed venture.
- The languages(s) of official correspondence.
- The total amount of the investment and registered capital.
- The amount and breakdown of each partner's capital contribution.
- Each party's time limit in paying registered capital.
- The ratio of profit distribution.

- The composition and powers of the board of directors.
- The powers and method of hiring the manager, deputy manager and other senior employees.
- Labor management, welfare and insurance information.
- The type and sources of equipment and technology to be used.
- The method of purchasing raw materials and selling finished products.
- The ratio of products to be exported to those sold on the domestic market.
- Land or building sites to be used.
- Foreign exchange balancing methods.
- Insurance provisions.
- Assignment of taxes, tariffs, and fee provisions.
- Finance, accounting and auditing measures.
- Confidentiality clauses.
- Dispute resolution procedures.
- Force majeure provisions.
- Merger, acquisition and dissolution provisions.
- Liquidation procedures.

The attitude to contracts: the negotiation

The attitude of foreigners and Chinese to the negotiation, approval, implementation and enforcement of contracts is different. During negotiation, the Chinese may try to keep conditions vague where the foreign side can benefit, but precise where Chinese interests are at stake. If they are successful in their endeavor, the foreigner's future position is weakened.

Generally, the Chinese feel that during negotiations they are working towards a long-term relationship rather than merely discussing the draft contract on the table; the foreigners on the other hand feel that they are working towards signing this specific contract. Despite the common Chinese attitude that the contract is not the target, you should still try to get detailed clauses in the contract, even if the Chinese do not want them. When it suits them, the Chinese side is likely to follow Western attitudes and insist that contracts have to be followed scrupulously. On such occasions, with their strong interest in detail, they may tend to take the contract very literally.

During negotiations, it is wise to keep notes of all items agreed that will go in the contract later. Summing up what has been decided by reading the items out at the end of each meeting is a good idea, so that both sides know where matters stand, which can avoid future disputes.

When a disagreement arises, the Chinese partner is more likely to look at the whole history of the relationship between the two sides, rather than turning to the contract for a solution. If they ask for a change, perhaps a higher price or new delivery date, they may well cite something said earlier, so that you have to be prepared. If there is any conflict about what was decided earlier, you must go over the record of discussions and at this point every piece of paper counts. This paper trail record can be seen by them as more important than the legal contract and an appeal to it can be more valuable than pointing to the contract should a dispute arise. This is a powerful reason for you to keep good notes, hand over details in writing of all agreed points , and give them a copy of your first opening speech (see p.83, "Your introductory speech – start off in the approved fashion").

The attitude to contracts: the approval process

The approval process can be drawn out and painful. In coastal areas any project over $30 million requires central approval, which means all documents have to be sent to MOFTEC and then everyone must wait until they return. This is supposed to occur within 90 days but may take longer. This process is set to change, so keep an eye out for new regulations in this area.

It is quite common to find that after the contract is signed by all those directly involved, some higher and outside body, like MOFTEC, SETC or the central bank, intervenes and demands renegotiation of points it does not like. It can be infuriating as well as time consuming to be forced back to the drawing board in this manner.

The attitude to contracts: the implementation

With regard to implementation, contracts will be followed wherever possible but the attitude of each side is not the same: the Chinese feel that contracts should be observed because of the status and respectability of the parties who signed, not because of the legal implications. The foreign side usually assumes the contract will be observed because it is a legal document.

It is sometimes difficult to implement a contract because of the sprawling bureaucracy and the difficulty of finding out who is responsible for causing the delays or the apparently insurmountable problems. New fees may be imposed, input prices suddenly increased, or instructions given to you to purchases from a certain province or unit, which will usually not be the cheapest source and it is not always clear to whom you can appeal.

Expect that the Chinese side might ask for changes in a contract; they see nothing wrong with seeking a few amendments. You can never assume that you have finished once it its signed and remember not to get irritated should the Chinese raise the question of making a few alterations. In extreme cases, you can find something you agreed to in the morning session being raised for renegotiation the same afternoon! The Xerox Corp found this out when discussing the establishment of a joint venture to make photocopiers with the Chinese.

The Chinese have been reported to offer to sign a contract that they have not yet even seen, knowing that they can change it later. They have also terminated contracts early, on the basis that they feel that a signed contract means both parties have a mutual interest and can work together to decide what is a better outcome for each side.

This view, that signed contracts are flexible documents, on occasion has dismayed foreigners in the past. At the end of the 1970s, when China unilaterally canceled contracts for the Baoshan steel mill near Shanghai, they were clearly surprised at the depth of the antagonism of the foreign partners. Similarly, there was great consternation in the companies involved when, in 1993, China refused to pay the contracted price for Australian wool.

Bear in mind that the general Chinese attitude allows *you* to ask for amendments to be made to the contract you signed some time ago. With a Western background, you will probably not automatically think of doing this when local, national or international market conditions alter. If you decide to request a change, you might find that an appeal by you to the earlier agreed general principles is powerful. They will understand and sympathize with you, even if they are forced to object to the change for business or political reasons.

The attitude to contracts: the enforcement

The enforcement of contracts can be difficult. In the eyes of the people, the law has never been very important in China (see p.120 What is this thing called law?). When disputes arose between the parties and they found it impossible to reach agreement, the issue was usually sent not to the courts but to arbitration by a third party who was deemed acceptable to both. During negotiations, you might find that the Chinese object to binding arbitration clauses, because they are more comfortable with a freewheeling system, just as you might fear that your rights are not fully protected without them.

Generally, you should always try to run the business without appealing to the contract, and instead adopt an approach of building up a set of personal relationships as the core of your operations in China.

Although this approach is usually more profitable, the number of contract disputes that reach Chinese courts is surprisingly high, reportedly reaching 3 million as the millennium approached. One reason for the large figure is the variety of fragmented rules and regulations, rather than a unified law for contracts, which has resulted in misunderstandings. In August 1998, the Chinese authorities announced that a new law of contract had been drafted and was under consideration. It appears to be substantial, with some 441 articles that, when in force will codify the existing fragmented laws and help curb contract fraud.[45]

The contract appendix

If you regard something as important, try not to let it be relegated to the appendix of the contract. That is the place for putting details and perhaps expanding the main principles agreed; all important matters and principles should appear in the main body of the text.

Accepting the model contract can be a mistake

You might be handed a model contract early on with the suggestion that it be adopted with little discussion. You should not automatically accept it. The existing standard contracts tend to favor the Chinese on things like shipping dates and penalties, and are certain to exclude much detail you want to see included. If you are told that this is the only contract that can be accepted or approved by higher levels, you should not automatically believe this. It is often merely a ploy and if you stand firm and insist, they might well give way.

Help! My joint venture partner won't stop renegotiating!

They might ask for changes in an agreed contract for several reasons. One is that contracts are regarded differently in China from the West. As mentioned, they are regarded not so much a legal document as an expression of good intent of the partners to the agreement. In addition, they know that foreigners place great store on the contract and if the Chinese feel like helping you, they might want to change it to fit altered circumstances so that they can continue to "observe the contract". Another possibility is that a new government policy may have been introduced and the old contract is not in accord with the new rules. Requests to renegotiate the contract emerge so often, that some foreigners feel that, rather than seeking agreement, the Chinese believe in the theory of continual negotiation!

The casual attitude towards the rule of law can affect anyone. Even a company as big as McDonalds found that a valid twenty-year lease on its site in the heart of Beijing was abruptly canceled and the store was forced to move to a new location. A two-year fight to prevent the move failed and the flagship store was closed in December 1996.[46]

After a few years have passed, it is unlikely that any contract signed earlier will exactly fit the changed Chinese or international conditions. Under such circumstances, the Chinese attitude is often simply to ignore the contract and go with the new circumstances. In some cases, they will ask to renegotiate the terms of the contract to meet the new conditions. In 1981, the Cummins Engine Company signed a ten-year license agreement with the Chinese National Technical Import Co. (Techimport); a few years later the end user, the Chongqing Automotive Engine Plant, said that it could no longer meet some of the terms of the original contract and wanted to change them. The American side, although initially shocked at the request to tear up a legally binding document, agreed to the request and both sided managed to reach an amicable resolution.[47] The common factor in both courses of action is that the old contract should be abandoned in light of the changed market or other conditions.

With our Western approach of the rule of law and sanctity of contracts, if a partner broke a term, we would normally appeal to the contract. If you try this in China, your partner might think you are merely an ignorant foreigner who does not realize that words mean little in the society. At the worst, he might look for hidden meanings in your behavior and conclude that you are trying to break the relationship and telling him this in a subtle and indirect way. In Chinese culture, if a partner in a joint venture has to appeal to the contract signed earlier, it is often a sign that a serious problem already exists. The situation is not unlike a marriage when the possibility of divorce is being considered - any prenuptial agreement is brought out for detailed examination. In China, once they are signed, many contracts are thrown into a drawer and forgotten; they have served their purpose in finding out about each other and determining that both partners will do business together to the best of their ability.

Laws, regulations and politics

What is this thing called law?

In China, the attitude towards law is not identical with that in the West and there is a strong preference for nonlegal conciliation rather than litigation. Historically the Chinese have avoided recourse to the law courts, which were a fearful institution. A popular saying was "go to the law, go to the devil". The courts were part of the magistrate system, which had the job of governing the huge population and keeping order for the Emperor in a huge country with poor communications. A major function was to keep the peace and prevent rebellion, which often meant holding down those who might prefer to rule themselves. The law courts were concerned with these greater issues, rather than being a means of considering a case in an objective manner under the rule of law as in the West.

In a traditional Chinese courtroom, a person could be treated harshly and even tortured in an effort to get at the truth, so there was good reason for this anti law attitude. There was often an unofficial presumption of guilty unless proven innocent, on the grounds that the person would not have been arrested unless they were bad. In China, society was based on a Confucian system of ethics, in which group relationship and proper behavior mattered the most; the law became involved only when the proper Confucian relationships had broken down. This meant that the law was invoked only when the situation was already evil, so that it was felt that someone must be guilty of something.

Such attitudes persist to this day; ethics and moral principles are more important than law; disputes tend to be handled at first through "friendly consultation", and then by arbitration by a third party. Conciliation is always preferred to arbitration, while litigation is disliked.

Chinese culture contains a deep sense of ascertaining what is correct conduct and then doing what is right. The people have little sympathy for individuals acting against the group and shattering conformity. Lawyers are frequently regarded with suspicion or active dislike, and in the view of many, are no more than bad people who make a living by defending criminals.

The Chinese legal system and laws are in the process of being reformed and where there are conspicuous holes they are being filled. During the Maoist period, the law was largely put in abeyance and was regularly broken with impunity by official organizations and groups. During such ultraleft periods, a newspaper editorial could possess more strength than any law. This situation slowly began to change after the introduction of reformist polices in December 1978; many new statutes have been drafted, lawyers trained, and the status of the legal system and profession raised. It is still the case, however, that many laws are vague and there are gaps in the legal coverage.

There is now increased protection for trademarks and copyright, especially with the patent law of 1 January 1993, but in practice the law is not always obeyed. The protection of American intellectual property and copyrights was enhanced with two Memoranda of Understanding in the 1990s.[48] In an effort to increase compliance with the law, China established a Copyright Protection Center in 1998 but poverty is likely to continue to pressure consumers to buy the cheaper pirate versions of software, videos and books.

The country is now a global center for the faking of produce and some specialist counterfeiting companies previously operating in Taiwan and Hong Kong have reportedly moved their location to China. Just about any well-known branded item produced in China can be copied, including hologram security patches! Even commonplace articles like soap, shampoo and razor blades are illegally copied and sold. These are marketed throughout China and there is a thriving export industry to Russia and East Europe. It is believed that currently only half the "Nike" products sold in China are genuine and the country has the worst problem of counterfeiting products in the world.[49]

In addition to national laws and regulations, many local governments have produced their own. These are often expressed in broad, vague or ambiguous terms, some are mutually contradictory, others are not internally consistent, and on occasion they might conflict with stipulations from higher levels. It is fair to say that the law is still regarded in traditional fashion by many, i.e., something to be avoided and to be ignored if useful, as it is not of overriding importance.

Internal secret regulations

One problem in China is that internal and secret regulations exist, that cannot be revealed to outsiders, but which in ignorance it is easy to break. There is now less of a problem with national rules because China has agreed to enforce only published laws and regulations, as part of its effort to join the World Trade Organization (WTO, previously GATT). However, at the provincial and city levels, some authorities continue to issue secret rules and regulations.

Despite the traditional Chinese antagonistic attitude towards law, they will still quote it at you for their own purpose, and during negotiations they might tell you that secret regulations prevent something you want from being done. Even if it were not true, there used to be little that one could do about it. At least these days you can point to China's entry into the WTO in 2001 and the central government's agreement not to allow secret regulations, and you might prevail.

The implementation of the law varies with region and time

Many new laws have been passed in the last few years as China strives to join the international business community. Despite this, not all provinces and local areas actually implement the nation's laws in their entirety. You can sometimes turn this to your advantage, should the other side point to a law that prohibits what you seek. You might delicately raise the issue of the possibility of setting aside the central government view in the light of strong local circumstances and needs. You can emphasize that this would not be something that you would necessarily feel it essential to publicize. It might need a concession on your part in exchange, but it can sometimes be done. It is a tricky area in which to operate and this not an action that I personally advocate.

As time passes some parts of China that used to implement a central rule may quietly drop it while others might suddenly start to follow it. This situation does make dealing in China more difficult than in most countries.

Lax laws and safety

Local officials, especially those located far from Beijing, can be a law unto themselves. Although it is uncommon, a few people have fallen foul of some local official and paid a high penalty.

James Peng, an ethnic Chinese with Australian citizenship, found this out in the early 1990s when he was illegally abducted by police from the Peoples Republic of China when he was in his hotel room in Macao, at that time a foreign colony. He was forcibly taken back into China.[50] He had earlier fallen out with his joint venture partner as well as some local officials who apparently instigated the kidnapping. He then languished in jail for two years before being sentenced to a further sixteen years and then deported. All this occurred despite regular protests from the Australian government.

In another example, in 1995 the American company president of a small biochemical firm was prevented from leaving his hotel by the executives and shareholders of a local corporation, to which he allegedly owed around half a million dollars. This incident occurred in Hefei, Anhui Province. Such is the power of local officials that the police refused to intervene or to help him in any way. His passport was confiscated and he became virtually a prisoner of the town. Only after intervention by the US Consul in Shanghai did a judge order both sides back to the table to negotiate. As a result of this, he was finally freed.[51]

A similar incident in July 1998 involved the Chinese CEO of Asia Electronic Holdings, a major Chinese company located just outside Xian, home of the terracotta entombed warriors. He was reportedly detained for twenty-two days, without being formally charged or even allowed to consult a lawyer and, in addition, five of the senior management were fired by the local town mayor. The firm's shares are listed on the American National Association of Securities Dealers Automated Quotation System (NASDAQ) and when the news broke the company shares dropped 32 percent in value. Not unreasonably, the incident was worrying for those thinking of investing in China.[52] It is likely that similar cases will emerge from time to time.

Politics still matter

Politics are still regarded as being of prime importance in China. A sudden political change in people or policies may result in actions being taken that are technically illegal. Under such circumstances, appealing to the law or constitution serves no useful purpose. Officials are afraid to act until the situation clarifies itself, public order is reinstated, and they are instructed what to do. Until this happens, the situation may freeze and you might find it impossible to obtain a decision.

Chapter Six: MEETINGS AND NEGOTIATIONS: YOUR TACTICS

Your introductory statement

You need a substantial and flowery "brief introduction" (opening speech) to deliver at the first meeting (see p.83, "Your introductory speech – start off in the approved fashion").

What do they want?

You might find that it is surprisingly hard to pin the Chinese down on what they are seeking. You might start to suspect they do not really know themselves! Be careful not to look surprised if they mumble, prevaricate, and seem unable to tell you what they wish to buy. When they are selling, it is usually easier for them to get to the point.

When you start negotiating, it is important to present your product, technology, or case clearly, simply, and always without condescension. At this point, it might start to become clearer what they might actually be after. You could indicate the sort of things the product is good at or can be used for. If you can demonstrate that it proved valuable in a third country, with a few examples of problems and solutions, it can sometimes help to elicit comments from them that suggest what their troubles are or what they are really seeking.

Don't trumpet your expectations abroad

While explaining your hopes and expectations clearly and carefully to the team opposite, it is desirable not to go public with these, and in particular not to talk to the press. The Chinese side often keeps the negotiations quiet to the point of secrecy; you might find however that they encourage you sign an early memorandum of understanding with full publicity. If you do this, and many do, the Chinese are aware that it is harder for you subsequently to break off negotiations and face the risk of public embarrassment.

This is particularly a danger if your CEO goes to China and signs a quick memorandum of understanding, publicizes it internationally and then departs, leaving the detailed negotiation to underlings. The Chinese side is then aware that you will not wish to break off negotiations, which gives them an edge. If you walk away from the deal, it is not only embarrassing for your company, but your CEO is likely to pull you in and demand to know why you were incapable of negotiating something he had already agreed in principle. It would not be a good career move for you to talk to the media; wait until the final contract is signed, when you can advertise it safely.

That frustrated feeling

Expect to be frustrated in China. Many things happen that are inexplicable and annoying, and constant delays are common. It is just about impossible to find out why you are being kept waiting for days on end, probably hanging around the hotel waiting to see someone or for a decision to be passed down.

There are many possible reasons for delays, including the following.

- In China, time is not seen as money so there is little effort to accomplish things quickly.
- It could also be inexperience on their part, although this factor reduced during the 1990s; it is still common when dealing with people from the interior.
- Inefficiencies abound in offices and factories, in part owing to overstaffing.
- Maybe your host company is a weak one that does not have the power to secure what you both want.
- Someone who has to approve the idea may be sick or has gone abroad on a visit, and nothing can happen until he or she returns.
- Perhaps the team opposite is full of insecurity and the leader fears that they might be criticized for making a mistake through undue haste.
- Possibly the other side fears that you might be trying to exploit them, so they are gathering information from international sources about you, your product or technology, which takes time.
- It is possible that the Chinese have begun to negotiate with a rival firm of yours and are comparing your proposition with theirs.
- Owing to the shortage of interpreters, the one you were using might have been suddenly reallocated to another set of meetings, so that your group is unable to meet and negotiate.
- It may be a deliberate tactic should the Chinese feel you are an impatient person or are eager to return to your own country.
- Once you are established in China, delays can also be caused by breakdowns in the ancient and ill-maintained machinery, especially in state operated enterprises. Goods are frequently not delivered on schedule.
- It could be that several different bureaucratic bodies are involved and

mutual agreement cannot be reached, perhaps because of power bound-
ary disputes, or because scarce assets will need transferring to another authority, which few are willing to do.

All organs in China guard their possessions jealously and refuse to
help another unless forced to do so by higher levels. China is a huge
country and communications have always been poor. A giant bureaucracy ran China and held it together as a nation for at least 2,000 years.
With that kind of history, each unit, such as a factory, regional office, or
ministry, looks after its own interests first. With the traditional "insider-
outsider" differences, no organization ever willingly helps another and
many will actively hinder others.

The bureaucracy is huge and impenetrable, and Ministries demand a
variety of regular reports from every institution beneath them. When
American Motors were negotiating their joint venture, Beijing Jeep, they
discovered that the team with which they were talking was reporting to
ten different sectors of government - and each one had to place a seal of
approval on the points agreed![53] Once the factory was up and running, it
got easier, but the officials there still had to report to their Ministry once
every five days on average.

Patience, the supreme virtue

Coping with such frustrations requires patience and you might have to
work at being polite and avoiding rudeness. The culture sees politeness
and human dignity as virtues, and it will be to your advantage to strive to
achieve both. Recall that withdrawn quiet behavior is valued; slapping
people on the back, putting your arm around their shoulders, or engaging
in "big" behavior is anathema to the Chinese.

A fine example of delays, misunderstandings, frustration and rage is
provided by The Great Wall Hotel in Beijing. This was a joint venture between the E-S Pacific Development Company and China International
Travel Service. During construction, the two sides had major disagree-
ments, with the Chinese alleging that foreign managers were impossibly
impatient individuals who persisted in the arrogant attitude that they always knew better than the Chinese. These and other factors delayed construction work by several months.[54] The venture ran into further difficulties and the situation deteriorated until the owners finally decided that
they needed more expert help. In 1984 they signed a deal with ITT-
Sheraton for a ten-year management contract and changed the name to

The Great Wall Sheraton.

Never interrupt

Do not interrupt anyone, or it will harm your position:

- It demonstrates arrogance.
- It breaks up the harmony.
- It interferes with the growing relationship.

You set your cause back by interrupting, however much you feel the urge. Calm patience is needed - you will get your turn.

Gloating is bad

Do not openly gloat or act like a winner. In Chinese eyes, this would be bad mannered and if you appear to feel that you have won something they would naturally feel they have lost. Their leader might be concerned that an opponent of his might report the event and suggest that a team under his or her leadership could have done better. This would cause the leader problems in the arena of normal Chinese office infighting. In his eyes, you would share some of the blame for the situation and this bodes badly for his future cooperation with you.

That self-effacing man might have much power – he might even be the real leader!

Do not ignore any member of the Chinese team, as it is rarely if ever clear who has responsibility for what. Remember, everyone involved has to agree in order to make a deal but it takes only one person to stop it. You should not automatically assume that their leader, who appears to be the most senior person present, has the most authority. That quiet self-effacing person in the corner might actually be the most powerful person in the room. He or she might be concealing this because they wish:

- To watch quietly in order to gain an edge.
- To follow a deeply held cultural tenet to be quietly well mannered.
- To have a nominal leader who has a good capacity in the English language which the person himself lacks.
- To train up someone by letting someone act as leader while he quietly observes.
- To see what actually goes on with foreigners as s/he is too high up to

be involved directly in negotiations but is curious to learn about these strange visitors.

If someone formerly silent interrupts anyone on their team, especially if he interrupts the leader, immediately suspect that the new speaker is *really* powerful and may be much higher up the bureaucratic ladder than anyone else present. This means that you should listen to him seriously and go out of your way to do him any favor you can.

A long term presence

A long term relationship

Keep in mind that you are working for a long-term relationship. The Chinese approach the process of negotiation not merely to sign a contract but to develop a relationship which will last and hopefully lead to more business over the years. Westerners often have a relatively short time horizon and you must beware of letting the Chinese think you are not in it for the long term. You are striving for an in-depth relationship and becoming "an old friend", and not just a quick profit from one deal.

Friends, but...

Although you are likely to keep hearing about your friendship, it is wise not to take the remarks too seriously. Although the Chinese are often sincere when talking about friendship, on occasion it can be nothing more than a polite phrase that the person using it deemed to be appropriate at the time. "Old friends" are esteemed, and such a relationship can be valuable, but be aware that some "old friends" have been dumped when another company comes along with a better offer. This means you need to become friends but cannot rely on that alone.

If you find you are getting along with your opposite number and a friendship is developing, this is good. However, your intention should not be to become ultra cozily friendly with the Chinese team, as this might limit your ability to be tough when needed. Although they may appear friendly, the members of the team opposite are primarily doing their job, which is to gain the best deal for China at the least possible cost.

No room for high pressure selling

Try not to talk fast and engage in high-pressure salesmanship, which is inappropriate and will probably annoy the Chinese. It is at odds with their approach of harmony and quiet style; they often feel disquiet about those with a fast-talking, "snake-oil salesman" approach.

Do not spring a surprise to try to gain an advantage.

The Chinese dislike surprises, so if you suddenly announce something new and different, you are unlikely to gain anything. They will normally merely take it on board and report back to you at a later meeting. It is often a good idea to put your suggestion in writing and submit it before the meeting as this can save time; any new proposal has to go through collective consideration and decision behind the scenes before they can even begin to discuss it with you.

Invent no figures

You should never invent a figure off the top of your head, even for illustrative purposes or to use as an example. It will be noted down and may be used against you in later discussions, with the argument that it is the price or whatever that you offered earlier. This may be partly the result of poor interpretation, but if you float hypothetical figures in this way, it fits awkwardly in the culture. It will probably be understood as a genuine offer on your part, made indirectly in the expected way of a cunning negotiator. In all probability, all you meant to do was illustrate what might be involved and you might have taken a low but easy number in order to make the mental arithmetic easier for you to do.

Even if someone on their team knows enough about foreigners to realize that your illustrative figure was not in any way an offer, and has explained this to the team, they still might use your earlier mentioned figure as a deliberate tactic and demand that you keep your word.

You should never try to speak "off the record", as nothing in China is ever off the record even if they agree it will be. It is normal practice for a Chinese individual to report to his or her organization (as an insider) what you (the outsider) have said, whether it occurred at a formal business session or during some leisure period. He or she will unhesitatingly place loyalty to the unit above a request from you to keep something a secret.

No ultimatums, please!

It is almost always counterproductive to force a showdown or deliver an ultimatum. Try to leave a door open for negotiations and not back people into corners.

If you ask for some information and they are being cagey, it is a bad idea to persist and try to force them to divulge the answer. If, for example, they do not know the answer they would lose face if forced to admit this. Or else they might feel the information is secret and they do not have permission to tell you. They could be seriously punished for passing on unauthorized information, including a possible death penalty if it is judged to be a state secret. On the other hand, perhaps they merely find it difficult to explain to you why they cannot get access to the information and so they are keeping quiet.

When you definitely need to know something, you could try writing down the request and transmitting it to the Chinese side, via your contact person or an interpreter, asking them to pass it over to their leader when he or she is alone. This avoids any loss of face to their side and yours, but informs the Chinese side that you are truly serious about receiving an answer.

If in the end things get desperate, you still cannot get the information you need, and the negotiations look like stalling as a result, you might try quietly indicating that you are prepared to leave without an agreement. Do this without making it a threat. Something along the lines of "it would be a pity if I had to leave without being able to sign the agreement" has a clear ring about it, but avoids intimidation. The Chinese will then understand you really need the information and might feel pressured to act on it.

The use of language

Why will no one tell me "No"?

In the culture, getting a straight refusal means a distinct loss of face for the recipient and so people prefer to avoid it. They seek other ways to indicate refusal, including words like "perhaps" or "it might be possible"; such a phrase, particularly if it is responding to a suggestion by you and they look at each other before they reply, is almost certainly a polite refusal (see Table 6.1).

Table 6.1 Phrases and words that can indicate "no"

That might be difficult
It could be a problem

I can foresee problems here
I am not sure about that one
It is certainly worth thinking about
Possibly
Maybe
We will think it over
We must think about that
Let us discuss this another time
We will have to check with others first
It is not an attractive proposition (strong!)
Leave it with me and we will consider it
I will consult with my superiors
It is not convenient
There is no responsible person
This is the first request of this kind we have had
The matter is under consideration

If you ask a question and they sit in silence perhaps not looking at you, it usually indicates a refusal. Similarly, if you make a written request or write a letter and receive no reply, that is also a polite refusal.

Body language can also help to reveal a "no", for example a sharp waving motion of the hand near or across the front of the face, or sucking in breath between clenched teeth before speaking are very negative gestures. When they really have to correct someone, a Chinese will often say "no" rapidly three times, as "No, no, no", which indicates they actually mean it.

Never say "never"

You too should avoid saying "no" in a direct fashion. If you know it is impossible to agree to something that they want, a way around is to say you will think it over carefully and let them know; or you could tell them that you will discuss it with your colleagues after the meeting; or else you might respond that you will go over it in detail with the important people in your company HQ. It is quite acceptable to say you will take it on board and the matter can be discussed at a later stage or use any of the phrases in Table 6.1.

What if they demand the impossible?

Do not be surprised is you are faced with an unacceptable demand. You should not reject any preposterous suggestion out of hand but at least discuss it, however briefly. They could be using it as a ploy, floating the idea then agreeing to drop it in order to get a concession from you. If you are faced with this situation, it sometimes helps to say you will report back to HQ for guidance (if you are not a one-person firm).

A blunt "no" to an unreasonable suggestion is best avoided unless you have decided to cut your losses and leave China. If you reach that stage, it is worth informing the Chinese through an intermediary that you are considering leaving, in which case they might back down in the light of what to them is a strong message. It rather depends on how seriously they wish to do business with you.

Note that if the Chinese continually push for things that seem outrageous, you might be getting the signal that they themselves wish to stop negotiations and are trying to force you to break them off. Your liaison officer can probably find out quietly if this is the case.

Indirect is "in"

Be alert for the use of indirect signals. Much in Chinese society is done in a roundabout way, to avoid the possibility of confrontation that would cause someone to lose face. Any unpalatable truths are best done through an intermediary wherever possible. Signals in body language abound, but you should also be aware that if nothing seems to be happening, it might itself be a signal.

When answering a question, be brief

When negotiating, do give the shortest reply possible. The more you say, the more you might tend to make concessions or reveal a lever that the Chinese will pounce upon and use. They also tend to distrust big talkers and fast pitch salespeople, having had some bad experiences with such types. Save your long speech for your first proper introduction at the first proper business meeting; make it flowery, general and full of what you might think of as banal statements (see p.83, "Your introductory speech – start off in the approved fashion").

Body language: But he nodded "yes"

The Chinese often nod when they do not mean "yes" at all! Nodding usually indicates "I am awake and paying attention" or "please continue", but it does not signify agreement with anything that you are saying. It is easy to believe that you are doing well merely because everyone nods encouragingly, but it could easily be the case that they are united in opposition to your statements and merely indicating politely that they are listening to what you have to say.

Prices and pricing

Setting prices

Try not to set or even mention prices until you know exactly what is involved and what you will be expected to do. There may be unacknowledged expenses that you will later be required to meet, such as running training schemes, providing manuals, or paying for a trip to Beijing or to your country for several people. If you agree a price before knowing all the costs, it can prove very expensive!

Once you get around to discussing prices, you might find the Chinese argue strongly and dig in their heels. You should take care to allow yourself enough leeway. If you set your selling price too low, then various unanticipated requests or unexpected costs might eat away all your profit. If you try to set prices at too high a level, you will not be competitive and the Chinese will almost certainly know this, as they check international markets carefully. They are not short of labor to undertake detailed investigations of a mundane kind.

When American Motors were negotiating the joint venture for producing jeeps near Beijing and turned to discuss prices, the American negotiators observed that the Chinese were familiar with Jeep prices from all round the world. They discovered that Chinese embassies in countries such as Mexico and Venezuela were obtaining price lists of goods and parts from distributors and relaying the information to Beijing, as well as undertaking their own surveys as needed.[55]

When talking prices, there is a problem is that you cannot rely on current prices remaining unchanged. If you do your sums on present prices, you will get a nasty shock if the price of your raw materials or parts suddenly increases sharply. China is gradually raising state-set prices to the market level, and in this process the price of a particular good or service can increase several fold overnight. Should the team opposite produce a feasibility study, remember to ask if the prices used in it are freely floating market prices, or were administered prices and set by the state in some way. If the latter, take care!

If you can, it is desirable to get agreement that your selling prices can be flexible if sudden changes force up your costs. The Chinese economy grows through a series of boom and bust economic cycles, which it has not proved possible to eliminate. During the boom periods, prices in urban areas can increase at over 20 percent a year, although the official statistics may misleadingly report a lower figure. After one or two booms, the earlier selling prices you agreed may look very poor indeed and cause you continuing losses. If you are negotiating a joint venture, rather than just buying or selling on a one-off basis, try to get the contract to stipulate "market prices", as this gives you the ultimate in flexibility.

A recommended approach to convincing them your price offer is reasonable

The Chinese have a horror of being duped by foreigners and they are liable to bargain heavily on prices. A way that has proved successful for several companies was to demonstrate that they were really honest. This not only removes a deep Chinese fear, it demonstrates you are sincere about cooperation and allowing mutual benefits. They are likely to accept a price in the same general area and an additional benefit for you is the rest of your negotiations may be speeded up.

Nike Inc. is a case in point. When they were negotiating the price they would pay for athletic shoes to be made in China, they adopted the simple expedient of opening the books and revealing the price Nike were paying in other countries for similar products. Having seen these figures, the Chinese side accepted the Nike price as reasonable and the process helped lead to a quick agreement.[56]

Why are they charging me more than the others?

You might suddenly discover that the price you have to pay for something is higher than the locals are being charged. Many services, such as travel and hotel accommodation or telephone installation, run on a sliding price scale, with local Chinese having access extremely cheaply, Overseas Chinese paying more, and foreigners paying more again. Within the foreign group, some pay more than others, depending on who they are: e.g., students can buy at a low price, "expert advisors" pay more, and tourists or business people are forced to pay the most. Resentment over differential pricing is strong among the foreign community. Over the years, people have complained steadily and the practice of differential pricing is starting to erode, especially as China has joined the World Trade Organisation and its rules prelude the practice. If you encounter the problem, this could be gently pointed out.

Making sure they all understand

Say it again, Sam

You might find it helpful to keep repeating your needs clearly. The

Chinese may not fully understand what you want and repetition does no harm. If you cannot get agreement for something, or an item you have asked for fails to appear, it is often caused by the ponderous nature of the bureaucratic system and the lack of horizontal coordination. Requests often have to be raised several times before action occurs and you might find that you have to hound them in a quietly persistent way. You should keep pressing gently for what you need.

While waiting, you can use the time to do something else. You might find it worthwhile to prepare a wish-list of things that you never seem to get around to doing, and bring it out if there are intervals when you are left to your own devices.

A summary is always a good idea

After a negotiation session, it is a commonplace that one side believes that something has been agreed but the other thinks it was merely discussed then put aside (see "Keep careful notes or live to regret it", p.93). At the end of each meeting it is a valuable habit to sum up what has been agreed, what the next action will be, and who will take it, so that both sides know where they stand. Keep a clear record of the summaries in case there is a dispute later.

Their really senior people are beyond your guanxi

It is usually not possible to establish *guanxi* with a senior official if he is well above your level. It comes down to a question of hierarchy and rank. Relationships work on a quid pro quo basis, and (unless both people are Chinese and one is a protégé of the other) usually take place between people of reasonably similar rank. As there is probably nothing you could do in return for any favor he does you, a high level official might feel insulted if you try to enmesh him or her. It is best to friendly and polite and show deference to their status - which goes with the job rather than the individual.

How well am I doing?

For several reasons it is easy to misjudge how well negotiations are proceeding. China is very different from Western societies, the bureaucracy is vast and unfathomable even for most Chinese, and much information that would be public knowledge in the West is kept from the people. Secrecy is the norm for the rulers and bureaucrats, so you may not be told about what is happening elsewhere, what is not happening, and why this is the case.

Secondly, the Chinese negotiators themselves may not know what their superiors really want, and so do not know how seriously they should tackle things. They may be keeping the talks going as a way of marking time until the situation clarifies.

Thirdly, many foreigners have difficulty reading Chinese features and can gain little sense of the depth of the relationship. In China the body language is different, so that your Western experience and training is of little value in determining what is going on. Misinterpretations can easily occur.

Fourthly, Chinese negotiators tend to deal either at the level of global and rather bland generalities ("friendship between our two nations", "strengthening the bonds between our companies" and the like) or else with specific and concrete matters of detail. Neither level reveals much about the rate of progress being achieved.

Finally, you may well lack experience in dealing in that province of China or with that particular team, and so are unfamiliar with what is "normal" there. You might find things go slowly, then suddenly speed up; or you might feel things are progressing well, but not much is really happening.

If the Chinese suddenly want publicity, it is often a signal that the end is in sight. Nevertheless, be careful that they are not encouraging you to go public with broad details of the agreement merely to increase the pressure on you to concede important points. They are well aware that you will wish to conclude the agreement rather than back out once it has been well publicized.

Easy on those concessions!

Do not concede anything too easily. Despite the recommended approach of staying calm while smiling and being friendly, it is important to be a firm negotiator. You should be well prepared, know what you can give up, what your costs are, and what is your fallback position. The Chinese have a well deserved reputation for negotiating and can sweep you along without letting you see how much you are giving away in total. Be particularly careful not to make a series of individual concessions, each small in its own right but in total adding up to a significant loss. This is a well-known tactic in China where the approach is known as "ants gnawing away at a bone" where we might use the phrase "salami tactics".

If you are suddenly hit with a request you have not previously considered, it is best not to agree at once, in case there are important implications. You can ask for it to be considered at a later session, thus gaining time for you to think it through or discuss it with others.

If you get into an impasse and someone of high status has to fly in from your HQ to handle it, there is a danger that he or she will simply agree to the concession and leave. The onus then falls on you to pick up the pieces. The visiting chief should be forewarned that this is not a good idea and will lead to future problems for you and the company. This was discovered by the American Motors Corporation, when it was trying to negotiate the details of establishing a joint venture to build its jeeps in China. The concessions made on the short visit by a high company official made the subsequent negotiations considerably more difficult for all involved.[57]

Gift giving

Gifts are important in Chinese culture and have several functions:
- They show esteem and liking.
- They are to repay a favor or gain the chance of a favor, either now or in the future.
- They are mementoes.
- They are expected in certain social situations, such as when invited to visit a home.

You should take a large quantity of gifts with you to China and choose them carefully. Gifts from your team to the Chinese side are of two kinds - there may be one large gift that goes to the group or institution itself, and a small gift that is given to each individual member of the Chinese team. Depending on the size and wealth of your company and the size of the deal, the large gift might be:

- something that typifies your country, perhaps in silver or crystal;
- a memento of your company with your logo on it;
- a "coffee table" book that is related in some way to your or their area of interest (e.g., a book about ports of the world, given to a shipping company); or
- electronic items, e.g., a portable computer, again with your logo.

If you give a book, ensure that your Company Chairman or other suitable VIP has inscribed it before you leave for China; this shows respect and impresses the other side. If this was not possible, or you forget, the team leader must sign it before handing it over. The final banquet is often a suitable moment to pass over your large gift.

Small individual gifts are mementoes only and should be inexpensive. Everyone in their team gets an identical one, including the interpreters, and if you had a regular driver, he should be given one too. Remember that their team might be a dozen or more in size and you might be seeing more than one team, so take plenty of small items with you. Chinese groups going abroad often give something like a tiepin costing a few cents to the members of the foreign team opposite. With these small mementoes, it is always the thought rather than the value that counts.

When planning your trip, you might examine the catalogue one of the cheap office supply companies in your country. Look for cheap items that they the supplier will personalize, putting on your company name and logo. The sort of things that you might consider are:

- Pens and pencils.
- Leather drink coasters (a lot of tea gets drunk!).
- Bookmarks.
- Document wallets.
- Pocket diaries.
- Management diaries.
- Pictorial calendars.
- Inexpensive electronic devices such as a calculators.
- Your company plastic brief cases or the like.

Be careful with the colors you select (see p.18, "The meaning of colors") and remember that red color with gold lettering is highly regarded, so reserve that for the "special" gifts for individuals. It might look like overkill if everyone on the team got this.

Your supermarkets and cut-price shops back home also have many small inexpensive items that are often unobtainable in China and hence prized. Try to ensure that whatever you give is clearly labeled as made in your country and in particular it must *not* have been made in Hong Kong or Taiwan.

You might find that bringing a few cheap toys pays off, as they may prove useful as gifts, especially if invited to a home were there is a child. It is the thought counts, and given the value Chinese place on their family, a present to a child is very well received. Even if the age-group is wrong, it will still be much appreciated and it might get recycled within the family group at a later date. Brand new magazines in English, of a noncontroversial type, are also enjoyed and make a decent gift.

It is better not to wrap any of these small gifts up, but if you do so, never use white paper and try not to carry them in a white paper bag, as this color is traditionally associated with death. Black or blue paper is also a bad choice, but red is always excellent, while pink or yellow are not a problem.

If you wish to make a gift to someone on a personal basis, it is best done in private. A bottle of foreign spirits is fine. Overseas Chinese often prefer brandy to whiskey, as many believe it is strongly "male" or *yang* (in the *yin-yang* system), i.e. can work as an aphrodisiac, but in China there seems little preference so far. Good foreign chocolates are also well regarded, as are imported dried fruits. A carton of cigarettes is an acceptable gift and because they can be used as trading goods, nonsmokers also accept them happily. Other good gifts are cigarette lighters, good quality pens (but not with red ink in them), small portable electronic devices (it is a good idea to supply a spare battery or two as good ones may be hard or impossible to get locally), or something typical of your own country, state or city *and* made in your country.

Bad gifts

Certain items are better not given as gifts. These include knives (symbolizing fighting and antagonism), cut flowers (symbolizing funerals and death), watches or clocks (also death-associated reminding us that our life is passing), anything completely pure white in color or blue/yellow in combination (death), and underwear or anything remotely connected with sex. That said, watches are now prized by the younger generation, who are generally less superstitious than their elders. Handkerchiefs are also best avoided as a present.

The size of gifts

It is better not to give expensive gifts, unless your company is a rich, well-known international one or something expensive is clearly being requested. Large expensive gifts to individuals are best avoided as they smack of bribery and the Chinese will feel an obligation to repay the gift, which could be difficult for them. Something like an automatic camera or notebook computer puts an onus on him or her that cannot easily be repaid. You should be aware, however, that attitudes in this area are changing rapidly and larger personal gifts are becoming more acceptable. It is quite proper to present a large gift to the whole organization rather than to an individual.

If you are clearly being asked for a large personal gift, in effect as a bribe, then you must do as your conscience dictates.   If American, be aware that the US Foreign Corrupt Practices Act makes bribery of foreign government officials a crime with severe penalties attached: you could be fined up to $100,000 and spend five years in prison, while your company could face a fine of up to $2 million.[58] The USA is so far unique in this respect, although in 1997 the Organization for Economic Cooperation and Development (OECD) drafted an international treaty that requires member states to enact similar legislation. Many in the States argue that the US law has disadvantaged American companies when seeking Chinese contracts.   Others believe that it can help US companies, because it allows them to refuse a demanded bribe - they can point out that it illegal and something for which they could be prosecuted back home.   Hong Kong business people are very skilful at making large gifts in a suitably quiet and backstage manner, in an effort to gain business and it seems to work well for them.

If they politely refuse a gift – they do not really mean it!

If a Chinese person is offered a gift, it is polite for him or her to refuse, occasionally up to three times, so when you offer your gift, you might experience a refusal with smiles and gestures. You should persist, also smiling and making small offering motions with the present.   Remember when you are offered a present, it would be nice if you declined once before accepting.

Presenting the gift

Hold the gift in both hands, as this is considered polite.   One-handed gift giving shows a lack of respect. You will find that Westernized or well traveled Chinese will frequently offer gifts to foreigners with one hand, as they have learned our customs too, but among themselves, two-handed is still the civilized way. They notice every time you do it and appreciate that you understand something of their culture, of which they are proud.

Paying for their visit to you

Do accept you may need to invite the leaders of the Chinese side to visit your country or pay for a local trip for them in China, particularly if yours is a large well known company. Some companies have found that they were expected to pay for a large delegation that stayed for a considerable time. Kaiser Engineers of California found that they had to accommodate three such groups on visits to the States, averaging ten members each, one of which stayed for nine months![59] Most visits are considerably shorter than this. Although they are ostensibly for business familiarization and learning, you might find that the group rapidly indicates a wish to go sightseeing, perhaps to Disneyland, a Movie World, an Oceanarium and the like. If yours is a small firm, then they might let you off lightly: you could find that you are only expected to pay for a domestic trip for the Chinese, perhaps to a local holiday area or Beijing.

It can hit anyone. Years ago when I was leader of a group of students studying advanced Chinese we went on a short holiday break to Emeishan in Sichuan - and were forced by the college to pay for a handful of Chinese students we had never even met to accompany us!

Some other pointers

Offering training is well received

You can expect that unless you are simply selling raw materials, the team opposite will negotiate hard for free training and the transfer of skills. You might find that they do not place a money value on much information that in the West could carry a substantial price tag. You need to be aware of what it will cost to bundle in overseas visits, free manuals, and technical training or seminars, so that if they request these things, or you offer them as a negotiating point, you can include them in your price. Indeed, you need to build in some slack for what you will be forced to concede later.

When you are attempting to set a the price for any services you will supply, or other intangible items, you should be prepared to face close questioning on how you arrived at the figure you propose. A little homework before you leave for China can pay off: make a list of arguments justifying what you are asking. Possible arguments include:

- That is what you have charged another company, or firm in another country.
- That is what your competitors normally charge.
- That is the recommended price from a trade association or similar body.

If you can think of any other arguments – good! Make sure you have the necessary evidence with you, for instance, a copy of the trade association recommendation. What you have to avoid is mumbling that it seemed like a fair price to you, that these things cost money, or some other vague statements which is not backed up by some sort of hard evidence.

   If rather than waiting to be asked and then trying to bargain, you make an offer to train their people, this will be well received. You will have to feel your way: an early offer might help build trust quickly with benefits to you. On the other hand, real concessions tend to come late in the Chinese negotiating process and you should not give away too much too soon, in case the concessions become one-sided. Remember also that they might make a concession, then reopen it later and try to retrieve part of it. You will find it very useful if you have kept good notes of the earlier decision and can point out that this was something they offered in exchange, so that your earlier concession also merits reconsideration.

Be wary about handing over any confidential information or proprietary technology

   Although China is a secretive society, it is common for confidential information given by foreigners to be widely circulated. If you tell someone something in confidence, there is no guarantee that the person will not use it as a lever when negotiating with you, or with one of your competitors.

   Similarly, technology handed over may not stay with the company involved, and could be passed to other firms or trickle into other parts of China. Reverse engineering can occur, with the result that foreign firms can and have patent rights infringed. With proprietary technology, the danger is no less real, but the results may not be too damaging. Technology is changing rapidly, so that the bit of your own technology that you supply may soon become outdated, as long as you continue to innovate.

China's problems might be your gateway

   You might benefit if early in the negotiating process, you enquire about China's current problems and policies. Asking about national priorities and the current five-year plan, then turning to local Provincial or city needs and their current development projects demonstrates an interest. More importantly, it can open up good topics of conversation, help develop your relationship with local officials, and might well reveal unexpected areas in which you can do business. Although economic issues are more likely to reveal interesting areas, it can be worth asking about any local social problems, pointing out that you might have suggestions or solutions. If you adopt this I-can-help-you approach, it can assist in offsetting the Chinese habit of not saying exactly what the problems are, or what they really want, but leaving it to you to offer your wares.

Try not to give them leverage

It is a good idea to avoid informing them that you have urgent business back in your country and must leave China by a certain date. You might think of it as a way of trying to speed up negotiations, but they are just as likely to respond by delaying meetings and procrastinating. Then suddenly, a day or two before your departure date, you might be given a well designed proposal that does not exactly favor you but, given the shortage of time, it is tempting to sign. They can be adept at using your pressing commitments to their advantage.

Another way you can inadvertently supply them with leverage is to tell them that they have your company's undivided attention and you are not negotiating with others. This might look like a tempting gambit during the early stages of negotiating, as it reassures the other side that you are working hard to establish and build the necessary friendly relationship. If however they understand that your are not talking to others in or outside China, it increases their bargaining power.

Parallel negotiations

It is quite likely that the other side is involved in parallel negotiations involving the same project with other foreign companies. If yours is a major corporation and the project is large and costly, this is more likely than not. They may not tell you they are doing this until your talks are well advanced and you have made a series of concessions. The first you hear about it might be when they inform you that a rival company has made such and such an offer and are you prepared to match it?

Parallel negotiations allow them:

- To check on some of the information you are providing or arguments you are using.
- To get alternative bids.
- To play one side off against the other.
- To obtain a better deal for their institution and China.

If yours is a small or medium sized company there may be little you can do, but if you are a major corporation, you might consider starting your own parallel negotiations in a different part of China. Inter-regional rivalry is such that one local authority is unlikely to inform another about business negotiations so the chances of you being able to keep it secret are good.

Be kind to those officials

Hard though it sometimes may be, it is a good idea to treat bureaucrats sympathetically. Some have immense power, although it will probably not be apparent to you how much each person possesses, or even which official is responsible for what functional areas. This means treating them all kindly. If you offend someone with power, a series of things can go badly for you without any apparent cause.

The extremely successful Thai tycoon Dhanin Chearavanont, who among other things owns the Lotus hypermarket in Shanghai, strongly recommends being cooperative with government officials because the un-specific nature of many rules and regulations allow for personal interpretation. This means you need them on your side rather than being obstructive. He follows his own advice and over two decades has met many officials including President Jiang Zemin and Premier Zhu Rongji and numerous provincial governors and city mayors. Although he argues his success is not merely the result of having the right connections, he puts a great deal of effort into maintaining his contacts and has done very well.[60]

Stick with it

Perseverance and persistence are crucial when dealing in China. It can be a good market, but in many cases the rewards do not come quickly or easily. You can slog along for months apparently getting nowhere then, if the Chinese really want to deal, they might suddenly offer major concessions. The stories say that this has been know to happen on the team's last day, when they were in a cab on the way to the airport! There is probably an element of urban myth about such tales but you will hear such anecdotes when expatriates get together to drink and yarn.

Keep your options open

The Chinese are tough negotiators. It would be a mistake to reveal that you are pinning a lot of hope on this deal or that it is crucial for you to en-sure the project goes through. That would immediately reveal your weak bargaining position and they could take advantage of this. You can keep stressing that the deal is important to both sides, mutual benefits should flow, and put over the idea that there is a balance in the gains. This has the dual advantage of not giving them leverage and reassuring them that you are not trying to exploit them or China.

Why won't they let me rest?

Many negotiators have faced marathon negotiations with little respite. There are several reasons why this happens. Traditionally China sees keeping an opponent active and allowing no rest as a valuable part of warfare. Business, to twist the Von Clausewitz phrase, is sometimes seen as an extension of war by other means. If the Chinese with whom you are negotiating see the talks in an adversarial way, then they might try to wear you down. Sudden switches from going slow to going fast, then suddenly finding a reason for delays, are a familiar story in Chinese history, notably in the novel *The Water Margin.* Cunning is valued when pitted against a superior and formal force, rather like the Robin Hood myths familiar to America and Britain.

Another reason for marathon sessions is that China is a poor country, those working there are used to long days and, at least until May 1 1995, six-day working weeks. At that date, the five-day week was enacted. The older staff learned years ago to endure long meetings, stay awake, and concentrate under Mao Zedong's regime. At that time, the personal loss of not doing so could be tremendous. Relative to them, you may find you become tired, a result of both the pressure of work and culture shock, which can be severe on your first visit or two.

What level should you be relying on?

You should not rely solely on a high level contact, as that is not where the actual recommendations are made. You should start at the top when seeking something, then use what influence you can gain to help you when negotiating at lower levels. You should not be surprised, however, if an agreement made by a top institution subsequently fails to be carried out, as units have been known to change their minds.

Can you deliver?

Do not promise more than you can deliver. The Chinese might tempt you to do so by indicating that if you do something they want, the contract is likely to go to you, rather than to some other company. You should be careful not to promise something that you *think* you can achieve when you return home, unless you are certain of it. The Chinese note all concessions carefully, will remind you of them, and expect you to honor your word.

Honesty is the best policy

You should always be sincere, and tell the truth. The Chinese make a practice of checking up on people and their statements. They tend to be suspicious as a result of their treatment in history as well as more recent rather outrageous events after foreigners were allowed in to do business. If you are found to have lied, either your business will not be wanted, or you may have to make major concessions in order to be allowed to continue.

But misleading them can be profitable

One way of improving your position is to use your liaison officer or interpreter deliberately to leak your "final offer", "lowest selling price", or fallback position to someone in the opposing team. You can rely on them to transmit the message. You might be able to arrange casually slipping in the information at a banquet or other social occasion. Of course, you should ensure that the "minimum acceptable result" that you are letting slip contains a margin in your favor. You might need this cushion to enable you to get a reasonable deal as negotiations progress.

Favors build relationships

Where you are able, you should do small favors for people and develop the relationship between you. Partly this gives face, but more importantly, favors must be repaid; in both their business and ordinary existence, everyone works in a network of favors owed and owing. Any time you want to obtain an item or get something done, it speeds up the application through formal channels if one goes go though this network at the same time. Without such a network very little can be achieved, with it the results can be surprising (see p.15, "*Guanxi*, the secret of being successful in China").

For the Chinese a relationship can be built on such things as a shared background in school, college, a military unit or even coming from or having worked in the same province. It helps if you knew them personally at that time, but the coincidence can still be enough to develop *guanxi*. They are members of an insider group, however tenuous. If a Chinese individual is looking for special help, he or she will normally first look for a relative before thinking about other possibilities.

For you as a foreigner, you have less material with which to work, but a relationship can be built on shared experiences: perhaps you have done business together before, have both visited a certain country. Or it might be something in common such as enjoying the same hobby, having the same number of children perhaps of the same sex, possessing a mutual friend, studying the same subject at college, or liking the same movie. It may be a bit insubstantial but it is a start and you have to work with what you have.

The easiest way for you as a foreigner to acquire a set of contacts is to hire the son or daughter of a powerful local official to work for you. This can be guaranteed to open many doors.

Should you ask someone to meet socially at your hotel?

If you want to organize a social get together with someone, you could tentatively mention your hotel but ask if the person could suggest a more suitable venue. If you thoughtlessly ask a private individual to come to your hotel, it might be difficult for them to get there, even though they would enjoy it. The newly rich entrepreneurs have cars and they enjoy flaunting their status symbol, so there is no problem with them. However, few officials or ordinary managers have easy access to one. The public transport system is often crowded, the routes might not be well arranged for the journey, and the family bicycle might be needed by some relative. You could casually ask if they live near your hotel and how they get to work, to try to ascertain if it seems a reasonable venue.

If it's bad news, send a messenger

If you have to pass on bad information, such as something will not be possible or an important shipment date must be changed, consider using a "go-between" to transmit the news. This avoids you having to say "no" personally which helps sustain your mutual relations. It is the acceptable way in Chinese culture. As an example, during Mao Zedong's reign, the ever-popular Zhou Enlai was often chosen to announce bad news, such as major harvest failures during the Great Leap Forward (1958-60). This helped to preserve Mao's position as a godlike person who could not be seen to make mistakes. Your local go-between might be a good person to function for you here.

How they might see you

In general terms, expect to be treated rather as if you are a supplicant from a weak tributary state to a powerful emperor. This is the old model of China's relationship with the world, and things have not changed much, especially if you are meeting with government officials. The Chinese know they are the best, and have the best culture and history, but feel they have been dogged by an inability to modernize and cope with the impact of foreigners since the mid 19th Century.

Chinese institutions do not cooperate

You can expect to encounter rivalry between organizations. These are not coordinated horizontally and all requests and orders simply go up and down. When dealing with China, it is crucial to ascertain which other bodies will have an interest in the project and to make sure that either they are involved in the meetings or the discussions are being communicated to them. Some projects have been held up for lengthy periods because no one bothered to secure the cooperation of the electricity supplying authority or the like.

You might find insecurity

Do not be surprised to meet insecurity or uncertainty among officials. It can be based on several factors, including their leader being new to the job; an awareness of past foreign exploitation of China and a dread of being deceived; unclear orders from above on what is expected of them; a change in the local power structure that is leaving them more vulnerable; or a fear that a future policy change may render the present negotiations pointless.

Leave the abacus alone

You must never touch an abacus should you come across one sitting on someone's desk. Many foreigners find it tempting to slide the beads around, perhaps invoking a distant memory of their childhood. You should be aware that it is common for people to leave off in the middle of a job, and there may well be a complex sum, half completed, sitting on it. If you casually fiddle with the beads or even alter just one of them, it might destroy hours of work. This will not make you friends or influence people!

Closing the deal

A sweetener may be necessary

Observe that the Chinese often expect a "sweetener" to be thrown into the deal near the conclusion of negotiations. The way business is conducted in China often involves suddenly speeding things up as the end grows close and the time for signing the contract is nigh. If they suddenly start to focus on details and the actual words to be expressed in the contract, suspect the end may be in sight.

There is a clear cultural difference between Westerners and Chinese on making concessions: we think in terms of negotiating one point and moving on to the next one, and so to the end. In contrast with this, the Chinese tend to roam from point to point, going back and forward, and may save up their concessions to the final stages. Be prepared for this and make sure you have kept something up your sleeve to give up - perhaps a price concession, some free seminars, or a training trip abroad for a few of their people.

The sportswear company Nike Inc. did well in this regard. After they had concluded the main negotiations and had reached agreement on producing sports shoes in China, in order to help build their relationship, Nike Inc. agreed to send three well-known US basketball coaches to China to hold a 10-day clinic and offered to bring 10 Chinese coaches to the States.[61] This suggestion was very well received by the Chinese. Notice how the offer was closely related to the product with which Nike was involved. If you could think of something related to your project that you could offer, then as in the Nike case, it might bring you a lot of business. If you are going to have to pay for a trip anyway, you might as well make it one that will pay off for you, rather than be a simple freebie for them.

Other large companies have supported the educational and health system, by providing free equipment to colleges and schools, giving money to build or extend school buildings, providing training facilities, or supporting hospitals. Examples of companies doing this are IBM, Motorola, and Xerox. A few thousand dollars can easily build a small school, and the rewards in terms of publicity and receiving special help can be great.

If you are selling to China on credit, towards the end of the negotiations when they are almost ready to sign, it would be a good time to announce something like a lower interest rate loan or perhaps a grace period before repayments need start. The Chinese often find such offers more alluring than a simple lower price. You might even hint at a major gift that you are considering giving to the organization with which you have been negotiating, in order to celebrate the signing - a powerful refrigerator, a good computer, TV or hi-fi set might be appreciated. Whatever you promise here, you must of course deliver and preferably be there to present it formally with due ceremony.

What if they spring a high official on me?

Do not be surprised if, without any warning, you are suddenly invited to meet a high official. The Chinese sometimes wheel one out to try to impress you and increase the pressure to make a concession. Alternatively, it may indicate that they are taking the negotiations more seriously, for instance, someone high in the bureaucracy may have upgraded the priority of the project. They could also be signaling that the end of the negotiations are in sight; if you suddenly see such a person, particularly after negotiations have been drifting along for some time, it can be a good sign.

Send Mr. Big to conclude negotiations

You should try to send a senior person to conclude the negotiations and actually do the signing. If this is done when the negotiations are at an advanced stage, it raises the quality of the agreement in Chinese eyes and they are likely to treat the deal as being more important. Status is extremely significant in the culture, which is sometimes difficult for people from more egalitarian and recently settled countries, such as North America and Australia, to appreciate. After the signing, the senior representative must host a dinner to celebrate and seal the friendship. He or she should not just leave China, however pressing other engagements may seem, as the Chinese side will feel slighted and insulted.

If your firm is small and you feel might not have a person of the requisite image to come and sign, you might consider looking further afield. One small family company based in Sanford, Florida, successfully negotiated a joint venture to assemble helicopters in Guangzhou and, knowing the need for a high level personage, actually managed to get Vice-President Bush to go to China and sign the deal![62] Another example is provided by the company Celestial Yacht Ltd., which succeeded in getting former President Richard Nixon to attend their opening ceremony in Xiamen.[63] If you can persuade your country's Ambassador or Consul to attend the signing ceremony and/or banquet, it could help to smooth your path in the future (see "Banquets", p.156, for what to expect.)

If things do not go right, you just might have to walk away

The Chinese will usually press hard to gain the maximum number of concessions and if they manage to push you down to your minimum position, you should stand firm. You have to be prepared to walk away from negotiating if necessary. It is usually better to do this and cut your losses, than to accept a deal that will cost you money.

The exception is if your company is large and has sufficient reserves to take current losses in the hope that business will be profitable in the long term. Many Western firms have done this and eventually make profits. While they proudly announce these, one wonders how long it will take to make up for earlier losses, particularly if the loss of earnings of the possible alternative use of the investment, and the trouble involved, are considered. If you see an encouraging survey of foreign firms making profits in China, it might tend to gloss over how long it took before the profits actually began. Few business people like to admit to mistakes and they may put spin on their statements. Keep in mind that there are markets other than China where money can be made.

One company that walked away after a feasibility study cast doubt on the project, was Europe's Airbus Industrie. Together with Singapore Technologies and Alenia of Italy, the company was contemplating building 100-seater airliners in China, in collaboration with the state-owned Aviation Industries of China. They bravely but sensibly abandoned the idea in 1998, despite the project having been publicized and effectively endorsed by former premier Li Peng on a visit to Paris in 1996, then publicized by President Jacques Chirac when visiting Beijing in 1997.

Some foreign companies have gone through the whole laborious negotiating process, actually established a firm in China, and *then* decided it was not worth it! The French Peugeot motor car company set up a joint venture in Guangzhou in 1985 but despite high initial hopes ran into severe problems. As early as 1989, one Peugeot official admitted that if they had the chance to make the decision again whether to come to China or not, they would have stayed away. By early 1997, the French company finally decided to cut their losses and pull out.[64] They still run a joint venture in Hubei province, producing Citroen vehicles, which did not suffer the severity of problems encountered in the Guangzhou joint venture.[65]

A report by Andersen Consulting and the Economist Intelligence Unit suggested that if a joint venture is not making profits by the end of the fourth year of operations, it should examine its performance carefully or consider if it should get out completely.[66] This is good advice, but many companies hang on in there, despite little or no profit, on the grounds that they have already invested so many millions that it is difficult to pull out and admit that mistakes were made. Others feel that the company simply must be represented in China or it is somehow not internationally respectable. A case in point is the French company Total SA, which is involved in a joint venture for an oil refinery. They faced so many problems in the initial period that the venture could not even start, and was forced to keep postponing the opening. Once in business, they refused to close down, despite many technical problems and poor international marketing prospects.[67]

Pepsi Cola was widely believed to have gone into China largely on the grounds that Coca Cola was there, and Pepsi could not be seen to have no presence in the country in the world with the largest population and good growth prospects.

Chapter Seven: SOCIALIZING AND PROPER BEHAVIOR

Invitations

You must accept all invitations

If you receive an invitation to go for lunch, dinner or some outing, you should accept. If the Chinese issue an invitation they have a reason, and it is part of their system of doing business. You need to be really ill to turn it down; otherwise your refusal can confuse them, upset the system, and leave them unsure what to do next. This can lead to delays while they discuss the matter behind your back, sort out what they believe your (probably cunning and inscrutable) motives were for refusing, and decide how best to continue the business process.

Going out for dinner or traveling with them on a trip offers a valuable opportunity to get to know your opposite number and his team. You can build up the relationship by asking questions, swapping information, showing photographs, and exchanging views.

Useful opening questions can include:

- Is he or she married?
- Does the person have children?
- What sex and age are the offspring?
- What school do they attend and how well are they doing?
- Are they are at college or have they started their career, and if so, in what line?
- Has s/he lived in this area all his or her life?
- Where else has s/he worked in China?
- Where is his or her original family home?
- Did he or she go to university and if so where?
- What did s/he study there and how long was the course?
- Did s/he get allocated to the first job, or did s/he have a free choice?
- Has he or she been abroad and if so where?
- How did they like it and what impressed them most?
- How many times they have been on foreign visits?
- Do they or their spouses have a particular interest, hobby, or sport they play or watch?
- What hobbies do their children pursue?
- What career options are possible for their children?
- Is anyone in their family studying English?

You naturally volunteer information about such matters also, and can then compare the situations. Look particularly for anything that you both have in common and stress this. If it is a shared hobby, visit to a country, or child-related issue, try to move to a more in-depth discussion if the other person is willing. This can really help to develop trust and friendship; and friendship involves obligations.

Taking photographs

It is a good idea to take photographs of their team members, especially the leader, when engaged in social activities or trips with them. Your first photograph should be of him or her. If no recreational visits are suggested and the negotiations are kept formal, you can still ask if they would assemble for a group photograph, which usually pleases them greatly. It is a good idea to warn them in advance that you would like to take photographs, as they may wish to dress up in special clothing or perhaps use makeup .

You should definitely aim to take memento photographs before you leave. After you get home, make sure you send each of them a copy of all the photographs, not just those that they personally were in. The photographs should preferably be mounted in a small album rather than sent in an envelope. A set of loose photographs might be taken as an indication that you do not really care or have not tried hard enough.

You might wish to blow up the set of group photographs that you will personally keep, in order to have space to annotate the back. As soon as you can, you should write the name of each team member in the appropriate position so that you can easily tell who is who. This will be very useful to you when you return to China or some of them visit you in your country. It acts a quick reminder of faces and names. If you can add a few facts about each one (such as number of children, particular hobbies, where they were hoping to go abroad and which trips you did together) it will help you to ask the right personal questions and reminisce when you next meet. When you do this, it demonstrates that you remember and like them. If you use standard small photographs that have insufficient space on the back, you can put the names on but keep the details in a small notebook or in a computer file - with backups on floppy discs!

Chinese homes

Few Chinese will invite you to visit their home. Instead, it is normal to be invited out to a restaurant. By Western standards, most homes are of exceptionally low quality and, aware of this, many Chinese prefer the anonymity of the restaurant. If you are invited to someone's home, you might be surprised or even shocked at the low standard of living - if so, you should hide it. Even by Asian standards, quite powerful people often live in relatively humble surroundings.

Your behavior in someone's home

When you arrive you will be greeted at the door, invited in and asked to sit down. You should take off your shoes at the door, unless your host tells you not to bother. Do not forget to change your socks before the visit, and make sure there are no holes. Using a foot spray is a good idea! You must take a gift, which you give immediately, holding it in both hands and saying something like it is just a trifle, or it is a small present, or it is not much at all. Do not expect to be shown around the apartment or house, as you might do with a visitor to your home. Your visit will probably be confined to the one living room, which they will have made a special effort to make as nice as they can. You should make a favourable comment on the decor as a whole, the way that the furniture is arranged to give a feeling of space, or how nicely they have arranged small items. Keep the praise general and be careful not to strongly admire any particular item, as the host might feel obliged to present it to you. In most cases, they will be poorer than you, and it would be embarrassing for you and certainly painful for them.

If invited home, it is more likely that you will not be given a meal but you might be offered biscuits, fruit or sweets. It is polite to eat one or two. If a meal is served, you should admire and praise it fulsomely. You might find that the wife serves the food but then disappears and does not to eat with you, which is a traditional practice. If this happens, it is best simply to ignore it and not ask where she has gone or why she is not eating. Later, she will dine off whatever is left over, so you should leave some of every dish on the communal plate, however much you are enjoying the food.

It is the duty of the host to offer drinks and keep your glass charged, which means you should never ask for a drink, as this would be an insult to your host. You will probably eat early, perhaps 6.30 or so, and finish by 8 or 8.30 p.m. If you make noises about leaving about ten or fifteen minutes after the meal has ended, it will be appreciated. Remember that the wife has probably not yet eaten and cannot do so until you have left. Ignore their protests that you should stay, this is merely polite behavior on their part, and insist you must be off. You can explain that you have things to do before tomorrow's meeting.

Before you leave China, you should reciprocate the invitation and invite them to a meal at your hotel if this is reasonably accessible; if it is far off, a splendid meal in a superior local restaurant might be better, as it will be easier for them to attend. Your liaison officer should be able to ascertain if there is anywhere worthwhile nearby. If there is not, then a good central restaurant near decent public transport is probably your best choice. Get your liaison officer to book a table and order in advance.

Gifts when visiting a home

If invited to visit a Chinese home, remember that you must take a gift with you. Exotic fresh fruit is nice, if you can find some locally, perhaps in your hotel. You can hardly bring some in on the off chance of needing it! Spirits, chocolates, fancy imported sweets and books in the English language are also very acceptable. Someone in the family is almost certain to be studying English. Perfume and cologne are much prized, but men's aftershave is not valued, mainly because Chinese men shave rather infrequently and the habit of using aftershave has not caught on.

You should wrap your gift and if possible in red or gold paper. You will probably find that the family will normally not open it at once but wait until you leave, which is regarded as good manners in China. This custom is related to the importance of face: it saves face all round if your gift is somehow inappropriate, perhaps too cheap, or too expensive. If you wish, you can explain it is the custom in your country to open it at once and they might take the hint, but you should not press the issue. Generally, they will respect you more if you let them do it their way. Some Westernized Chinese might mention the fact that in your country presents are opened immediately and proceed to do so themselves, but it is uncommon.

If the host smiles deprecatingly and refuses the gift, persist with your offering, holding it in both hands and use a repeated urging motion with your arms, pushing it gently at him. He might refuse once or twice, to show good manners before finally accepting it.

Banquets

Two sorts of banquets

Banquets fall into two: the major ones that mark something important, like the start of negotiations or the end of them, and the minor ones that crop up more often. The minor ones are less formal, the meal will probably not be ordered in advance, there will be a polite quarrel about who will order, and eventually the most important person will either order or tell someone else to do this, and the Chinese will fight to pay the bill at the end. These minor banquets are more like a normal business dinner than the formal ones. Much of the description here refers to formal banquets, but the advice holds good for both kinds.

Banquets really are important

Banquets play a unique part in doing business in China. They are a means of introducing new people to you, they help to develop your relationship, and they celebrate an event, such as the conclusion of a deal. China is a poor country and low salaries for powerful people are common, so those free banquets are an important part of their salary package. When you get to China, a banquet will be organized by your host unit. The more importance the Chinese place on your business or project, the more important will be the senior host. All those present, who may be from a variety of different units, will at once take note of his or her status and evaluate your importance accordingly.

Banquets have a hidden agenda of making you feel warm and welcome as well as putting you under some obligation. You wipe the obligation slate clean by giving a reciprocal banquet for your host unit after a decent interval, which might be a few days or up to a week. Good manners require you to do this in any case.

The banquet is usually held at a popular local restaurant. The Chinese eat early so expect it to start somewhere between 6 and 7 p.m. and last for about two hours or so. Your team should arrive as a group and be on time. The food will be served shortly after you arrive.

Towards the end of the meal, fried rice is often served because in some parts of China tradition dictated that a guest must not leave hungry and this dish really is a filler! Sometimes a whole fish might appear, marking the beginning of the end stage, and soup is then often the last hot dish. You will know when the meal is finally over, as a bowl or basket of fruit will be put on the table and in summer cold towels will usually be given for you to wipe your hands and face. In winter they may be very hot indeed, so take them by the edge in the tips of your fingers and wave gently once or twice to avoid burning yourself. After the towels come, the evening will be over in about ten minutes. In China, it is traditionally the function of the guest to initiate leaving, but some Chinese hosts now rise and use a phrase like "it was nice of you to come" indicating the evening is over.

Greeting and seating rules

The host greets the guests as they enter and then, if the numbers are small, indicates where they should sit. With large numbers, someone else may show you to your place. It is polite to suggest that the main guest sits first, and the older people next, with the normal Confucian reverence for age. The leader (you) will be placed on the immediate right of the principal Chinese host. The "best" seat, or seat of honor, is the one facing the door with your back to the wall, and you and the main host will probably sit in that position. The seat to the right of the host is considered superior to the one on the left. If numbers warrant it, there may be several tables, with a representative of the main host sitting at each and in charge of it.

Where are the wives?

Traditionally a wife ate apart from her husband, and although this did not apply to the very poorest section of society, it is unlikely that wives will be present at the banquet. Everyone you see will be business oriented, although one or two may be receiving a payback for a favor done, and may have relatively little to do with you or even nothing. You should never ask a Chinese person why he is present or why he has not brought his spouse. If you are in China with your spouse, and he or she is specifically invited, they should attend. If women are present at a social gathering, you might find they try to sit together. If you should meet someone's wife, it is wrong to compliment her on her beauty, which would seem impertinent. You may praise her for something she does instead, such as cooking beautifully or speaking English well, whatever seems appropriate.

Banquets tend to follow a set format

After seating, there will usually be light conversation, perhaps the cracking and eating of melon seeds and the serving of cold hors d'oeuvres. When the principal host picks up his or her chopsticks, it is the signal to start. Grace is never said. During the meal, you should wait for the principal host to start on a dish before you sample it. Often it will be offered to you first as a mark of respect and you should accept gracefully, with a smile and slight inclination of the head. Remember that a slow nod is a respectful gesture and can mean thank you. Traditionally, the host has the duty of serving both food and wine to guests, but these days serving the wine is usually delegated to the waiters. The host will normally be the one to break into dishes like whole fish, using a fork and spoon or a set of serving-chopsticks, and serve the nearby (hence important) people. If using his own chopsticks, he will reverse them and use the blunt end that has not been near his mouth. If he serves you in this way, you should offer to do the same for him (and use the serving spoon or reverse your chopsticks) as this is polite. He might well decline - equally politely. You should learn to use chopsticks properly, but if you cannot manage at all, then quietly inform the host and you will get Western eating implements.

Be careful not to eat too much

Try to pace your eating, and sample only a small bit of each dish, especially early on. There may be more courses than you imagine: eight to twelve is common, and some special banquets might offer fifteen or more. The host will often have a list by his side in Chinese - each complete line represents one course, so if you can surreptitiously count the lines, you know the number of dishes to be served. The list may be written from top to bottom rather than left to right; the ragged ends on the lines of characters indicate the bottom so you can tell which way the list is written.

It is wise to start slowly because traditionally it is considered rude to stop eating in the middle of the banquet, even if you are feeling bloated. If you stop, it can be taken as a silent criticism of the food, of something just said, or perhaps of the Chinese side in general. Although they will certainly realize that you have simply eaten enough, they often feel uncomfortable that you have dropped out, and will keep insisting that you eat a bit of every dish. If you find your host starts putting food on your plate that you do not want, do not finish it all but leave a little - this will probably dissuade him.

"Charge your glasses and drink a toast"

In an ordinary restaurant in the interior, the first thing you should do is surreptitiously check that all of your glasses have unchipped rims so that you do not cut your lip. In good city restaurants the glasses should be fine. Now you are ready to toast! Early in the proceedings, the host will rise and toast the main guest, the delegation, and perhaps your country of origin. After a few minutes, often after the next course has been served, you as the main guest, rise and respond, toasting their leader and delegation in return. It is best to follow the toasting line established, and toast to success, the business at hand, the friendship of your two nations, cooperation between the two companies, and such like. This is a good time to wheel out all the platitudes you can call to mind. You must toast the Chinese team itself and if the host toasted your country, you have to do the same for theirs. Always refer to China in full as "The People's Republic of China". Mention of Taiwan is probably best avoided, although it is no big deal these days. If you must refer to it, always remember to call it "the Province of Taiwan", and not just "Taiwan", in case it sounds as if you are referring to a country.

Particularly at the first banquet, you should listen carefully to their speeches in case they indicate anything special about the project - for instance, they might mention a speedy start is desirable, or it would be nice to go into production quickly.

There will be several glasses on the table, one reserved for toasts, usually filled with a strong spirit such as *maotai*, a traditional "wine" going back to 135 BC. Be on your guard, for sometimes individual members of the Chinese team have a sort of game, whereby they toast your health one after the other with a brief delay. They of course take one drink each, but if you have to cope with eight toasts, you get an awful lot of strong spirit. If they say *ganbei* ("bottoms up", where you empty the glass in one swallow) you can get drunk very quickly. It varies with the individual but many Westerners find that more than two full glasses is acceptable but five or six make their head spin. Hardened visitors have sometimes gone to nine glasses or so, but if it is your first experience, it would be wise to stick to three! When you know your limit, you can increase. There is a macho feel about the amount of *maotai* a person can drink - the more the better. It is felt vaguely polite for the host to try to get the guests drunk, so beware!

One way out is to reply *suiyi* ("sway-ee") when they try to *ganbei* you; this means "let's please ourselves on that", and allows people to sip rather than empty the glass. Some people feel it makes one look a bit like a wimp and prefer to go with the flow. Another solution is to return the toasts in lighter wine, beer, or even the ubiquitous orange juice or Coca Cola. If you are drinking alcohol at all at the dinner, you must return a toast in alcohol, not a soft drink. *Shaoxing* is a pleasant wine, normally served warm and tasting a bit like sherry; it is less strong than *maotai*.

It is acceptable to sip at beer or soft drinks as you wish, but it is not acceptable to drink hard liquor, like whiskey, brandy, or *maotai* on your own. If you drink spirits, you must raise your glass and toast someone silently each time before you drink! Remember the hierarchy while doing this and start with the top person or someone important, and not with the lowly placed gofer. In fact, it is better not to toast the least important members of their team, but repeat your verbal or silent toasts with the important ones instead.

If you are a woman, it is not felt quite proper that you should drink like the men: alcohol consumption has a macho feel to it. You might do better in the negotiations if you stick to soft drinks during the meals as they will perceive you as behaving in the correct manner. You can always get stuck into the duty-free back in your room later!

The Chinese will describe all kinds of alcoholic drinks as "wine", a common translation of *jiu,* a generic word for alcohol. A word of advice: avoid any bottle of "wine" that has some object in the bottom of the bottle – it is usually some nasty part of a poor unfortunate animal, is felt to have medicinal properties but it will probably not do you much good.

The worst drink I have ever had in China was called "Swatow Rice Wine"; it tasted like low grade paraffin smells and it burned with a clear blue flame, leaving no residue. I discovered that it did not remove the paint on the window sill although, going by the taste I had half expected it would. It might have been better to cook with it. Different alcoholic drinks can be a useful topic of table conversation with your neighbors.

There are some poor local beers in China, some of which are reminiscent of soapy washing up water; I have encountered these especially around Chengdu for some reason, but if you stick with the brands labeled "Beijing", "Qingdao" ("Tsing Tao") or "Tianjin" you should not be disappointed.

If the Chinese host should rise and walk around toasting people individually, when he gets to you, rise to your feet and reciprocate the toast.

As with eating, pacing matters when you are drinking. It is important not to start the evening on alcohol, find you are drinking too much, and then switch to fruit juice. This would probably, if inadvertently, pass the symbolic message that you have suddenly been annoyed or insulted in some way.

Traditionally, it is impolite to pour your own drink, as it is the responsibility of the host to watch your glass and refill it when necessary. This view still lingers and the waiter should keep an eye on glasses and top them up. They usually do this with some gusto before your glass is empty, and consequently, it is easy to drink more than you think, without noticing. If, or perhaps when, this happens to you, retire to your room as soon as you can, drink lots of mineral water and swallow the recommended two paracetamol tablets and sleep it off. I personally prefer aspirin and take three of them, but then I was greedy even as a baby I am told.

If your glass does get empty and there is no waiter around, it is impolite for you to fill your own glass first. Instead, you offer to fill the glasses of those nearby, and finish with yourself. You will observe that when pouring the drinks, the glasses are often filled to the top. This is a mark of respect and signifies something like a full and friendly relationship. If you are used to partially filling wine glasses and stopping for esthetic reasons, as I am, remember to pour more than you normally would. You can gauge how much to fill the glasses by quietly observing what the host did, or failing that the waiter.

Business and banquets

It is best not to raise matters of business at the banquet. You should be particularly careful if they choose to raise a business issue, as they may be trying to take advantage of the relaxed atmosphere or the alcohol you have drunk, to gain an edge. You should never make a promise to do something, or agree to a clause that you might later regret, even in laughing jest. If you do, it will be taken seriously and it could be raised at a future meeting as a definite commitment by you.

It is wise to stick to the safe topics of conversation, unless the Chinese initiate something, and avoid the unsafe ones (see the discussion of "Safe topics of conversation", p.51).

At banquets, food is inevitably discussed. The Chinese love talking about it and comparing dishes, restaurants, and the various provincial styles of Chinese cooking. The more Westernized and traveled person may compare France with China and you might encounter a discussion on whether Marco Polo took noodles from China to Italy and called them spaghetti (they will probably insist he did!) or brought them to China in the first place.

At the banquet, it is best if the team does not keep chattering together in English. This would in itself be bad manners and leave the Chinese isolated with no opportunity to participate. The people you bore one evening might be making decisions about you the following day. It can also be dangerous if a member of your team becomes a little indiscreet - someone at the table might speak fluent English unbeknown to you and is carefully monitoring every word you say.

You will have to make a speech.

Be prepared to make a gracious speech referring to matters such as the warm and continuing relationship between the two sides, the intention of both to do business together, China's excellent economic progress, your hopes for China's future, the past and present friendship between your two nations, the mutual benefits of the project, future friendship and harmony between the two companies, and the like. This part of the speech is normally banal but it is expected; it plays an important role in the culture by reassuring the guests about you and the relationship.

In the speech, you should praise all successes achieved and any agreements that have been reached. If things went badly and no agreements were signed, you must ignore this and dwell solely on the positive aspects. You can refer to fruitful talks, the way the team members have grown to understand and like each other, how you shared a wonderful visit to some place, what you have learned about their institution's and China's needs, what you have gained from the other side (i.e., as part of your personal development) and finally express hopes for the future. Remember to avoid all jokes in your speech, speak slowly, and keep it relatively short.

You might even have to sing

Once the Chinese get to know you, you might find that at more relaxed banquets, or at the farewell one, they produce a singer or two, often specially brought in for this purpose. If this happens, take it as a silent advance warning that they will shortly ask you to sing in return and probably they will insist on it. It is a good idea to practice something beforehand, or at least to have worked out who in the team will sing what. A typical song of your country, a folk song, or sea shanty is quite acceptable. Avoid anything from *The Sound of Music* as too many foreigners have sung such selections for years (especially "Doe a deer a female deer" why is that?), the Chinese are bored with it, and some might feel a little cautious about it because it was reputedly a favorite film of Chiang Ching, the politically disgraced wife of Mao Zedong. This is a good opportunity to recall your interest in pop music when a teenager, and see if you can still remember the tune and words of some suitable song.

If you are living and working in China, you should try to learn one verse of a Chinese song by heart. It will endear you to those with whom you socialize. After a few glasses of *maotai*, I can usually be persuaded not only to sing in Mandarin, I am even prepared to sing an old song in Cantonese, just for the southerners in the group! I find that it helps to bond the group together.

They finish early

Do not hang around after a banquet or expect after dinner entertainment, despite the hour being early. The Chinese will indicate it is time to go, usually by some obvious remark, or the leader shuffling and standing while smiling and thanking you. You might choose to return to your hotel where there is a bar, probably a disco, and possibly a nightclub. Nightlife now exists in all major cities, but some of the establishments can be rather dreary. Karaoke bars were very popular in the early to mid 1990s; taking a private room complete with sofa and huge TV screen was particularly attractive, but the hostesses even more so. Still favored, the karaoke places seemed a little less fashionable in the latter half of the decade.

Table manners

Table manners: chopsticks

Many countries have their own distinct table manners and China is no exception. The food is cut up into small pieces in the kitchen so that everything can be eaten with chopsticks without you needing to cut it up. There is no need to touch the food with your fingers and indeed that is considered to be very bad mannered. There are a few exceptions to this, including eating steamed buns, large shellfish, and sometimes chicken or duck legs and wings. If these are served, it is best to wait and see if the host picks up in his fingers before you do. Do *not* lick your fingers afterwards.

If you cannot use chopsticks, you can ask for a fork and spoon, which are the commonly used implements in South East Asia. You should not ask for a knife because this could prove embarrassing. The waiter will probably look disconcerted and check with the host first to see if he approves. A knife on the table is a symbol of violence and is unsettling for those present, many of whom will be superstitious. You will not need a knife as the food is cut small anyway. If you are living in China, you must learn to use chopsticks or people will look down upon you.

Your personal chopsticks should not be put in the communal bowl, so use the spoon or special serving chopsticks provided. Reversing the chopsticks and using the blunt end in the communal dish is quite acceptable. When placing food in your mouth, ideally the end of the chopsticks should not actually enter your mouth but merely brought to your lips and the food then taken in, but few foreigners aspire to such niceties.

If you are left-handed you have a problem, because when you are eating your left elbow will probably knock into your neighbor's right elbow, so both your chopsticks can open and the food fall out. Chinese parents force their left-handed children to eat with chopsticks in the right hand for this reason. If you are left-handed and cannot cope with right handed chopstick use, you will just have to be aware and extra careful. If you do inadvertently send someone's food flying in this way, smile, incline your head gracefully, and apologize profusely for your clumsiness.

Try not to drop your chopsticks, as many people believe this to be unlucky and would feel bad about sharing the table with someone apparently determined to call down curses upon them.

Foreigners frequently misuse chopsticks in a variety of ways. It is quite wrong to spear food with one chopstick, even in desperation and if you make a joke about it. You should not use the chopsticks to point at anyone or anything, nor should you wave them about or gesticulate with them while talking. Foreigners tend to do this, probably because having finally managed to hold them properly, they are often reluctant to let them go. Put the chopsticks down first and remember that in any case it is not good manners to use arm gestures when you talk.

It is best not to lay chopsticks across your bowl as it is not the best of manners and again some people feel it brings bad luck. In a good restaurant, at the end of the meal you place your chopsticks on the small rest provided, which is where you found them originally. In less expensive restaurants with no chopstick rests, you can place the chopsticks on the table when you are through.

It would be particularly bad to stick your chopsticks upright in the rice and leave them standing up. This is a part of Buddhist funeral ceremonies and strongly symbolizes death to those around the table.

Table manners: bowls

Try to conceal your surprise when someone slurps soup or tea, which in China is not considered to be bad mannered. You will encounter people who burp, but not everyone feels it to be truly polite. The less educated and those recently arrived from rural China tend to do it a lot. You may put your elbows on the table with impunity, however, and, unlike in England, you may move your soup spoon towards you in the bowl when eating.

It is not thought to be bad mannered to pick up one's personal bowl and eat from it, and many Chinese think it strange that foreigners do not do this. They sometimes pass a comment in Chinese along the lines of "honestly, one would think foreigners' bowls were glued to the table!" If you do not pick up your bowl occasionally, those present will probably notice.

It is regarded as bad manners to sift through the communal dish looking for a particularly nice bit - you should first select by looking carefully and only then pick up your chosen piece.

You do not have to eat everything provided, so that if you get a piece of food that you do not like the look of, maybe a duck's foot or chicken's head, just leave it. In cheap restaurants the unwanted bits of food, as well as bones, and gristle, may be placed on the table by your plate, but in decent restaurants this is considered bad manners and any unwanted bits should be placed in the special dish provided, or failing that on the small plate under your personal bowl. This will be emptied by a waiter from time to time.

Be careful not to put too much rice in your personal bowl in the beginning. It is considered a cardinal sin to take more rice than you need and then leave some at the end of the meal. This is the result of centuries of poverty: the rulers were aware that they had to feed a large population and families had to feed all their children. Parents still bring up their children to empty their bowl and you should remember to examine yours at the end and finish any odd grains of rice that you have left.

Waiters serve and clear from either side in Chinese culture, unlike in many Western countries.

Table manners: other

Most Chinese people use a toothpick after a meal and this is considered a proper thing to do. If you follow their example, remember to cover your mouth with your free hand and use the toothpick surreptitiously. You can keep your eye on the way their delegation does it, and copy them.

Should you ever handle a teapot, which is perhaps unlikely, remember not to put it down with the spout pointing at anyone. It is a widespread superstition that doing this will result in a quarrel between the pair of you and the opposing team might feel uneasy about doing further business.

The return banquet

Hosting a return banquet

After you have been invited to and attended a banquet, you must reciprocate. Ask your liaison officer which is a suitably good restaurant and if s/he seems unsure you could tactfully approach the contact person on their team. You should discuss how best to organize it and your liaison officer will probably suggest s/he can do it and will come back to you with a price or two. Ask how much would be about right - it is always arranged on a price per capita basis. It can be expensive - a good place ran above $100 a head in 1998 for a top meal at a top restaurant! You can find good places cheaper than that.

Choose the guest list carefully and take advice from your liaison officer about who should be there. If you have no such officer, try the contact person on their team. Not inviting someone who should be there would be an insult that could damage your prospects. The restaurant should be booked for the correct number, several days in advance and you will normally be given a private room. Most restaurants choose the menu for you, and usually only need to know how much per head you are prepared to spend.

As host, you must ensure the guests are met at the door and escorted to the room where you personally wait to welcome them. The seating must be strictly by protocol, with the principal guest on your right; this is where your liaison officer or the interpreter can help decide the best seating arrangement. Recall that any lists of names the Chinese supplied earlier will be in protocol order and examine these if you need help. Should you be entertaining people from different organizations, take particular care: getting it wrong will result in someone feeling insulted. The hosts and guests sit alternately; some of the guests might have relatively little English, which means that some of your team members as well as theirs are likely to have a boring time. Many present might speak and understand more English than at first appears, so take heart.

Place cards with names in both languages are used, and you should show each person where they are to sit, not expect them to wander around looking for their name.

At the close of the evening, you escort them to the door. If there are many of them, you and your team can stand at the door in a line arranged in pecking order and make your farewells.

You settle the bill after all the guests have departed, never in their presence. Note that there is no concept of sharing the bill even in ordinary restaurants, for someone is always the host and all the others are guests. If you are out for a meal with the Chinese and it is not a formal banquet, they will usually fight to pay, which technically makes them the host, and they feel that this gives them face.

Chapter Eight: HOW TO TREAT VISITORS TO ONE'S OWN COUNTRY

You have to do a lot with them and organize a lot for them

When a Chinese delegation visits you in your country, you can assume that you will have to make very detailed arrangements and look after them thoroughly, more so than for most visitors, foreign or otherwise. Back home in China, everything is arranged for them when they are visiting on business, as it is for foreigners. They are simply unused to the freedom of deciding for themselves where to stay, where to eat and what to visit. A really Westernized and well-traveled Chinese person can cope with it, but might still feel insulted that you had not bothered. It means there will be a lot of work for your PA or secretary and you should keep a watchful eye on things to ensure that what is organized is appropriate.

Meet them in at the airport

You must ensure that your Chinese visitors are met in at the airport, which is a basic courtesy. If possible, do this yourself, as this gives them face. If you have a tame corporation President whose function it is to do such things, this would be even better, and if you both go that would be best. When you produce a high-ranking figure from your firm, it shows how seriously you are taking the visit and gives them much face. Remember that China is hierarchical so that leader greets leader first, before moving on to second stringers. It is a good idea to remind yourself of the names before they arrive - business cards and the photographs you took, (hopefully by now annotated on the back) will help you a lot. If there are members of the delegation whom you have not met previously, it would impress them if you have learned their names beforehand.

The Chinese know things are done differently elsewhere and will make allowances for not getting things they would expect to receive at home, but it is human nature to be easily flattered or insulted. If they are a diplomatic group rather than business people they *must* always be met in and escorted, and if they are a business delegation, it is still an extremely good idea.

Give them a liaison officer and photographer

It would be a good idea to allocate a specific contact person for them. He or she should accompany them, pick them up at the hotel, bring them to your office, and take them to lunch or out in the evening. Either an Overseas Chinese or a speaker of the language is useful for this. This will make them feel comfortable and probably more inclined to cooperate.

If you can manage it, get the company photographer or some in-house enthusiastic, competent amateur to take plenty of shots of them as they go around. You must particularly make sure that they are photographed when they meet with your CEO and other high company officials – and with local city dignitaries if that could be arranged. Those shots will give them much face when they show them back in China and they will be grateful to you for this. Remember, favor for favor operates! Before they depart, have the photographs mounted in albums, with the company name and logo on, and present one to every member of the team. If the albums are not identical, their leader should get the best one, for example one with a red cover while the others are blue or it might be embossed in gold rather than printed in black. You can get the average cost down by ordering more of these empty albums than you need at the one time and keep the surplus to use for future visits by other foreign delegations.

Other time slots

It is a good idea to leave their calendar with occasional empty slots in which to relax so that you do not overwork them. Often they like the idea of a break during a strenuous visit and they usually have a detailed daily diary to write up about where they went, what they did, whom they met, and what their impressions were.

Your own team members will be pleased too! It can be tiring going out night after night with the visitors, and some delegations expect such conduct. The members of your own team will begin to miss quality time with their family and might start to grumble about it. Your liaison person in particular will probably be grateful for the time off. If s/he is forced to leave them for a period for reasons of business, s/he can suggest "perhaps you would like to rest" which will normally be understood.

In the evening, many delegations are happy to stay in together, watch TV, talk, fill in their diary and amuse themselves, but they will expect to be taken out sometimes. Depending on how long they will stay, you should arrange an evening out, perhaps to a local restaurant, theater or movie show, at least twice a week. Although they can be left alone for the weekend, it would be better if you could arrange something for them to do. Without local transport and probably being a bit out of their depth, they are likely to become bored and then resentful if left totally alone.

Different visiting delegations have different expectations, but in general they want to be taken out and about more rather than less. They are unlikely to organize anything for themselves, because their culture dictates that the host will take proper care of his guests as long as they are around.

Often a few books in Chinese, such as novels or detective stories which are available cheaply in Hong Kong, are enjoyed and you could leave a few in the hotel room or apartment for their use. You should get a local Chinese to glance over them first and ensure they are not pornographic, which might prove embarrassing. The Chinese often enjoy such light-weight rather trashy novels, as they are not commonly available in China and are sometimes banned.

It is not worth organizing a cocktail party for them. Chinese visitors are rarely comfortable at cocktail parties and hosting one for them could be counterproductive. At a party there is the problem of a lack of a recognizable hierarchy, and strangers (outsiders even!) coming up to address them, both unannounced and uninvited. Nor do they like barbecues much, which can be painful for them. To most Chinese, huge slabs of meat look gross; they do not care to eat with their fingers; and barbecues are an alien concept, which are too informal and uncivilized. The so-called "Mongolian barbecues" that some Chinese enjoy are quite different and are eaten indoors using chopsticks and seated formally around a special oven in the center of the table. If you are ill-advised enough to hold a welcoming barbecue, you might find they stand in a silent group, and are rather unresponsive. Basically, they feel threatened and a bit out of their depth.

Both cocktail parties and barbecues lack structure and are too free-wheeling for the Confucian integrated hierarchical society in which they were brought up. A formal dinner is the thing, and one rather splendid banquet before they leave is so desirable that it really must be considered to be essential.

On long stay visits they like to live together

You should let the Chinese live together if they are staying some time in your city. For short visits of a few days, a good hotel is now desirable. Only a few years ago it could have been of moderate or even low standard, unless the visitor was around ministerial rank or you were really trying to impress. Those Chinese who have traveled abroad a few times have now become accustomed to top hotels and these days may feel slighted if put in a cheaper one.

If however the Chinese are staying longer than a few days, perhaps for training lasting a month or more, you should let them share and live together in an inexpensive place. It may seem spartan accommodation to you, but they will be more used to this, and less bewildered by the change of scene. Expect them to live cheaply and economize. They will be unused to your high prices and will often prefer to save money where they can and cook for themselves. They might well be horrified if you were to supply a cleaning and cooking service, and could even question the way you waste money and start to wonder whether you are in fact a suitable person with whom to do business. Similarly, if you put them in an expensive modern hotel for a long-term stay, they might start to worry about your attitude towards costs. This said, the more traveled people are rapidly raising their expectations and it is better to err on the side of better treatment than worse.

For such longer stayers a few simple rules help. Few Chinese can drive a motor car so that easy access to safe public transport is essential. If the traffic in your town permits, and they are relatively low grade technicians or engineers who are there for training, rather than high level company presidents, you might suggest to them that, if they wished, you could buy them a bicycle each. This might be appreciated, as it is the normal form of transport for most people in China. Senior Chinese rarely stay for an extended period, but for them a motorcar and driver is usually necessary.

The meetings

If your company has a special meeting room, it would be a good idea to use this. They find it normal to meet and talk with you in such a room rather than at your desk. You should serve tea, coffee or soft drinks without first asking if they want them. Make sure that your team drinks the same things the visitors do and discourage your staff from wandering in with their own cup of coffee or your visitors might feel they are being discriminated against in some crafty foreign way.

Food matters

Restaurant meals

You should entertain them in a good Chinese restaurant before they depart. A quality place that specializes in seafood is usually a good choice. If it is a formal banquet, recall the traditional seating arrangements; it is nice to observe the customary Chinese etiquette as far as is practical. Do not forget to begin the toasting when entertaining in a restaurant, as this is a duty of the host. The first toast should be to the guests themselves. You should keep supplying them with food, so watch carefully and if eating Chinese food never let their personal bowl get empty. Similarly with the drinks - an empty glass is a reproach to the host. In

China, it is customary to settle the bill after all the guests have departed and you should certainly never do so in their presence. The best way is to discuss the matter in advance with the restaurant and get them to bill you at work. If this is not possible, then you might choose to go quietly over to the desk to pay, rather than lay a credit card or cash on the table in front of those present.

Should I invite my visitors home?

Although taking them to a good Chinese restaurant honors the visitors, if you have met them before they will probably be pleased and interested to visit your home to see what it is like. After their mean housing standards, they will undoubtedly find it palatial and well furnished, and may well ask if such a big home is typical of how people live in your country.

Home meals

If you invite a team to your home, you should serve a full meal and not just snacks and nibbles which would appear insulting in their culture. The Chinese prefer their own food, which they are used to seeing cut small before they receive it. Remember that they often have difficulty with the appearance of large joints or slabs of meat, which typically look repulsive to them. It is in your interest to avoid trying to impress them by serving large steaks! In my view it is usually better to offer a decent and suitable Western meal than an ersatz Chinese one which will probably taste peculiar to them.

Pork is the favored meat, but beef, chicken and duck are very acceptable. It is best to avoid lamb or mutton, which to many Asians smells and tastes disgusting. Only in the northwest of China is mutton popular and those eating it are from despised minority groups and your Han visitors would not be impressed by your action. Fish and seafood of all kinds are always well received. Chinese people tend to eat a lot of vegetables rather than meat, largely a product of historical necessity in a poor country, so more vegetable dishes than usual would not go amiss.

When the group departs

When the visit is over, you must accompany them to the airport if possible and go with them as far as is allowed by the authorities, not just drop them off at the concourse or in the bar. If all went well and substantive things were agreed, it would be helpful to you if you can get your company president or some other senior official to accompany them, in addition to you.

In 1983, when American Motors were in the middle of protracted negotiations concerned with setting up a joint venture to assemble Jeeps
near Beijing, they flew the visiting Chinese delegation from America to
Cairo to see how AMC operated there and to talk to the Egyptian partners. This was a smart move and helped to reassure the Chinese that
AMC were a good company with which to deal. What really impressed
the Chinese, so much so that Chen Zhutao kept mentioning it in
speeches and toasts for the next two years, was the fact the leader of the
AMC team, Mr. Clare, got up and saw them off at Cairo airport at 3
a.m.![68] These things count for much in China.

Before you go

The right person

It is important to select the right sort of person to go to China. Professional and technical expertise is high on the list, as he or she will have to cope with the unexpected and make fast decisions. This frequently necessitates a detailed knowledge of the product and manufacturing process. Secondly, you need someone who is mature, flexible and likely to fit into the local scene with understanding. Patience and gentle stubbornness are essential requirements. Thirdly, someone with previous overseas experience, in Asia for preference, would be desirable. Fourthly, experience of living amid poor and trying circumstances would be an advantage. Finally, the ability to speak Chinese is useful, but it is less important to success than possessing normal business skills and having a genuine interest in China and its culture.

Ex-military people, or those who have survived a boarding school, might have an advantage, in that they have been trained to endure privation and perhaps intense periods of work followed by prolonged stretches of boredom.

Establish the ground rules before departure

The company must decided in advance what the manager is expected to achieve and make clear what exactly is expected. "To run the branch properly" is not enough. Is the selected person expected to make profits or raise them? Or increase sales? Or total revenue? Or market share? And in each case by how much? Is it envisaged that new product lines should be initiated or plans developed for expansion into a different part of China? These and other expectations should be discussed and clearly understood on both sides. That way, some idea of what constitutes success or failure will be apparent, and the manager will be more certain about the priorities to be attached to different duties. Sending someone off based on "just do your best" is never good enough and can almost be guaranteed to lead to dissatisfaction and problems later.

Reassurance about career paths

Everyone should be aware of the manager's career path, and reassurance should be offered about his or her position in the firm. A problem that expatriates often have is a fear that they will be forgotten, overlooked in promotion considerations, or lose out to rivals at HQ. They may also have concern that when they return the overseas assignment may count against rather than for them. The manager will function better if he knows that such fears are normal and widespread among expatriates, and in his or her case are groundless. You could appoint a mentor or guide to look after the absent manager's interests at HQ while he or she is abroad. Although this method is relatively little used in Western companies, it is common in Asian ones, where it has been found to work well.

Train before they enplane

Investment in suitable predeparture training in order to minimize culture shock will pay off handsomely. At least three months before departure, the manager and family should be involved in a preparation program. Anyone going to live and work in China can expect to suffer some degree of culture shock. Such extended training is desirable, despite what may seem to be the high cost involved; predeparture training actually saves money if the firm manages to avoid having a manager floundering out of his depth for some months. In the worst outcome, he or she may have to be recalled early because of problems; this is not only costly, it also probably results in a black mark going on someone's file in the organization, and it will not impress those in China with whom you hope to do business. Predeparture training can reduce this danger.

According to one source,[69] in the late 1990s, a full compensation package for an expatriate based in China costs around $250,000-$350,000, including salary, moving and relocation expenses, modern housing, annual leave, home leave, children's education expenses, and a hardship allowance. A different author suggests $300,000-$500,000,[70] quoting a survey of 100 manufacturing and 100 sales companies by William Kent International Inc. This also revealed that, typically, there is one expatriate per 100 local staff, and large companies with sales exceeding $500 million keep about 90 expatriates in China. Some companies have found it can cost up to $700,000 a year for each expatriate. All in all, it can get very expensive! It is believed that about 25-30 percent of expatriates fail, in the sense that they either do not achieve their set goals or else have to be pulled out ahead of the scheduled end of their posting. In view of the costs just mentioned, you should consider predeparture training as a good investment.

The initial posting of executives used to be around two years, but because of the high costs and the length of time it can take to function at full capacity, many companies are beginning to find it desirable to extend this to three, four or even five years.

Predeparture training might take several forms.

- The company can issue selected brochures and handouts about the country, its history, culture, standard of living and ways of life. Photographs might be helpful here.
- Videos and films about the country can be borrowed by the company and loaned to the family. This could usefully include commercial films made in China, which often reveal attitudes and aspects of the culture that might be missed.
- Discussions with anyone in the company that has visited and in particular lived in China can be most valuable. This method might best be done over a dinner in a private home, when people are relaxed and more likely to speak freely about the lessons they have learned.
- Enrolling the husband or wife, as well as the manager, in any locally available night classes or day courses on China or the language at company expense can be worthwhile.

A lone expatriate will face problems

Culture shock can be a worse problem for those living on their own, and some people find it hard to survive. This is particularly the case if posted to the interior of China. Your manager is cut off from normal surroundings and friends, and it is extremely unlikely that there will be any suitable recreational facilities. A married couple may be best, for at least they have each other. Against this, the experience could put a strain on the relationship and it might founder. Perhaps for such reasons, the majority of expatriates in China seem to be single.

Don't forget to keep in touch!

All must agree on the need to communicate with HQ. The manager and spouse should be made aware how often they are expected to report in. This might include a fortnightly telephone call to a specified person in HQ, accompanied by a regular monthly and quarterly report by fax. It should be made clear that if a really urgent matter arises that ought to have HQ approval or knowledge (e.g., rioting workers that could turn into an international incident) then the manager must fax or telephone immediately.

The early days

Your company will probably need to place someone there

If you open a joint venture, you must accept that you will need to base an expatriate in China to manage the firm. The level of Chinese management is not high and it would be risky to rely on a local manager, especially with a new venture. You are putting up the capital and skills, and need to keep a close eye on events. Later you can and should consider training your Chinese managers and eventually replacing all your expatriates. This is justifiable on cost grounds alone. Some of the more successful companies have found that localization (using locally hired people rather than expatriates hired abroad) is not only cheaper, it is an important factor in making profits.

If your business lies in the area of growing or extracting simple primary produce, you might find it easier to dispense with using expatriates more quickly, because there is likely to be little processing involved and the business is probably relatively simple, with less to go wrong.

On balance, it is probably better to send a male to live and work in China. As in many countries, the Chinese are essentially male chauvinistic by tradition and although the Communist Party and the government have made strong efforts to alter this, including putting equal rights into the Constitution, the legal situation does not exactly coincide with reality. In rural China, women are not regarded or treated as true equals; in urban China the attitude towards women depends in large part upon the level of education - the more educated males are more likely to be tolerant and egalitarian. Those who work in state run enterprises may also be more tolerant, partly the result of "education sessions" they have been forced to attend, and partly because they see personal benefits from having two incomes in the family. The attitude towards women became clearer in the 1990s when SOEs were forced to release workers to increase efficiency and rectify conditions of overstaffing: it was usually the women who were the first to go.

The inequality situation has improved but it is still far from perfect. A survey released in September 1998 revealed that 71.6 percent of Chinese managers would not hire a woman, even if she were the best person for the job.[71] The report went on to point out that of the nineteen members of the Politbureau of the Chinese Communist Party, not one was a woman.

In general, the Chinese with whom you will deal will probably be less worried about a foreign manager being female than would be the case in Japan .

Post arrival training

Training after arrival is desirable. It takes time to settle in, feel reasonably at home, and begin to function efficiently. Local orientation is essential. If a manager is replacing someone, a good way is to allow an overlap, say of one or two weeks, for the change over. For business efficiency, this allows the new manager to get in to the job, see how it is done, and note any differences from the methods that are used at home and discover why this is a sensible way to proceed in China. It also allows him to be introduced to the right people, such as powerful local officials, important business people, and influential expatriates.

It is particularly valuable for the incoming person to be introduced by the outgoing manager, and not merely to take over the branch and rely on introducing himself. Trust in China often starts with an introduction, when an "insider" vouches for someone and brings that person into the fold. It does not arise automatically from the position the individual occupies. Respect on the other hand can come with the position, and often does not have to be earned, unlike in most Western countries.

A more formal induction process could include training and orientation sessions, preferably for manager and spouse together, with lectures, films, slides, or videos about what to expect now they have arrived, how to behave, and what to do about the common problems that will be encountered. If the existing manager or company has put together any pamphlets, brochures or hint sheets, these should be handed over and explained. If such a compendium does not exist, it would be a useful task for the spouse to put one together. This could provide an interest and purpose in life, and prove a valuable asset for those arriving in the future.

After a few days to get over jet lag, a large reception could usefully be hosted by the company, to introduce the new couple to both expatriates and those Chinese who really matter; this would be appreciated in the culture as a nice, enjoyable way of making the necessary introductions. Chinese are not comfortable trying to eat standing up and balancing drinks and plates, nor do most of them tend to drink a lot. A sit-down dinner is therefore preferable to a buffet-style one or a drinks-only party.

Some one to watch over me

As early as possible the new manager should try to meet other expatriates who have been there for some time and know the ropes. He will have a hundred and one problems, so their experience and advice can help enormously. If you are a newly arrived manager and your predecessor or company does not immediately introduce you around, ask if they could do so.

The sort of help needed includes finding housing and servants, obtaining a Chinese driving license, getting started in a good language course, locating a reliable doctor who can speak English, and finding where to shop. Several commercial firms that specialize in relocations have been established in the cities; using one can provide a quick and convenient way for the manager and family to settle in.

Coping with the conditions

Things are different

China is quite different from most countries, even other Asian ones. There is much that will delight and fascinate but there is more that will surprise, and might even shock. The first few months can be a trying time, especially if this is your first experience of living abroad.

Facilities

You cannot automatically assume that all normal Western facilities will be either required or available. In China, there will be no need at a factory for a huge car parking lot, but a bicycle storage area will be essential. In large parts of China, the electricity supply is frequently erratic and also suffers from fluctuating voltage, so that many companies have found that it pays to provide their own generator to keep the factory or office running properly. You will probably notice that your light bulbs seem to burn out more quickly than at home. Maybe it is the fluctuating voltage or perhaps just the usual problem of low quality standards locally. Water and gas supplies can be equally unreliable, and if these are essential to your production process, you should sort out a reliable means of supply at the negotiation stage.

Domestic help is not expensive, but the standard is below what you would expect in countries such as the Philippines, Thailand or even Indonesia. Unless you are particularly lucky, their level of English will vary from nil all the way up to little. Think about it: if you were a local, with good English, would you be happy sweeping and cleaning some foreigner's house, rather than working for IBM as an interpreter? This is a good reason why you have to start learning to speak Chinese as soon as you arrive, tones and all. In the 1980's people used to worry that their servants were really spies, working for the Public Security Bureau, which meant keeping sensitive documents away from them. Unless the cunning rogues were amazingly expert at disguising their ability to read English, it seemed improbable that, even if it were true, they could do much harm. Still, some people like to worry, and if you have incipient paranoia, China is definitely a good place to bring it out.

Getting about

Note that in China, as in the United States, people drive on the right. A few short years ago, it was essential to buy a good bicycle for getting around and it is still a useful investment, especially if you are there with your family. Chinese bicycles are poor - typically as delivered from the factory the spokes are so slack that the wheels will not turn, and the buyer is forced to push or carry it straight to a small local private shop where it is entirely dismantled and rebuilt. Such "repair shops" exist everywhere in cities - they also mend punctures and do other minor jobs. It is important to get it rebuilt before you try to ride it. It is possible to hire bicycles in all the large cities – but check carefully that it works properly, especially the brakes, before cycling off! You might find you have to visit a repair shop with a hired bicycle too! Perhaps the thing you really need to remember is that *everything* has right of way over bicycles and you must drive defensively.

Nowadays taxis are widely available and motorcars can be bought by expatriates. Locally made cars are cheaper than imported ones, owing to high duty that can be 100 percent or more, although diplomats can import duty free. If staying for only a few months, leasing is usually cheaper than buying and saves you a lot of trouble. If you hire a car for a short period, it normally comes equipped with a chauffeur.

Local driving conditions can be horrendous. Unless very brave you should not attempt to get behind the wheel yourself but should hire a local driver. Many expatriates are however choosing to drive themselves rather than use a chauffeur but if you have an accident, the hassle and bureaucratic procedures can be a nightmare. If the victim should die, the problem can be extremely serious, whether the driver is foreign or a local. A Chinese drunk driver involved in a hit and run accident in Zhuzhou City, Hunan Province, which caused the death of a woman, was sentenced to death in 1998.[72] If the worst should happen, it is strongly rumored that it is not unknown, even in such serious cases, for the judge to be swayed in his decision by the provision of an excellent dinner in a top restaurant.

Eating

Eating out is possible in all the larger cities where fast food is proliferating. You will find well-known names like KFC, McDonalds and Pizza Hut. American, French, German, Italian, and Japanese restaurants opened during the 1990s and although the quality at first may be lower than you are used to, after a time it starts to seem quite acceptable.

The local Chinese restaurants vary from very good at the top (although often less good than you can find in New York, San Francisco, or Hong Kong) down through a decent standard in the middle, to street stalls at the bottom. Some of the latter are surprisingly good and dirt-cheap. Sadly, many of them have low standards of hygiene and, if you are unlucky, an upset stomach or even a bout of hepatitis could result. Ask a long-term resident where they prefer to eat and if there are any clean food stalls that they can recommend. Otherwise, take care!

When eating at home, remember that all fresh produce should be carefully washed or peeled before eating. Washing fruit and vegetables in one of the liquid sterilizers, like Milton, seems to kill germs effectively and doing this is a particularly good idea if you have children.

Shopping

Until recently, Chinese department stores tended to look old fashioned, with rows of goods simply displayed under glass-topped flat cabinets. The range of goods on offer was small, and much that was on display was not actually available for sale, so that a department store was sometimes more like an industrial display center than a real shop.

Shopping is still not particularly enjoyable but is rapidly improving. Supermarkets and department stores have been established with foreign assistance and they are spreading rapidly in all the cities in coastal areas. Wal-Mart has warehouses in Shenzhen (Shenzhen Wal-Mart Super Center), and Shanghai has the Yaohan department store (Japanese), Shanghai Jusco (Japanese), Bilho, and Tops (Singapore). More large foreign stores keep opening. By the end of 1997, there were 1,000 store operators in China with 15,000 outlets, representing a 43 percent growth in twelve months. The retail sector was opened up in 1997, as part of China's attempt to enter the World Trade Organization.[73]

This has made life considerably easier and many brand names familiar to Westerners can be found. These have often been made in China and can be of lower quality than you are used to, as some of them were originally intended for export but rejected as not good enough. In the cities, cheese is now readily available, as is milk. Fruit and meat are now more plentiful, thanks to free markets, but the prices can be high. Fresh fruit and vegetables are obtainable all year round, but the variety is restricted in winter.

Many Western shopping malls have appeared, often located on the ground floor of office complexes. Many of these shops are probably technically illegal, as hotels and offices with foreign investment are so far not allowed to sublease, but the rule is widely ignored.

Small local Chinese stores can be fun, and you will find that the prices are often not fixed and some bargaining is expected. If you wish to buy clothing or shoes however, you might find a problem with sizes (see "The clothing you can buy will probably not fit", p.59)

Antique shops exist but are often run by the state, which means that prices are very high. Nothing more than about 150 years old can be taken out of the country without special permission, which limits the range on offer.

Shopping in Hong Kong is still superior to China proper. Try one of the China Arts and Crafts stores, which have a much better range of produce, higher quality, and lower prices than you can get in China itself. The one by Star Ferry at Kowloon is good, but locals often seem to prefer the one up Nathan Road near the Jordan Road ferry, or the Wanchai or Causeway Bay ones on the Island.

Things to do: the boredom factor

Boredom and feelings of isolation are common problems for spouses - there is nowhere much to go, while travel can be uncomfortable. There is no public cinema with films in English, nor any theater except for the traditional Chinese type, which is best described as an acquired taste for a small minority. There are no swimming pools or country clubs, and few bars in which one can meet people except in the top hotels. Once one has seen the local temples, the Great Wall and so on, there is not a lot to do, particularly during the day.

There is now a reasonable nightlife in the major cities. Nightclubs, karaoke bars, regular bars, discos, cinemas and theaters exist. In Beijing, fads and changing tastes have seen the rise of karaoke in the early 1990s, followed by a disco boom in 1995, to be succeeded by pubs in 1996 as discos began to wane. Tenpin bowling became popular in the new millennium. The Beijing Recreation Center at the Asian Games Village offers swimming, bowling, billiards and video games.

The family would be well advised to take lots of novels, books, cassettes, and videos of films[74]. A good short wave radio is an asset and allows you to stay in touch with the outside world. Perhaps one or two computers and lots of games would help - more than one person may wish to use the computer at the same time. A laptop with lots of batteries is an advantage. Unfortunately, it is unwise to run a laptop on AC with the battery in as a backup as this fries the battery quickly. Recall that the electric voltage tends to vary a lot without warning and this can damage or destroy really sophisticated hi-tech equipment so it needs to be sturdy as well as good. The dust storms that blow around the north of China also do damage.

It would be beneficial to have a friend in your company HQ regularly send out things like new videos, CDs, books, magazines, and the latest computer games. It is possible to access the Internet via an Internet Service Provider (ISP), but the authorities worry about locals having the freedom to visit any sites that they want. These can include not only pornographic sites, but any sites or newsgroups that might encourage the fledgling democratic dissident movements, advocate freedom of speech, or supply information in Chinese (like the British Broadcasting Corporation). The authorities block access to them. It would be wise to sign up with an ISP before leaving home, then sign up with an ISP in China, and use it to telnet over to your home account. So far, this allows you to go where you like. Cybernet cafes have been established in Shanghai and will undoubtedly spread, unless the government decides to ban them entirely, but are subject to similar restrictions. Some of these cybercafes have turned out to be fronts for porn parlours and may not even be on the 'net!

Pass your address around early

It would be helpful if you were to send your address in China to all your friends and relatives a month or so before you leave home, rather than wait until after arrival. The company address will suffice until you have a private one. Mail can take two weeks or more to get through and a strong sense of isolation from the real world can easily develop in the first month while you are waiting to receive letters. Regular correspondence is a valuable commodity; it provides a great outlet for emotions and stops people feeling unwanted. It would be possible to make a small rubber stamp of the address in Chinese, or alternatively print up hundreds of sticky labels, for grandparents or other close relatives to stick on the envelope. This can speed up the delivery in China, as letters addressed in anything but Chinese tend to be held up in the post office, waiting perhaps for the return of the only person who can read the language who is currently off work sick.

The staring game

When in China one should not be surprised to see adult males or adult females walking along holding hands; this simply shows close friendship and has no sexual connotation whatsoever. At first it is tempting to stare, but one gets used to it. In Westernized Hong Kong, however, such hand-holding, particularly in the case of males, would have a clear homosexual feel about it.

One must expect to be stared at as an unusual object and should try not to become annoyed. It is common for parents to draw the attention of their children to you, or one adult in a group to tell the others, in case they have not noticed the presence of such a strange being. This is not considered rude in China. The more remote the district, the more likely it is to happen, but it can occur even in cosmopolitan Shanghai when away from the main tourist area.

If things go wrong

Given the difficulties of living and working in China, the company needs a fallback position in case major problems occur. It should be prepared to move the wife and children to Hong Kong if things get desperate, and the manager could be allowed to go down and see them, say, every two or three weeks or so. Alternatively, the wife and children might prefer to go back home and return to China on visits, perhaps once or twice a year.

Health

Health can be a problem. Before going to China to live, you should have a complete physical and dental checkup and fix any problems. China is a country in which it is easy to get sick – many visiting Westerners seem to go down with ailments like upper respiratory tract infections, colds, or tonsillitis. This is worse in the north and west when the dust storms blow in from the desert. It is essential to take plenty of medicines, especially if you have children, to cover all normal "visit the doctor" situations in your country. If you have any special medical needs, make sure you take a copy of the prescription with you. You can hand this to a clinic in the big cities and get it filled, but make sure you keep the original for future use.

Health insurance is a good idea. Road accidents are common and you might consider insuring for medical evacuation by air to Hong Kong or the States in case of serious illness or chance event.

The major coastal cities usually have clinics with a few Western trained doctors. You can go and introduce yourself before anyone in the family gets sick because it is useful to establish a relationship with the clinic or hospital doctor in advance. Severe illness can be a problem - if it looks serious or could develop nasty complications, it is essential to fly to Tokyo or Hong Kong at once.

You should be aware that stocks of blood in China could be infected with hepatitis or even the HIV virus so that even a minor operation can be dangerous if a blood transfusion should become necessary. Some poor people sell their blood on a regular basis in order to survive and testing is poor. One youth who admitted to having sold blood on forty occasions was HIV positive.[75] The selling of blood is now banned, but the law will be difficult to enforce where hospitals cannot obtain sufficient voluntary blood donors and people are poor. Even Hong Kong, generally reliable, had a scare in 1998 that local stocks of blood might have become infected with syphilis.

Dental care is not generally good and teeth should be fixed in your country before departure. Even Beijing could be better in this regard, although the treatment costs little by Western developed country standards. Spectacles are also cheap, widely available, and I have not heard their quality criticized.

It is easy to feel isolated in China, cut off from home and unable to communicate with the majority of people you see around you. Depression can strike: keep an eye on family members for sudden and uncalled for mood changes, irritability and lack of sleep. Stress can be a problem for the working members of the family because most jobs can be frustrating and take longer than expected. Travel can be tiring and regular visits to other sites or cities might be part of your job.

If you are going to be in China for an extended period, consider taking regular Rest and Relaxation (R&R) breaks in another country, once or twice a year.

Schools

Children face special difficulties. They will have only a small peer group speaking English - probably none if you are outside a major city. They will have to learn Chinese to communicate or they will lead a greatly restricted social life. The major cities now have Western schools, but it is not always possible to get your children enrolled, owing to the pressure on places. You should make enquiries before leaving for China.

If the posting is to the interior then you can assume that there will be no Western schools in the area. Depending on your children's age, it might be better for their education to leave them in your country in a boarding school, as colonial people often did in the past. If the nonworking spouse is a teacher, he or she could consider setting up a small school for other local expatriates. There is a need for education and expatriates from non-English speaking backgrounds are often keen for their children to attend an English speaking school. This would not only help your children, but it would also establish their place in a social group, and give them needed playmates.

Spouse issues

The accompanying spouse will probably be a wife rather than a husband. She should also be considered when the decision on who to send is made; she needs to be flexible, open-minded, tolerant, and able to adjust. As loneliness is apt to be a problem for the spouse, someone who is self-reliant is preferable. If the spouse is unhappy, the manager will probably be miserable. If the couple's marriage is already going through a bad patch, it would be unwise to send them. The China experience *could* cause a rallying round and solidify the relationship, but it is far more likely to aggravate tensions and lead to breakdowns of marriage and possibly people. For some people there is an immense stress from merely living in China.

If the children are experiencing difficulties at home or could in any sense be considered to be "problem children", it would be better not to send them to China. Your company would be well advised to select a different family, rather than increase the danger of premature withdrawal of the manager for family reasons.

Poverty

China is a poor country, and poor to a degree that can startle. In China, people who share kitchens or bathrooms with other families are not regarded as poor, but as quite well off; after all, they must have living accommodation of their own to be able to share such facilities. Many sleeping around railway stations would envy them.

Accommodation

Accommodation can prove to be difficult. A few years ago it was normal for no house to be available for rent, and the family was forced to spend the whole period in China living and working in one or two hotel rooms. This is still the case in remoter parts of China, where there may not even be a hotel, but you might have to live in a government "Guest House". These vary in quality.

In the cities, things have much improved. Hotels have been built, and five star hotels are now common but not cheap. Living space and office space is currently (late 2000) relatively easy to find, because of the real estate boom of the mid 1990s. The availability of commercial office space in Shanghai continues to increase. There may still be waiting lists for housing in new complexes, but as new buildings come onto the market the list shortens or temporarily disappears. In some areas rents can be expensive by international standards and at times may be dearer than in Tokyo, New York or London. The building boom and the Asian financial crisis have caused rents to fall: at mid 1998, the rent on a two-bedroom apartment in Shanghai had fallen by around 30 percent over the previous 12 months to a more affordable level (see Table 9.1).

Unfortunately, high rents often go along with poor Third World standards of fixtures, fittings, and power supply. The power supply can be intermittent, as can water; plumbing standards are low, so that leaking taps or broken fittings are commonly encountered. A typical example is provided by the experience of technicians of American Motors when they were working on the Beijing Jeep joint venture. They were not pleased when they found that in the hotel in which they were staying, the lavatories leaked and the bathrooms were not caulked.[76] You might find that when negotiating a lease, the owner or managing agent requests that some or all of the rent be paid offshore in US dollars. This is frowned upon by the state, is currently still legal, but may not be so for much longer. Keep checking!

Table 9.1 The approximate rent per month on a two-bedroom apartment in various international cities, in US $

Hong Kong Mid level/South Side	6,495
London, Hampstead	3,570
New York, Upper West Side	3,000
Paris, 16 and 17th Arrondissements	2,440
Tokyo, Aoyama/Hiro-o	2,440
Shanghai, Putuo District	1,510
Sydney, Bellevue Hill/Point Piper/Vaucluse	1,510

Source: *The Hampstead & Highgate Express*, London, weekly, September 4 1998, Property Express, p1.

If your enterprise is in the interior, engineers or technicians who have to stay for a period could find conditions spartan. Your company might decide that it needs to supply air conditioners, heaters, and even a generator if the local electricity supply is inadequate. Your people need to be comfortable if they are to function adequately. Toho Titanium Company Ltd. of Japan found they had to do this when it sent technicians to a site only about thirty miles from Beijing to build a catalyst plant for a petrochemical company. In another example, Kuraray Company Ltd., a Japanese textile maker, built two plants at Chongqing in Sichuan Province, where it gets very hot in summer. Kuraray supplied its own air conditioners for its technicians' housing and noted that some Western engineers working locally and living without air-conditioning were adversely affected.[77] Depending on the time of year and where the enterprise is located, temperatures can vary from permafrost conditions, to over 100 degrees Fahrenheit for weeks on end.

Privacy

You will probably find you have less privacy than you are used to. It is partly an attitude of mind; in China the group is regarded as important and neither individual liberty nor privacy are considered a really serious matter. It is also the result of long-standing overcrowding forcing people to live and operate closely together. Politics had also played a role: during the Maoist era (to 1976), neighbors were encouraged to watch each other and report on any unusual behavior, including the comings and goings of visitors, which limited the freedom of residents.

You will probably encounter behavior that you feel infringes your personal privacy. Your Chinese colleagues and neighbors are interested in other people, and many would think it quite acceptable to pick up a private letter from your desk and read it. You might notice that people will enter your room at work without first knocking. Most hotels have now managed to train their staff not to do this to their foreign guests. Apart from in one's own home or hotel room, it can sometimes be difficult to feel and be alone.

The bureaucracy may not tell you what is happening

It is not unusual to feel that one is constantly engaged in a battle with an invisible but all-powerful bureaucracy, along the lines of a novel by Franz Kafka. Dealing with the officialdom can be an infuriating part of being in China. Even ordinary matters, like organizing a trip, can be time-consuming and frustrating at the least; at the worst, after a request has been tabled, no reply might ever be received. Just getting permits to do something can take days of effort.

Try not to get upset if the bureaucracy does not inform you of something you should know about. It is usually the result of inefficiency rather than a deliberate ploy but sometimes it may be an individual bureaucrat protecting his back. In China it is always safer not to say something that should be said, than actually to say something that should not be said. Secrecy, rather than communication, is the norm.

HQ might start to wonder whose side you are on

Once the manager understands the job and has learned enough about the business culture to function properly in China, the staff back at HQ will probably begin to wonder if he has "gone native". They may start to feel that the expatriate has begun to consider the interests of the Chinese more than those of the company. The gradual assimilation into Chinese ways, which is needed in order to be more effective for the firm, often means a cultural clash between the expatriate and HQ staff. For his part, the expatriate will probably start to feel that HQ does not understand either him or the difficult situation on the ground, and keeps asking the impossible. If both the manager and HQ staff are aware in advance that this is a potential problem, it can perhaps more easily be minimized.

Coping with the realities of China

China is a poor country, lacks a good basic infrastructure, and many of the things usually taken for granted can be of low quality, function badly, or be entirely absent. There are far more things that can surprise and shock than can be mentioned here, and it is impossible to know what will startle a particular person. Such things as lack of drinking water from taps so that all must be boiled, the unavailability of known brand-name goods, the limited range of food and fruit in the market outside major cities, the inability to read labels on jars or medicine containers, or the TV that cannot be understood, upset some. The lack of familiar music on the radio, the noisy throat clearing and spitting that will be encountered, the sight of men pulling small carts loaded with human manure, or women pulling hand carts loaded with heavy goods, can upset others. The normal utilities such as water and electricity supply can go off without warning - in a large block or hotel, the higher the floor you are on, the more likely it is to happen with water, so that lower floors are often considered a better location.

Letting off steam is important as a safety valve but often this is not easy to do. Loud swearing or shouting in a soundproof room, or beating stuffed images with wooden sticks might prove to be ideal for many, but do not seem to be common outside a few Japanese companies. Frustration will be felt, and some way of alleviating it must be found. Some have found taking a "treasure box" into which each family member puts a few personally selected reminders of home, helps. Possibly watching videos about your own country or well-known films or a TV series would help.

In tackling the stress and culture shock there are two different approaches involved:

- Relieving the frustration in some positive way, e.g., by taking physical exercise, finding out about the culture, learning the language, studying *taiqui* or concentrating the mind on the good things of the new experiences; or
- Removing oneself temporarily from reality and living in a sort of dream world, which is a pretended return to one's own country and conditions.

The latter may be psychologically less useful, or even damaging, as it ducks reality rather than faces it. But whatever proves to help the individual the most is probably worth doing. The exception to that is developing a reliance on drugs or alcohol, which tends to be destructive.

Chapter 10: WORKING IN CHINA

Your partner and the structure of management

Starting off

If approaching China for the first time, it is a bad idea to jump straight in and establish a joint venture before considering all the options. It often pays to start with a simple buying or selling contract. In this way you can learn the ropes, make contacts, visit different factories, judge who might make a good partner for something more permanent, and get to feel comfortable in China. The slow approach also means that you do not have to put so much money up front and costs less. Further down the track, a joint venture might be the way to go, but they can be costly in terms of investment, and there is a long learning curve getting used to Chinese conditions.

Keep your liaison officer handy

When you have set up a joint venture using a go-between or helpmate, do keep him in the area long enough to make friends and teach you how best to operate. He should introduce you around and help you settle in. As an insider, he can bring you inside at once, rather than you spending long months doing it the hard way.

Ease your way in

The Chinese side of a joint venture, and the Chinese institutions around you, will expect you to start slowly and feel your way. If you immediately begin to make waves and show great zeal, it may upset your partner or perhaps a powerful local official. If you spend the first few days quietly talking to people, sounding out their ideas, floating your own but making it clear that nothing is set in concrete, you should find things go more smoothly and, rather ironically, more quickly.

Splitting joint ventures

With China possessing a fragmented cellular economy, poor transport, and lacking a national distribution network for virtually everything, it is tempting to try to run several joint ventures rather than one. This is not a good idea when you are just starting in China. If you choose to split a joint venture between cities, you will encounter endless problems of control as well as logistical difficulties in supply and marketing.

Once you are well established in China and wish to expand, a separate joint venture in another area may begin to make sense. Your joint ventures can then compete with each other, and you are able to compare their relative costs. It is generally not desirable to split one joint venture between two areas, as they are unlikely to cooperate, owing to intercity and provincial rivalry as well as possibly suffering interference by local officials. In such ways you could easily lose all the potential economies of scale.

Layout

It is a bad idea to agree to a factory layout that includes many small office cubicles. Over the years, Chinese workers have become used to sleeping, chatting, reading newspapers and playing cards in the office; if possible, go for open plan which renders such unproductive activity more difficult and can result in higher efficiency.

The partners in the joint venture may have different goals

It is a common mistake to assume without thinking that your goals and the Chinese ones are the same. Your intentions will be relatively narrow, probably focusing on profit, sales, and market share, but the other side may have wider and different intentions. These can include fitting in with or helping to meet the announced policies and goals of the nation; achieving something which they feel will help to make China strong; and protecting themselves against intrigue from a rival faction within their department, ministry, or company. These different goals can lead you and them to perceive and approach a problem in quite different ways.

Shanghai Volkswagen found that right from the beginning the German side wished to maintain German standards of product quality, whereas the Chinese side wanted to promote the localization of parts and components.[78] The Germans were successful in the struggle, and refused to purchase local parts until they were of acceptable quality, which took all of five years. Consequently, the quality of motor vehicles produced by Shanghai Volkswagen was notably higher than those from Peugeot.

Like life partners, the perfect business partner can be hard to find

It is difficult to choose a suitable joint venture partner but this is crucial to your future success or failure. There are many possible firms, and you might be approached by some that are quite unsuitable, so you should be cautious before making a final decision. Approaching CCPIT and your embassy is a good first step, but you should talk to other business people and keep your ears open.

Firms are organized on geographical lines or functional ones. Major decisions which need a lot of thought include whether to choose a national, provincial or city level firm, and where to locate e.g., in a Special Economic Zone, in Shanghai, or in the booming southern delta area around Guangzhou. In 1992, it was reported that joint ventures tended to do better in the major urban areas of Beijing and Shanghai and locating in the five SEZs; up to that time, inland cities had proved somewhat disappointing.[79]

When considering location, you should be aware that competition is intense in the coastal areas, and dubious characters and downright crooks have proliferated. The inland areas often offer greater incentives and support for foreign capital, and the standard of honesty seems higher. To be set against that are the poor transport and distribution systems in the hinterland of China and few facilities for Western style living.

The Board of Management

Before going to China, you should be determined to negotiate majority control of the board of management - a minimum of two-thirds is a good idea. If you are in a minority, you will have substantial, probably insoluble, problems later. You must never agree to an all-Chinese Board, which would leave you out in the cold.

The management structure of joint ventures

If establishing a new factory, just before you are ready to go into operation, take the time to examine the production processes carefully to see if they are complete. The Chinese have been known to do things like replacing a section of the foreign-designed production line by more labor intensive methods, in an effort to boost employment. If they have done so, you should put things back the way they should be, or you will face reduced levels of productivity and possibly quality.

If you have a 100 percent foreign ownership firm, you might find it beneficial to hire a local cadre to act as a buffer between you and the workers, rather like the old comprador system of pre 1949. Taiwanese firms in China tend to do this, find it usually works well, and the locals have no trouble understanding the system.

Two reporting systems may be needed

A joint venture must report its results to the Chinese government, via its controlling Ministry or other organization. At the same time, your HQ will require reports on events and achievements. Because the bookkeeping and accounting systems are different between the two countries, you might find that you have to keep two sets of accounts, one for each country. Shanghai Volkswagen had to report both to the Chinese authorities and to Volkswagen in Germany; not only did it have a bookkeeping problem, it was also forced to alter its management system more than once to cope with the dissimilar demands.[80]

People are often crammed in

You can expect to see large numbers of people squashed into rooms, when attending briefings or in training sessions. China is a poor country with a huge population, and space is at premium. People are used to living and working in conditions that might shock you.

Other poor conditions you might encounter include homes and offices that are extremely hot in summer and freezing cold in winter, factories with no safety equipment on high-speed cutting machines, and workshop floors slippery with grease. Industrial and mining accidents are common and China has the unenviable record of suffering the highest coal mining accident rate in the world.

The concept of fashion and style is becoming more accepted

It is quite common to find that style and fashion loom low in Chinese eyes, and time must be spent promoting the idea that such things matter. Although the Chinese have a long history of appreciating beauty and culture in art, the Manchu dynasty (1644-1911) had poor taste and favored the garish and the obvious. More recently, the central planning system, with its ethos of scarcity and a sellers market, meant there was no interest in quality and design, only the size of physical output. Even the political dictatorship and cult of personality under Chairman Mao was unhelpful, in that it caused the widespread distribution of millions of ugly political artifacts that people found it safer to purchase and display prominently.

You must keep an eye on production, and if you supply anything special to be used, such as distinctive buttons for particular dress designs, you must watch to see they are handled properly. You might find that the workers save time by not bothering to use them at all; or they might casually mix in local buttons with a different design, ruining the appearance of the dress. It is worth spending time training people properly, showing what you want and explaining why. A growing number of Chinese yuppies are tremendously interested in style, and on the quality front things are beginning to improve.

Prison labor

Rumors about the use of prison labor in China circulate regularly in the West. You should try to ensure that none of your parts or equipment comes from a source that could be associated with a prison, in order to avoid publicity and scandal in the Western press which could lead to an organized boycott of your products. The Chrysler Corporation suffered when its joint venture partner was accused of using prison labor but the complex web of ownership allegedly linking Beijing Jeep to the prison camp made investigations complicated and the truth difficult to ascertain.[81]

Management behavior

The shortage of skilled Chinese managers

It is difficult to find local managers of quality. In a joint venture, the managers can be expected to have excellent local contacts, but will usually have little or no experience of marketing. Under the planned economy, managers operated production units and handed over what they made to the state, which accepted it all, regardless of quality. You can expect to have to spend considerably more time on training in marketing and quality issues than you would back home.

Using Overseas Chinese managers

It is tempting to use Overseas Chinese managers on the grounds that they understand the culture and speak the language. It is not necessarily a good idea however. Although some Overseas Chinese work well in China, many suffer from the disadvantage of speaking a southern dialect that is totally incomprehensible to the majority of Chinese people. If such a manager learns Mandarin, it often comes out with a strong southern accent that tends to be universally despised. There is an old saying: "I fear nothing under heaven or on earth but I flee from a Cantonese speaking Mandarin". The accent does not carry respect, which in status-conscious China is a major flaw.

In addition, you cannot automatically assume that every Overseas Chinese person understands Chinese culture: some know almost nothing; others have a sort of bastardized version, heavily influenced by Indonesian, Philippine, American or other cultures; and none has *guanxi,* unless they have been living in China for some time. It could be a mistake to send them to China to let them resolve an identity crisis at your expense. It is a difficult issue and only you can decide if they are suitable for the position.

There is a further reason for not preferring an Overseas Chinese to run the venture in China or even allow him or her to select the managers who will do so. In either case, the person is likely to feel obliged to hire family members. This does not ensure that the most suitable people will be chosen and the probability is that they will not be appropriate or up to the task.

Keeping existing perquisites

You should retain any existing perks for managers, such as regular banquets or attendance at local or distant meetings. You may wonder why you have to fork out for such things but is part of their salary package: the food eaten and travel enjoyed cannot be taxed, and face is gained by attending such events.

Egalitarianism may not be a good idea

It would be a mistake to try to establish an egalitarian system in your company in China or treat the workers as equals. If you do, it will be a source of scandal and resentment when you mix together workers of different grades or skill, and it could easily demoralize the Chinese management.

In similar vein, you should not address important officials familiarly. China is a heavily structured society and proper respect must be shown to those higher up. It is important never to talk to an ambassador, for example, as if he or she were an ordinary mortal and an equal. You might feel he is charming and an equal, but he will feel you are impertinent if you address him as one. Egalitarianism has little if any place in China, despite the strong political rhetoric since 1949. High officials expect due deference, which they get in abundance from their own people.

Avoid public criticism

You should never criticize a manager or worker publicly as this would cause an extreme loss of face to him or her; you would not be forgiven or receive his or her support henceforth. Indeed, the person would be more inclined to oppose whatever seemed to be in your best interest. If you must reprimand a staff member, take the person into your office quietly and do it tactfully. Rather than saying they are bad at doing something, it is better first to praise them for something, and immediately go on to suggest ways their performance might be improved. Perhaps you could explain to them that an alternative way might work better than current practice, and ask him to try it.

It is even more important not to criticize high Chinese officials in public, for they can exact a terrible revenge. An example of someone who should have known better is Jimmy Lai, who in his magazine *Next*, attacked Premier Li Peng. Lai owned the Giordano clothing chain and in retribution, its flagship store in the national capital was ordered to be closed. Over the next two years, about one third of his 93 stores in China were also shut down.[82]

Making changes

It is a good idea not to jump in and make a lot of changes as soon as you arrive. The Chinese system is quite different from the Western ones to which you are accustomed; what works in New York or Dresden may fail in China. If the Chinese do a thing in a way different from yours, it may still be the most sensible way to operate. You might find your suggestions politely received and then ignored. Sometimes a refusal to do what you want is merely innate conservatism and rejection of a foreign idea; or it may be a failure to appreciate why you want it done that way and what benefits will ensure. At other times, you will be ignored because your way would simply not work well.

If your Chinese managers ever suggest something, you should listen carefully. There is often a good reason for what they want even if it is not immediately obvious to you. Ask your go-between, especially if he is Chinese, why they might want it done that particular way. However, you should keep watching for suggestions that might favor some other company more than you, for example, hiring in transport facilities, as the person suggesting it may have something to gain if you follow the advice.

When trying to alter something, try not to say that your way is better. "What about if we try it this way...." sounds a lot better in China than a bald "this is how we do it, because this is the best way." Many Chinese hate this, and feel that their country and its ways are being criticized and put down. They will see it as patronizing and arrogant behavior on your part. An acceptable approach is to explain the benefits, show them how it works, and in what ways it can be better for all concerned, without emphasizing any drawbacks of their present ways. If *they* choose to mention weaknesses in the existing process, it is an indication that they like or trust you. You can strengthen your suggestion if you are able to say that it has been scientifically proven to work better, or is cutting edge technology, as these appeal to the "only the best is good enough" element in Chinese culture.

Innovative thinking

Do not expect much in the way of innovation, lateral thinking, or creativity among the workers. They can be trained to do a good job, although it requires time and patience, but they tend to do exactly what they are told, and no more. It is worth regularly checking to see what they are up to and how things are working on the factory floor or in the office. You might find that you need to issue new suggestions or instructions in the light of operating experience. If circumstances have changed, the old ways that you laid down might no longer fit well and you may need to undertake some retraining or adjust the work practices. Many local workers will notice that a work practice is no longer sensible but few will think to point this out to the person above them, as it might be taken as a criticism and draw unwanted attention to the worker as a potential trouble maker.

Problem? What problem?

You should never admit to the Chinese that you have problems, even at managerial level; instead, you should quietly set about solving them. Culturally, the Chinese tend to see a person dealing with obvious problems as an incompetent, rather than someone facing up to and tackling the challenge, as it might be viewed in the West.

If you must explain some change that you will make, do it in detail and then relate it to the big picture, so that the interlinked process and system can be seen. For the Chinese, cause and effect often matter less than being able to appreciate the interrelationships and understand what and who will be involved.

External problem solving

Do observe that if you are having problems of delays with Customs or other local officials, inviting them to a good dinner and supplying them with a bottle of brandy and a carton of cigarettes is often a good way of ensuring the problems suddenly disappear. Such gifts are often an effective way of building up a relationship and greasing the wheels of the bureaucracy in advance of need.

A quiet gift of a bottle of brandy or carton of cigarettes may not come amiss for small issues, but major problems may require a bigger offering, such as a personal computer, TV or refrigerator. This is a difficult area and it may depend on how far you are willing to go ethically in order to work more efficiently within the local system. The system requires it to work well, but some people believe it wrong to encourage the behavior.

If you have a problem and call in a favor from a friend in the bureaucracy to help solve it, remember that it is important to keep a rough balance of good turns owed and owing. This means that you may have to build up a new credit balance with him or her.

Maintenance

Do not expect that equipment will automatically be properly looked after. You might easily find, for example, that machinery or valuable materials are left exposed in the open and no one covers them up when it rains. In the past, such items were communal property and were not the responsibility of any particular person, so everyone ignored the problem. The fact that the machinery is being damaged is clearly seen, but this is not recognized as an issue for the person who sees it, nor as something with which they should deal. You might need to supply instructions to cover such eventualities.

Sometimes the problem is simply one of lack of skills or true concern with handling the equipment. A helicopter joint venture in China, set up by a family company from Sandford, Florida, received a helicopter with a badly damaged rotor head and fuselage. This was the result of dockworkers in Shanghai managing to run it into an overhead projection when offloading! The Florida company then sent another helicopter to its joint venture, and this one arrived in such poor condition that a family member reported that, in all his experience, he had never seen damage like it anywhere in the world.[83]

Getting interviews and seeing people

You might be surprised how rarely important people plan far ahead. Even top officials rarely seem to pencil anything in for more than a week or so in advance. This means that there is no point trying to set up a meeting for a month ahead, say, because no one is likely to agree to this. Often you will not be told until the day before that you will be able to meet with a particular official and it might even be the same day when you suddenly receive notice. Should your CEO wish to visit in six weeks' time, and asks for an appointment to be set up, you are unlikely to be able to manage it. You might as well explain to him at once that the system does not work that way. If you inform the organization involved ahead of time, and then remind them a week before he arrives, they will normally be able to find someone of suitable rank to meet and talk with your VIP visitor.

You will find that keeping your own business calendar flexible is essential, if you are to survive in this short vision system. If you are not already used to flying by the seat of your pants, you will learn!

Respect the hierarchy

It is wise to observe the importance of hierarchy in the firm and treat the higher level Chinese managers with respect. In practical terms, age matters, so try to promote people who are older and do not put someone very young over someone middle-aged or old. If you break this rule, neither person would be comfortable and the system would not work well. Promotion by merit is something of an alien concept in China, but if there is no alternative to putting a younger person over an older, you might get by if you pay the older one the same salary as the younger. Note that it would be particularly unfortunate to put a younger woman over an older man as it would violate two Confucian values.

Those in supervisory positions get perks such as trips to other cities or perhaps to Beijing, and you should watch to ensure that all get a turn, and no one is left out while others go twice. If this should happen it can cause great resentment and loss of face; even those benefiting from excessive numbers of trips would think you were not competent to understand China or run the firm properly. You must accept the slight loss of efficiency involved in sending someone who is not the most suitable person for the task at hand.

Secret internal rules

Do not get annoyed if "internal rules" are cited at you. They do exist and the passion for secrecy, together with the "insider-outsider" attitude, mean you cannot even be told that there is such a rule, let alone what it says, until after you have broken it! Sometimes you might be told that there is a rule preventing something, when in reality they simply do not wish to do it. China is supposed to get rid of the secret laws under its obligations to the WTO but many unpublished regulations still seem to exist.

Introductions – "Why don't you call Mr. Wang in Wuhan?"

It is better not to try to introduce a Chinese person from one ministry or area of government to another. It tends to embarrass them, for it seems wrong for you, as an outsider and a foreign one at that, to know more about the workings of the bureaucracy and its personnel than they do! They may feel a distinct loss of face and you will be blamed for this. Similarly, it can backfire if you suggest that a Chinese colleague might like to call some other Chinese person you know who could be useful. It would put your him in a difficult position, having to cold-call someone like this. The proper way is to arrange an introduction and let the two meet first.

Why do they do not like making decisions?

You might find your Chinese managers are reluctant to make decisions and sign documents. Patience and training is needed to allow Chinese managers to overcome fear, develop a feeling of responsibility, and become decisive. If you go away from a joint venture on a business trip or holiday, on your return you might find that few decisions have been made during your absence, however pressing the problems. With time, effort and patience, this attitude can usually be overcome. Chinese managers are often reluctant to sign documents as in the past they could be sent to work as laborers for an unlimited period or punished severely in other ways, for merely signing something apparently innocuous which later was judged to be politically incorrect.

When they do send documents, the message is often short and may be peremptory in style, resembling a curt order with little if any semblance of politeness. This is in sharp contrast with their personal style of interaction. You might need to show them how to draft polite requests, perhaps supplying a series of template documents for different sorts of issues, to help them learn to overcome their abrupt written manner.

Using your influence

Do not hesitate to "use the back door" if you need something. "Going through the back door" means using pull, influence and contacts to get what you want, rather than doing it the formal, probably bureaucratic, way. Officially frowned upon, it remains a normal way of doing business, in government, commercial and industrial circles.

Love those details

You will get used to having to explain things in great detail. This is partly because although the Chinese love details, they also need to see how the picture fits together, they are unfamiliar with Western business practices, and they are often a little afraid and unsure what is required of them. You might find your managers as well as your workers are rather literally minded and do not do something that obviously needs doing, simply because you did not ask them. Anything that is not clearly laid down in their job description may be ignored.

As a boss, you may be expected to do some odd things

A boss has obligations forced upon him by the expectations of society. You might be asked to intervene in personal matters, perhaps as an arbitrator in a dispute, or to write letters of recommendation for a staff member's relative that you have never met, or to obtain some scarce (in China) item from abroad for one of your managers. Depending on what the item is, this last action may be legally dubious.

Housing problems loom large for many workers. Until recently, the state took it upon itself to provide heavily subsidized accommodation for all workers (but not peasants), normally providing housing through the employees' place of work. A change in policy occurred in the mid 1990s, when the State tried to divest itself of such responsibility, although the success rate so far is small. As and when the state manages to withdraw from the provision of cheap housing, your workers may pressure you for housing assistance. Because you are the boss, the workers are likely to approach you for help. Although you are not legally bound to house them, it might render attracting and retaining good quality workers easier if you provide assistance. Once they have a place to live in the city, they are much less likely to leave. Your company might choose to build its own dormitories (common in China), or else rent accommodation from the private sector.

Think very carefully before rejecting a request which seems strange or out of order to you; if you refuse, it can cause you later problems of cooperation from that worker and the staff member might even decide to leave your employment. Other staff, when learning about the issue, might also become demoralized if they see you as uncaring and not behaving in the proper manner.

Keep an eye on your inventories

If in a joint venture, watch for any tendency to stockpile the produce. During the centrally-planned era, all units tried to build up stocks of materials and spare parts in order to guard against the regular shortages and late deliveries. They also stockpiled extra output and hid it, in order to meet future targets more easily. The habit lingers on, and stocks may tend to build up unless you are watchful.

Mindful of the problem, the authorities announced in late 1998 that such surplus inventories could be bartered through a nationwide electronic network. The size of the problem was revealed by the estimated total of such unnecessary stocks which were estimated to be valued at over $360 billion!

Prices, quality, costs and profits

The quality of domestic supplies can leave much to be desired

You will face a complex but inadequate distribution system, with insufficient transport facilities and poor warehousing. Deliveries may arrive late or in damaged condition. If a reliable electricity supply is necessary, you should bring in your own generator and ensure that you have sufficient spare parts for it. If it breaks down, Murphy's Law guarantees that it will occur at the worst possible time and you need to get back into production as rapidly as you can.

Materials and supplies in China can be of low or variable quality and it is hoped you have obtained a contract that allows for choice of source. If not, you might find that the quality of your finished product is too low to be exportable and at the worst, cannot even be sold within China. Beatrice Companies, Inc., one of the large American food firms, discovered that their regular bottling machines caused the Chinese bottles to explode, owing to low standards of bottle manufacture.[84] Another company, McDonald's, foresaw that it would face the problem of low quality Chinese potatoes, and sensibly encouraged the development of decent potato farming *before* it opened its retail outlets and began making French fries in China.[85] The Xerox Corporation also faced problems, in their case caused by the low quality of Chinese paper. It had a nasty tendency to jam their copiers, which was only solved by a total redesign of the feeders on the machine.[86]

Packaging

Until recently, packaging in China was irrelevant: the state took all output and distributed it easily in the sellers' market which existed because of the limited supply of many items. With the increase in competition in the last two decades, packaging is starting to become important to people. Good, well-designed packaging can enhance the status of your product, which in a Confucian society can mean higher prestige and bigger sales. The Oak Tree Packaging Corp, New Jersey, has helped to create, and then fill, a lucrative market in cartons, using their Fujian Oak Tree joint venture. They managed to avoid the problem of not being paid which has been faced by some foreign companies in China, usually caused by the Chinese company not being able to get a bank loan or having no foreign exchange available. Much of the output from Oak Tree Packaging goes to other foreign firms located in China and they are generally not short of money or foreign currency.

If you are producing and transporting such desirable goods as hi-fi's, TVs or VCRs you will probably find that the pilferage rate is unacceptably high. To counter this, your bulk packaging materials should disguise the precise nature of the content, as this can deter thieves. If yours is a well-known brand name, irrespective of what you produce, you might find it advantageous to conceal the fact that the contents are from your company by not putting your name on the cartons.

Not only consumer goods are targets: the Hong Kong company Celestial Yacht Ltd. set up a pleasure boat building venture in Xiamen and found their materials disappearing. They would receive a delivery of teak and resin on one day and find that as much as half of it had been stolen by the next.[87]

Quality control

Do not expect good quality control. The central planning system and decades of sellers' markets have virtually ended quality as a factor in production. Chinese workers do not fully appreciate that international markets demand high quality. You will have to train people to take it seriously, and may be forced to monitor them regularly to ensure they do not backslide.

Nike Inc, for whom quality in their athletic shoes is of paramount importance, decided that they could not rely on local inspection being up to the standard that was needed. Instead, they chose to send their own quality control personnel to China where they examined production. They decided on the spot what athletic shoes were good enough for Nike to accept at full price, what were of lesser quality and would receive a lower price, and what were so bad that they should simply be destroyed.[88]

In this, Nike did a lot better than a small American buyer of equipment for the sand and gravel industry. He imported machinery from China at a price half to two-thirds of the American equivalent and sold it on to the end users. Sadly, the quality was lacking: the Chinese factory relied on cheap and dirty solutions to problems, including filling any cracks or indentations in gear box housing with putty! Unsurprisingly, when the machines were put into operation, the users found that "Bolts sheared, springs broke, bearings failed, metal bent and cracked, and railings and chains snapped."[89]

One US firm managed to impress the Chinese with the idea that quality mattered, by insisting that every single part be shipped back to the States for inspection before going into assembly. This was of course costly, and when the Chinese side complained about it, the US side agreed to drop the requirement. But by this time, the point that quality was important had been well established and henceforth it could then be easily maintained.[90] The latent threat of reimposing the original quality rule no doubt helped to focus the mind wonderfully.

Watch those costs!

You should be aware that costs can be higher than expected and the infrastructure is weak. Because of poor quality of materials, you might be forced to buy from remote areas or even import instead of being able to rely on local suppliers. The French company Peugeot Citroen established the Guangzhou Peugeot Automobile Corporation, and found that it could not get local spare parts of quality for its motor vehicles in Guangzhou. When it tried to buy in from another province the Guangzhou authorities refused to allow the company to purchase anywhere else in China! All the other provinces were seen as direct rivals who must not be helped in any way. Consequently, Peugeot Citroen found itself forced to bring all such needed parts from abroad. Importing in kit form in this way proved expensive, especially after the French *franc* appreciated against the *yuan* in the late 1980s.[91]

A similar problem was faced by the Xerox Corporation, which signed a contract providing that seventy percent of the components needed by its joint venture would be sourced locally. Afterwards, it found that *no* firm in China had the expertise to supply parts of the requisite quality, which put it into a difficult situation. In order to solve the problem and stay within the terms of the contract, Xerox had to spend several millions of dollars providing training and support for sixty local firms and then had to continue to monitor their activities. Even after transferring technology to them, Xerox found that the Chinese firms were not particularly efficient, and the domestically-made parts were still twenty-five percent dearer than imported ones.[92] What is interesting is that it is not clear if Xerox even contemplated asking for a change in the terms of the contract, which any Chinese firm would immediately have thought of as the obvious solution. Cultural ignorance surely can be costly!

Machinery in China breaks down regularly for several reasons: maintenance is not taken seriously, skilled technicians and engineers are in short supply, spare parts are lacking, and power fluctuations take their toll, as does the dust in the center and north, and humidity in the south. You might find that breakdowns push up costs more than in your home country.

Workers' costs may not be as low as you would hope, because low productivity can offset at least part of the low wage paid. The Chinese managers may ask for the same salary and package as the expatriates, despite lacking knowledge and experience, and may be little more than high level apprentices, learning how to do the job. They do this for reasons of face, as well as wishing to increase their standard of living.

Remember that workers may not actually receive all of the salary you pay them: if the government supplies managers, it may take most of their salary as a sort of tax on you. It is a good idea to try to write into the initial joint venture contract that expatriates are paid at international rates but locally hired staff at domestic rates, to keep this particular cost problem at bay.

If all the expatriates in the joint venture have a motor car or a notebook computer, it may pay you to give each Chinese manager one as well, even if they have no real need for the item. Motorcars and computers are both scarce items and symbols of power so that if the Chinese do not also have them they will feel a loss of face. This might lead them to become demoralized or actually obstructive. If you only issue such items to those with a real need, you can expect to waste a lot of time discussing the matter which is likely to keep cropping up. Costs are higher either way!

Other costs may arise from:

* Land use fees.
* Connection charges or establishment fees for public utilities, like water, electricity, gas, and telephones.
* Chinese New Year, which may require double monthly salary for all workers, or a present like a basket of food.
* Workers you have paid to train might suddenly be removed, to be replaced by new unskilled ones.
* The slow pace of negotiations, which can delay activity or necessary change.
* Banquets, "study tours" and free trips for officials.

Hidden or unexpected costs can suddenly emerge

Hidden costs abound and the Chinese may spring a range of expenditure on you after the contract has been signed which can come as an unpleasant surprise. Be aware that the feasibility study may exclude some outlays that will subsequently turn out to be necessary. In particular, it is wise to get worker services fully spelled out in writing. These can include training, housing subsidies, health care, a crèche or school, free lunches, and a variety of strange allowances e.g., for haircuts or ice cream in hot weather. In the mid 1990s, the Fujian Oak Tree joint venture planned to build a huge manufacturing and training center, which would include dormitories, a cafeteria, a park, a recreational area, an infirmary and a day care center; not all of these are automatically considered essentially in a Western business environment.[93]

Be aware that if you provide dining facilities you will require more than one cafetaria, possibly three or four. The managers will not eat with workers, and even among workers the office staff will feel superior to the manual, and below them, the skilled will be uncomfortable and resentful if asked to sit with the unskilled.

No one is automatically immune from sudden requests for money. Even a person with the international stature of Steven Spielberg was faced with a sudden demand for more money when filming *Empire of the Sun*. After being granted permission for him to film in Shanghai, local officials suddenly imposed a $10,000 fine for air pollution, which they argued was caused by smoke from the battle scenes.[94]

Fees of somewhat dubious legality can be imposed by local officials on top of the standard taxes. McDonalds is just one company of many that faced such unexpected demands: each of its thirty-eight restaurants in Beijing is said to be subject to thirty-one miscellaneous fees, but only two of these are listed in the legal code! Stratton pointed out that in 1997 the central government had to force twenty-one provinces and cities to cancel over 2,800 fees that they had unilaterally imposed.[95] This was only the tip of the iceberg: in 1998, the Minister of Finance, Xiang Haicheng, reported that some 20,700 illegal levies on companies had been called off and added that irrational or illegal levies would continue to be canceled.[96] Many are believed to escape the eyes of the Ministry however.

Blatantly false claims may be made against you in the hope that you will hand over money. Mats Engstrom, the president of Tsar Nicolai, a San Francisco-based food company, reported that he bought two Cherokee Jeeps outright for $19,000 for use in his Beijing caviar operation. He was subsequently pestered to pay so-called "rental fees" of $100 a day in order to use his own jeeps! He repeatedly had to reject the persistent demands.[97]

You may have to pay higher prices

Do not be surprised to find that you must pay more than state-owned firms for your fuel, raw materials, water, electricity, and telephone use.

State-owned enterprises are heavily subsidized and are widely regarded as inefficient, which many of them are. However, a large number of them are forced to sell at fixed prices, which are less than the cost of the material content, so that making a loss is the natural result of poor state pricing decisions. When a state operated enterprise makes a loss, it is not necessarily an indication of the level of its efficiency. Because of this topsy-turvy pricing system, in order to help state firms, the state allows many of them to pay less for their inputs than you do.

Other prices for things like travel by `plane or train, hotel rooms, or meals may be high simply because you are foreign (see p.134, "Why are they charging me more than the others?")

Cash flow problems

It is easy to run into problems of sustaining cash flows, especially shortly after setting up. It is common for your Chinese partner's earlier promises of easily available loans to evaporate, or at least take a long time to appear. Your suppliers will press you for payment, but those you are supplying frequently hold off paying you. This can be an ongoing problem. Many Chinese firms suffer from a shortage of working capital and might have to raise a bank loan to pay the invoices you send. The banks are often unwilling to lend, especially when under strong government pressure to extend loans to SOEs in order to keep them afloat. There may be little or no money left for private firms or joint ventures. The banks will insist on guarantors for the loan, but guarantors can be hard to find; not all banks are willing, or legally allowed, to accept the firm's assets as security for the loan.

There is a well-known "triangular debt" problem in China. This exists when an enterprise finds it impossible to collect from a Chinese firm, especially if it is a State Operated Enterprise, because that organization cannot gain payment of *its* outstanding accounts from other firms, or obtain finance from the bank as working capital.

Profits

China can be a difficult place to make profits. Procter & Gamble made a profit in 1995, but admitted that it was the first time since they began operations back in 1988.[98] Seven years is a long time to wait! Rockwell International Overseas Corporation says that its motive for going into China was to gain a foothold in a large and growing market. From 1979, when the CEO first visited China, to 1982, they were taking a loss in order to build for the future.[99]

Pilkington, a British company, found that after they opened their glassmaking works in China, they was unable to use the local raw materials owing to the low quality. As a consequence, they were unexpectedly forced to import them in quantity. Glass making is an industry that uses large amounts of low value, heavy materials, so the unforeseen burden had dire effect on profits.

I once visited a small joint venture in Shenzhen and during the discussions I enquired about profits. I was told by the Chinese partner that "of course we make profits!" in tones of great finality. In a subsequent discussion with the foreign partner he confessed that perhaps technically this was true but it meant little: the firm had made profits - but only in one month during the entire three years that they had been operating!

Price competition can squeeze your profits

At the time the decision was made to go ahead and invest, the estimates of potential profit were probably made on prices of the day. Over time, many retail prices have fallen and this can squeeze profits dramatically. Firstly, new firms have probably gone into production, increasing the supply on the market and placing pressure on prices. The giants Coca Cola and PepsiCo, which hold 57.6 and 21.3 percent of the cola market respectively, faced a sharp challenge from a local entrant in 1998. "Future Cola", made by Wahaha, a leading Chinese soft drink producer, hit the market with a major advertising blitz on TV, cunningly placed during the transmission of the extremely popular football World Cup, and also priced slightly below Coca Cola. Many observers feel the two giants will not have much to fear, but time will tell.[100]

Secondly, local firms have learned rapidly from the foreigners and, as quality improves, they are increasingly providing stiff competition in some markets. Skin care products is an example where foreign brands, such as Oil of Ulan, face particularly fierce competition from local producers. Beer brewing, too, suffered from intense competition in the late 1990s; because of this, Foster's Brewing Group Ltd. of Australia plans to sell two of its three breweries to reduce losses.[101]

Another company that suffered from increased competition was Shangling, which makes refrigerators in Shanghai. It once dominated the whole east China market, but got into serious difficulties in the mid 1990s, as new firms with better management and superior products came on the scene.[102]

A third source of price competition can come from parallel imports.

These arise when products produced in China for export are somehow sold within the country. If an item is to be sold abroad, import duty can be waived on the inputs; if the product is then illegally diverted to the domestic market by someone down the line, or is even properly exported but then reimported without high duty, the original producer may not be able to compete with his own product. A prime example is Singer Company that found that it was unable to sell the sewing machines produced locally in a joint venture) to the domestic Shanghai market; parallel imports of Singer sewing machines were undercutting its price.[103]

Despite the profit difficulties that some firms have experienced, a survey in 1991[104] revealed that only 12 percent of 306 US investment projects in China appeared to lose money, while 60 percent reported a return on investment (ROI) of 10 percent or higher. The same survey revealed that the four types of joint ventures (high-tech, export-oriented, domestic-oriented, and import-substitution goods) showed significant differences in ROI. Hi-tech and export producers did best (15.4 percent ROI), while the import-substitution companies did the worst (8.7 percent). China has a rapidly changing economy so that the information is indicative but no more.

A second study[105] reported that in 1994, 64 percent of 47 large joint ventures in China reported making profits. This might underestimate the number of profitable companies, as some observers believe that enterprises with foreign investment have been underreporting their profitability, in order to retain concessions or to avoid paying tax. Certainly, these results were lower than those found in another 1994 survey, done by the US-China Business Council. It examined those of its own members who operate in China, and of the thirty-one companies that responded, some 76 percent said they were profitable.[106]

A survey at roughly the same time from Taiwan, reported that only 38 percent of Taiwanese investment in China were profitable.[107] The same source reported that although twenty-five of the thirty-one factories owned in China by Japan's Matsushita made profits, they were only small.

A collapsing market

Many companies have seen their sales shrink drastically as competitors entered and flooded the market. Changes in government regulations can cause an unexpected market reduction or even its disappearance. During the 1980s and up to the middle of the 1990s, the Tianjin Automobile Industrial Group assembled small 0.98 liter Charade motorcars and Daihatsu minivans, and did so with reasonable success. Their market collapsed when Beijing banned small vehicles from its roads on every other day and Shanghai decided that no new taxi licenses would be issued for vehicles under 1.6 liters.[108] Toyota Motor Corp came to the rescue by establishing a new joint venture with the company. This was a brave move, for the motor vehicle industry of China was not short of capacity. At the time, the total capacity was expected to reach 900,000 units by the end of 1997 but demand was estimated at only about half that level.[109]

Competition forced down the price of motorcars in 1998 so much that the government stepped in and set minimum prices, refusing to allow market pressures full sway. Industry made its response and cartels began to appear to hold up prices; steel, flat glass, farm use vehicles and motorcars were believed to be involved. The steel industry generally was pressured by the state in 2000 to reduce output by 10 per cent, to try to restore profitability. So far, there is no antitrust legislation in force in China and the government encourages cartels to prevent falling prices .

Smuggling

Some producers have faced unexpected and illegal competition from smuggled goods. The Japanese electronic giant Matsushita established a joint venture with Hualu Electronics Corporation in 1993 to produce videocassette recorders. Most of the forty-five production lines remained idle, largely because smuggled VCRs prevented sales of legitimate products.[110] The motor vehicle industry also faces competition from illegally imported vehicles, which number perhaps as many as 40,000 a year. It is commonly believed in Hong Kong that their expensive and highly desirable motorcars are stolen to order for Chinese customers. Certainly the theft rate is remarkably high in the ex-colony - and right hand drive vehicles are commonly observed in Guangdong Province!

In 1998, a smuggling racket covering oil, steel and motor vehicles in South China's Zhanjiang city was valued at a minimum of $1.2 billion and involved the cooperation of the director and vice-director of Customs as well as border guards.[111]

The smuggling problem is taken seriously and President Jiang Zemin and Premier Zhu Rongji both delivered important speeches to a national conference on antismuggling work in July 1998.[112] Unfortunately, many Party, government and army organizations, as well as judicial and law enforcement departments, are heavily involved in the smuggling, so that it is no easy matter to tackle.[113]

The macro cycle of profits

The central government has poor control of the economy and lacks the means of fine-tuning by use of monetary policy. The alternative, fiscal policy, is a clumsy once-a-year tool invoked at budget time and is not easy to use. Much tax revenue is lost through easy-to-do illegal acts, including companies engaging in false reporting or keeping two sets of books, and provinces retaining revenue that they should hand over.

The economy progresses in a series of booms and slumps, which are usually investment based. During booms, the economy races along, perhaps at 10-15 percent p.a., and inflation accelerates sharply. The government responds to this by imposing a major credit squeeze, aimed largely at investment. Most companies can make money during the boom, but many find it difficult when the government tightens up and forces a slump. Those companies just starting up finding it particularly difficult. If the government has just announced an investment squeeze, you might consider deferring any start-up project you were planning.

The nation's foreign exchange situation can have its effects on economic policy: when exports slump or increase more slowly, the foreign exchange reserves cease to grow or fall. The normal response of the government is to cut back on imports and squeeze investment.

As an example of one of many companies that have suffered from the stop-go economic policies, the Shanghai No. 2 Textile Machinery Company was a star performer in the early 1990s. At that time it invested heavily in advanced machinery, anticipating that the good times would continue. The company then saw the market for its products collapse when the government suddenly tightened the economic screws in 1994/95.[114]

Problems faced by foreign investors generally

A survey of about one thousand foreign business people and 101 companies in Shanghai in 1997 indicated the major problems faced (see Table 10.1, p.213). Government red tape was the worst, followed by the tax system, which can also be regarded as falling into the area of bureaucratic nuisance. Living conditions were the least of the problems identified by the respondents.

Problems faced by some American companies

A survey by the US-China Business Council of those of its members who had foreign invested enterprises in China at mid 1994, revealed that among their operating difficulties, the worst were inflation and rising costs, and an inability to be paid by other firms for goods or services rendered. Quality was not an important issue for them, nor was obtaining licenses for importing needed items (see Table 10.2, p.213).

Table 10.1 The results of a survey into problems in Shanghai in 1997

1st	Government red tape
2nd	The tax system
3rd	Human resources
4th	Financial and insurance services
5th	Infrastructure
6th	Expatriate living conditions

Source: Wu Zheng "Shanghai Survey Finds More Red Tape to Cut", *China Daily Business Weekly*, Nov. 9-15, 1997, p.5.

Problems reported in 1997

A survey by The Economist Intelligence Unit in 1997,[115] revealed that most companies describe their China ventures as "long-term investment", which was merely a euphemism for making losses! More than half the firms questioned said they were disappointed with the results they had obtained. The most serious problem reported was obtaining local managers of sufficient caliber, so there was a forced use of expensive expatriate staff who could not easily be replaced by locals. Many also indicated that they had problems with their joint venture partners.

Table 10.2 Problems faced by twenty-one US firms in China, 1994
(Responses: 0 = severe; 1 = not severe; 2 = no problem)

Problem Item	Average
Inflation/costs	0.41
Rising accounts receivable	0.74
Bureaucratic interference	0.93
Transportation	1.04
Quality of locally produced inputs	1.04
Supply of RMB working capital loans	1.11

Supply of raw materials	1.13
Access to domestic markets	1.30
Production and quality control	1.30
Relations with partner	1.30
Electricity supply	1.33
Obtaining import licenses	1.40
Achieving export quality	1.42

Source: "Feeling Upbeat", *The China Business Review*, May-June 1995, pp. 39-44, selected items from Table 1.

Labor issues

Hiring workers

Many enterprises take workers from the state-run Foreign Enterprise Service Company (FESCO) the main state supplier, or one of its competitors, like China Star (Ministry of Labor) or China Intellectech. If you do this, you should not be surprised if some of the better workers, in particular those supplied by FESCO, are later recalled after you have trained them. The officials may wish to put them in state-owned factories, so that they can train others there in turn and thereby raise the average quality. If this occurs, you then have to train more workers to replace the lost ones.

This happened in a joint venture set up by Celestial Yacht Ltd. in Xiamen; the company paid to send its workers abroad to Japan and the USA for training but when they returned with their new skills, local officials promptly transferred them to work in a local Chinese shipyard. After complaints, the authorities explained that they only "borrowed" the workers for one or two months to help raise standards in the yard - and in any case, they only took five of the six, leaving one in place in the joint venture![116]

Other ways you can obtain workers include:

- Newspaper advertisements.
- Job Fairs, Labor Markets and Personnel Exchange Meetings.
- Using your partner's *guanxi* and connections.
- Establishing a relationship with vocational schools and university colleges that teach courses relevant to your line of business.

Increasingly, joint ventures hire their own workers directly, which stops the labor supply companies recalling them later. Even hiring in this way you might find that your workers are later headhunted by other foreign companies in the area, possibly including the company from which they originally came.

It is best to be polite to the official who supplies your labor; if you annoy him, he might fob you off with inferior workers in retaliation, or deliberately handle all your requests slowly.[117] It seems that bureaucrats the world over have ways of making you squirm!

The level of skills

Unlike North America or Europe, there is no pool of skilled labor easily available. Even basic skills, like driving a motorcar or being able to type, are scarce. When Peugeot Citroen began its joint venture in Guangzhou, it discovered that the partner's workers from the Guangzhou Automotive Manufacturing Company possessed skills far lower than the foreign company had expected. To bring the Chinese managers and workers up to scratch, it was forced to spend more than it had anticipated on training them in China as well as having to send some of them to France.[118]

This shortage of basic skills, and inadequate levels of existing skills, means that you will probably have to train your own workers, and then try to hang on to them. It is now slightly easier to hire workers, particularly in the Special Economic Zones to which workers flock from other areas.

You may encounter two problems peculiar to skilled workers. One is that a local engineer may be well trained and experienced, but not want to get his hands dirty. It can be difficult getting some individuals to deal with a problem like adjusting the speed of a machine; they prefer to issue orders to someone lower in the hierarchy to do this, even if they will not do it as well as the engineer would. A second problem is that it is often impossible to know what the person's paper qualifications actually mean. Despite this, many expats have reported that they find the local engineers are often good enough for the job, so you might be lucky and never face these particular issues.

Training your managers and workers

If you have gone into partnership with an existing firm, you are likely to find that any managers you inherit from your local partner will need extensive training in Western business practices. They may also require educating in any particular work ethos that your own company possesses.

level, this need not cost as much. For local staff, Li Wenfang suggests that because of different corporate cultures, it can take between five and eight years for them to have acquired all the necessary skills.[119] There are in fact more reasons than simple corporate cultures, including factors such as language, and differences in experience, skill levels, attitudes, cultural beliefs, expectations, and personal goals. In my view he overestimates the length of time generally required.

The training required can prove to be expensive. One US manufacturing company found that it spent more than the amount budgeted for training because it underestimated the number of training trips that would be required. The company also failed to realize that it would be expected to pay for *all* the expenses of the Chinese trainees brought to America. After receiving complaints that not everything was provided, they were forced to allocate more for subsequent trainee visits.[120]

Shanghai Volkswagen tackles the problem of a skilled labor force by getting its young workers direct from high school and giving them three years' training, before letting them loose on the production line. Secretaries and sales staff receive two years' training. In addition to local instruction, a number are sent on to Germany for one or two year's management training.[121]

Training can be divided into "hard skills", such as accounting or advertising, and "soft skills", like how to deal with colleagues and customers, or general problem solving.

Hard skill training is relatively easy and the Chinese are keen to learn. Choosing the language of instruction can be tricky. On the one hand, your own instructors will almost certainly not speak Chinese fluently; on the other, you might find that most of your managers, and even more of your workers, will have only a rudimentary grasp of English. In many cases, the best option is to hold the training in your own language, the one that you wish to be used as the medium of communication within the firm, which is probably English but it could be German, French, or Japanese etc., depending on where your company HQ is based. Then you need to use a good interpreter, supplemented by lots of visual aids, and copious clear handouts *all* written in Chinese.

The real difficulties arise with "soft training", because you are really trying to change an entire culture and work ethos. It is important to lay emphasis on people taking responsibility, thinking creatively, and generally behaving as a Western individual. You will probably find that certain traditional attitudes persist, such as waiting for orders to be issued and then following them unthinkingly, deferring to higher authority uncriti=

cally, and refusing to cooperate laterally.

One thing to watch out for is that you will encounter problems if you assemble managers and workers in the same training session, or even if you place skilled workers with unskilled. The Chinese view of the importance of status and hierarchy means that they find it offensive to be placed in the same group as people below them. If they are constantly worrying about the people around they will not be concentrating on learning what you are trying to teach.

With managers in particular, you might find it beneficial to keep telling them that you want to hear their views, including suggestions and criticisms, because deference to those above is strongly ingrained in society. This means that many will prefer to remain silent rather than offer a good idea because they feel it could seem like an indirect criticism of you and cause you a loss of face. For these reasons, people may fail to report a problem or even inform you that what you suggest will almost certainly not work. Their traditional attitude could cost your company money. Asians generally tend to be less assertive or pushy, and dislike arguing in public, unlike, say, Americans or the English, who are often trained at college to state their views and argue them persuasively.

Senior Chinese managers could benefit from spending time at your HQ back home in order to assimilate Western practices, or at another of your joint ventures in a different third world country to see how things can work on the ground. Alternatively, you could do what Fujian Oak Tree did, and send senior American managers to stay in China for extended periods in order to train local managers[122].

Keeping your workers: the poaching problem

Labor turnover can be a major problem for any joint venture. In 1993 alone, an estimated 15 percent of Shanghai's work force changed jobs.[123] This is not unexpected when you consider the type of person who is attracted to work for a foreigner: they tend to be ambitious, adaptable and footloose, all characteristics which encourage easy movement. As the economy expands and the demand for skilled workers rises, such workers find it easy to move to a better paying position, particularly if you have already trained them. The solution is not to refuse to train your workers, which would harm your company, but to attempt to build a sense of loyalty in as many ways as you can.

You could for example:

- Discuss the issue of labor turnover early, with your liaison officer and your local managers, before it becomes a problem.
- Ask other expatriate managers what their experiences are and what they have tried to do about the problem. Which ways were found to work better and which were ineffective?
- Establish a system of regular pay increases, according to length of employment.
- Ensure that your workers understand the financial benefits within your company of the regular pay increases, the value of working hard in training sessions, and the career paths that exist.
- Point out that any criticisms by you are to help them to advance their career (in case they wish to leave because they were criticized and feel a loss of face).
- Supply them and perhaps their families with other benefits, such as free housing, education facilities (perhaps English lessons for their children) or free health treatment. The Fujian Oak Tree, a packaging joint venture, has found it particularly valuable to give health benefits.[124]

Poaching of workers is commonplace, but it is a swings-and-roundabouts affair; you may lose workers to other local firms but you can try to attract workers from them in turn. In particular, you may be able to attract skilled workers from SOEs, where they are often badly paid; you can certainly offer better salaries and conditions than they currently enjoy.

If your company is in the interior rather than in one of the major cities in the coastal region, such as Shanghai, Beijing or Guangzhou, you might find that you lose trained staff and workers to firms in bigger towns or to the coast. The attraction of The Big City is real. You can help to keep them happy by improving your facilities. You might consider setting up an entertainment area for your staff, which could be equipped with TVs, videos, CD players, headphones and CDs, and maybe some computers and games. A small workout room or gym with hot showers might also help. The suggested ways of building loyalty also apply. Remember that a happy and contented staff work more efficiently, and are less likely to be poached. The expats, used as they are to better conditions, would also appreciate your efforts and expenditures here.

Redundancy and dismissing your workers

If forming a joint venture with an existing company, you can expect that within the other firm there will be overstaffing at virtually all levels.

Your partner will almost certainly try to persuade you to keep everyone on, which of course means higher costs. Partly your partner attempts this out of kindness, as it is felt to be the duty of a manager to protect his staff. Sometimes it is just that everyone is so used to overstaffing that they believe this is the norm. On occasion, it may be due to nepotism, and your partner is merely trying to protect the relatives that he or she hired earlier. Whatever the cause, you might face stubborn resistance to trimming staff and worker levels, and may have to pay money to dismiss those you will not need.

It may be a better alternative to consider keeping the surplus workers and retraining them in new skills, so that you can put them to profitable use. This will of course cost you, but if you intend to build and run a new cafeteria, for instance, then you have a natural outlet for some of them. Even if you have no need for them, the extra skills you give them may lead them to find an alternative position more quickly and get them off your books.

If you ever intend to dismiss people, you should first check out the individuals carefully with your Chinese partner, in case any are a son, daughter or close relative of a powerful local official. These must never be fired. Nepotism is common throughout China and a person is expected to look after his or her family. The press regularly criticizes the phenomenon but to no avail. If you sack someone with a powerful relative, he will probably take revenge upon you and your firm in a variety of ways, some petty but irritating, others potentially very damaging indeed. This could easily cost you far more than you would save by dismissing a bad worker.

Volkswagen's joint venture in Shanghai is so organized that it is unable to dismiss workers whose performance is unsatisfactory, and the company is obliged to find lower positions for them. The Volkswagen joint venture appears to have found a solution for the problem of the Peter Principle, as workers are moved back down to their level of competency! Only those who are judged to have made "a big mistake" can be fired.[125]

Work incentives

Worker motivation is often not high so that you might find you need to provide incentives. In most joint ventures, work incentives take the form of paying higher wages than Chinese firms, as well as a wide variety of bonuses. You could also consider adopting more Chinese ways of motivating your workers, such as posting signs on walls to encourage them. A notice board with slogans at the entrance, and on the front lawn, can encourage people to work harder, raise quality or pursue whatever goal you nominate. Putting the names of the "Worker of the Month" on the board, or pinning up individual photographs of successful workers along with their names, can be used with some success. This approach gives much "face". Methods such as these have been used for decades, seem to work, can be geared specifically to what you wish to promote (such as quality, fewer work accidents, attendance rates, or cleanliness), and can be altered as your needs change. Using such traditional methods can help persuade the workers that you take these things seriously. It is worth a try anyway.

The lower level of motivation can result in your workers tending to stop what they are doing perhaps ten minutes early in anticipation of a coffee break. Others, particularly if coming from a state run firm, may have got used to sitting around reading newspapers, playing cards, or even sleeping while at work and will have to be dissuaded from such practices. Remember that some workers might have been released from their existing job because they were not particularly good, and their boss wished to get rid of them. Most state firms try to retain their better workers and may refuse to release them. It is common within joint ventures to find that it can take a couple of years before the workers are really working well, but the low wage rates do tend to compensate for the initial lower productivity.

New workers from rural China usually lack experience and may have difficulty in accepting Western-style discipline and hard work. They may also lack what we regard as normal common sense. It has been known for recent arrivals from rural China to poke their fingers into a moving fan to try to see where the blades have disappeared to! It is not stupidity, merely ignorance of things that we customarily take for granted.

Worker discipline

Disciplining workers can be a problem, because it can prove to be difficult, and in some cases impossible, to fire them. Even if you manage to get rid of some inferior workers, their replacements will certainly need training, so think carefully about it, and also talk it over with the Chinese managers and your liaison officer, before taking action.

When you need to discipline workers but not fire them, the most normal punishments, in descending order of seriousness, are:

- Demoting to a lower grade or position in the company (the most serious short of dismissal).
- Imposing a fine (very serious).
- Issuing a *stern* warning.

- Issuing a warning.
- Quietly and privately suggesting an improvement in their work style.

You might achieve better results by not dismissing workers. The Thai magnate, Dhanin Chearavanont, prefers not to fire any of the workers in his group of Chinese companies. Like other companies that have foreign capital invested in them, he pays his workers more than they would receive in purely Chinese firms, but in return he expects them to work hard. When there is a problem with some workers, he first trains them, and then moves them to other divisions, which develop openings as his overall business in China expands.[126] It would appear that this action forces the worker to shape up, as s/he realizes that this may be their last chance. The threat of retraining to what will probably be perceived as a lower position is also a bit of an insult as it involves a loss of face. If the move involves physical location, it will be unpopular, particularly if the worker is currently in well-located, heavily subsidized housing, as many are. Whatever the psychological mechanism, retraining and moving seems to work well for this company.

Labor saving is often not seen as a virtue

With the difficult problem of finding work for everyone, it is hardly surprising that saving labor is often not a high priority. Local officials may demand that you overstaff in an effort to reduce unemployment. This happened to Cardio-Pace, a St. Paul-based company that makes heart pacemakers. The company was pressured to take on a number of totally unnecessary "assistant managers", but the company stood firm against these demands and eventually managed to avoid hiring them.[127] A Hong Kong toy manufacturer who set up a factory in south China was forced for a time to hire people whose sole function was to sit and watch the gauges on the air-conditioners to ensure the temperature did not alter.

Cheer up – things are getting better!

China was once an unattractive place to work, other than for dedicated Sinophiles or young people who felt a sort of cult need to gain "the China experience". It is now much improved and some have begun to suggest that it should no longer be considered a hardship post. Although I personally love China, I still feel it is a hardship post for most people and believe that it wise to negotiate a good salary package with decent allowances before agreeing to go and live there for an extended period. However, if you get the chance of a relatively short visit, grab it with both hands and enjoy the experience!

APPENDIX: CHINA'S HISTORY, POLITICS, ECONOMICS AND SOCIETY

China's History

The oldest Chinese books still in existence date back to almost 1,000 BC, although various myths and legends as well as archaeological evidence indicate that an earlier period might extend as far back as 5,000 BC. China has the longest continuous history and culture of any currently existing nation,[128] the people are proud, and they possess more awareness of the past than most Westerners. There are many stories and legends in China, some of which occurred a thousand or more years ago, with which any well-educated person is familiar. In contemporary discussion, reference to ancient events and long dead people is common; there is a tendency to look back on history to gain lessons of value and apply them to the present. This attitude provides wide scope for plays and stories, ostensibly about the past, which actually criticize current political leaders and their policies. Chairman Mao Zedong was reported to have been incensed in the late 1950s by historical dramas that could easily be taken as an indirect criticism of his regime. They probably were.

China was a stable empire for two thousand years, in the hands of a series of ruling dynasties. This system collapsed only in 1911 with the passing of the Manchu Dynasty. Its decline had been hastened by the impact of the West, especially from Britain, during the colonial expansions of the Nineteenth Century. The First Opium War (1839-42) had a traumatic effect on Chinese leaders, who began an intense search for the best way to organize China to meet these new and powerful barbarians. After the fall of the imperial dynasty in 1911, there was a brief flirtation with an embryonic type of parliamentary democracy that lasted for less than two years, before President Yuan Shihkai seized total control. His effort to establish himself as a new emperor failed, China collapsed into warlordism, and the nation began to fall apart. After 1916, many independent little "kingdoms" were established, and banditry was rife. In 1927, civil war broke out between the Kuomintang (KMT) and the Communist Party. In 1931 the Japanese invaded and rapidly took over control of all the important coastal areas. This Japanese presence sucked China into the Second World War and at the end of hostilities the government of China was handed to the KMT. The civil war between them and the communists was resumed in 1946 and continued until 1949, when victory went to the Communist Party. In that year, the KMT moved its seat of government to the island of Taiwan, from where it still claims to be the legitimate ruler of all China.

At least nominally, the civil war continues unresolved, although there has been no military action for years. In 1993, both governments began to talk in Singapore, and now relations are closer than they have ever been. There was a notable economic rapprochement during the 1990s, based on China's need for foreign investment and technology, and Taiwan's need for cheap labor. For many years, indirect trade between China and Taiwan was commonplace, largely via Hong Kong, and in March 2000, the Taiwanese parliament voted to overturn the ban on direct trade, investment and postal services between them and China. Taiwan has sent much foreign investment to China and in 1998 it was the fifth largest provider. In the decade to the year 2000, 24,000 Taiwanese firms had invested $24 billion in China[129]. The inhabitants of both areas accept the strong bond of ethnicity, despite major political differences.

The Political Scene

China enjoys government by geriatrics; youth is generally mistrusted with power. Following the views of Confucius, no one under thirty years of age is regarded as being mature, and few under fifty years of age exercise much authority at higher levels of government. Since 1949, anyone who took part in the famous "Long March" (1934-35), when the beleaguered communist forces trekked 10,000 km across China to a safe haven in Yennan in the northwest, has had immense power. He or she was virtually untouchable, however poor the performance. With the passing of time, few are left, but even being related to a deceased member of the group can bring social status and power.

The political system

China is an authoritarian, one-party state, under the control of the Chinese Communist Party. Eight unimportant noncommunist parties are allowed to exist and have grown but slightly in importance in recent years. In real terms, this means they have changed from having no power at all to possessing an insignificant amount. Attempts by "dissidents" to establish a true democratic opposition party result in those involved being arrested. The CCP is the central power in the land, and has mostly been run by a single person: in effect, this makes him a dictator. For a time during the Cultural Revolution (1966-76), Mao Zedong's wife, Chiang Ching, exercised much power, but as one of the Gang of Four, she was eclipsed shortly after the death of Mao in 1976. Other than that brief interlude, high political power in China has been in the hands of males since 1911.

At the top level of politics, there is the supreme leader, and under him the Central Committee. This is an important level where the leaders of the political factions are based. Power passes from one leader to another, and the members of their factions rise and fall with the top person. At the center of the Central Committee is a small Standing Committee which, unlike the full Central Committee, meets regularly. This is something like a Cabinet in Western terms but it possesses more authority as it is not restricted by considerations of democracy and does not have to please the people to seek reelection.

The legislative center in China is the National People's Congress (NPC), which until recently has been an obedient lapdog totally under the control of the CCP. During the 1980s it began to assert itself in minor ways, which seems striking to the Chinese and to some foreign observers. Nonetheless, NPC is hardly an independent body and cannot be regarded as possessing the power of a Western Parliament. Despite occasional (and well-publicized) critical speeches, the CCP is still able to dominate it without serious worries about opposition.

China is divided administratively into 23 provinces, 5 autonomous regions and 4 cities directly under the control of the central government (China includes Taiwan in this counting of provinces). Each of these levels has its own government. Below these are more than 2,000 counties, and various towns, each with its own local government. Because China is so vast, much power has to be decentralized to local levels; many important decisions are made here, not always in line with central policy or laws.

Since December 1978, the CCP has been engaged in a major effort to resuscitate and improve the economy. That was the year that Deng Xiaoping finally got the numbers and gained control, after two years of inner Party struggles. These had surfaced immediately after the death of Chairman Mao Zedong in September 1976, and involved two issues: who should run China, and along what policy lines. At the time of Mao's death, the country possessed an inefficient moribund economy and a people wearied of political upheaval and change. Deng Xiaoping set about modernizing China, cautiously at first, and then with increasing speed, as the reforms took root.

Domestic political policy

The overall policy of the current leaders of China can accurately be described as "communism with an acceptable capitalist face", although the official version is "a socialist market economy with Chinese characteristics". The socialist market economy was written into the Chinese Constitution in 1993 by a series of amendments. The thrust of policy since 1978 has been to reform a stagnating economy while maintaining the political monopoly of the Communist Party. Currently the leadership has no intention of moving towards a Western democratic system, but some observers feel that it will be pushed into doing so by the effects of economic reforms and growing affluence.

In more detail, domestic political policy since 1978 has included the following.

- To end Maoism and remove all strong Maoist sympathizers from positions of power.
- To replace such people with pro-market sympathizers and thereby reinforce the position of the ruling faction.
- To prevent the Stalinists from regaining control within the Party.
- To keep the CCP in power as the process of reforming the economy proceeds.
- To keep the People's Liberation Army on side with the pro-market faction and use them to support the reformers and to maintain civil order and control. This includes preventing provinces from drifting away from central authority or the country descending into civil war.

Over history, because of its size the country has traditionally been difficult to hold together. Typically, there has been a dynastic cycle, which started with a slow disintegration of central authority as the rulers gradually weakened; this descended into ever-increasing lawlessness until the dynasty finally collapsed in chaos. A new dynastic leadership then took over which led to reinvigoration and dynamism under strong central control, until eventually the dynasty began to weaken and decay in its turn. The current leaders, well aware of this pattern, are striving to prevent the traditional enfeebling process from appearing. This is one reason they were prepared to get tough in Tiananmen Square on 4 June 1989 and send in the troops against unarmed students and workers to maintain the status quo.

The political aims have been successfully achieved. Domestically, the Maoists have been whittled away until there appear to be none left. Underneath the political surface, they are thought to continue to exist, but lacking any real power base, they currently show no sign of resurgence. The Stalinists are thought to be well outnumbered, but remain hopeful, and probably have a few powerful backers in the Party. There is no sign that the pro-market leadership faction is going to lose power in the near future.

Politically there has been little fundamental change: the Communist Party is still in charge and allows no serious opposition, although its own power and stature have certainly diminished. The economic reforms have continued, and so far been successful. This is particularly so when compared with the situation in East Europe, especially in the former Yugoslavia or USSR.[130] In China, the state has been maintained, civil war avoided, and the Party kept in power. The political decision-making process is neither chaotic nor paralyzed. Firm control has been maintained, even as the shackles on freedom were loosened.

The movement towards increased use of the market has been relatively slow and careful: the rulers slackened power a little and monitored events closely. Different things were tried in different areas and the results compared. What had succeeded was then adopted as official policy. This bottom-up pragmatism has meant that policies have been appropriate to actual conditions, rather than being imposed from above and hence probably unsuitable. Relative to the cautious 1980s, during the 1990s the use of market mechanisms accelerated.

The reform process had been accompanied by features that antagonized many urban residents. These include corruption, inflation, a rise in the level of uncertainty, and a diminution of the standards of public and private morality. Disquiet turned into opposition and demonstrations. Those involved in Tiananmen Square were mainly students, plus a few workers, especially journalists. The latter kept encountering good stories but censorship and control prevented them from reporting, so they became resentful. Some of the demonstrators were protesting against the above unwanted features of the economic reform process; others simply wanted a bit more freedom; and a few others probably did not know what they wanted, other than a change of some kind.

The conclusion of the episode, when the army went in with its tanks, was to squash the hopes of a relatively limited number of Chinese, largely confined to the educated and literate, roughly equivalent to those referred to in Britain as "the chattering classes". The vast majority of Chinese are peasants and were uninvolved in any of the Tiananmen furore. In poor rural areas, the horizons tend to be limited to survival; in better ones, people are concerned about economic improvement. The peasants have little active interest in politics.

There is probably more concern about democracy and human rights abroad than in China, and the events in Tiananmen Square antagonized many foreign observers. The latter tend to identify with both Western values and middle class aspirations. Self-exiled dissidents, mostly in the United States, press steadily for democracy in China, but seem to have relatively little support within the country. The present students in China are regularly criticized by both foreign observers and dissidents abroad for not caring about such matters, in sharp contrast to the generation that preceded them.

In practical terms, the Tiananmen massacre caused few economic losses and these were short-lived. Economic growth rapidly resumed; the minimal sanctions imposed by foreign countries were soon abandoned; and the foreign tourists quickly returned. As early as 1991, the number of tourists visiting China, and the foreign exchange earned from them, exceeded the pre Tiananmen levels. Foreign investment also recommenced and in 1993, China overtook Mexico to become the largest recipient of foreign direct investment in the third world. Foreign investment continued despite a tightening announced by the State Council on Boxing Day 1995, that included measures which could have been expected to deter it. These included the ending of the right of newly formed foreign ventures to import equipment and raw materials free of Customs duties and value-added tax. The full measures came into effect on December 31, 1997, and along with the Asian financial crisis of that year, led to a fall in contracted foreign direct investment of 20.9 percent in 1999.

The PLA, once a Maoist stronghold, had generally been trained to fight guerrilla wars and possessed little modern equipment. It now has a brand new role: to maintain civil order and to become a more modern, Western-style army. Its equipment and training lag well behind its new role because China is too poor to allocate sufficient resources, despite some increases in the defense budget since the late 1980s. In 1997, the PLA had just over 3 million on active service, although it intended to cut back some half a million over the three years to the end of the year 2000.

The army has long been involved in marginal military matters, and operated over 20,000 companies in transport, hospitality, entertainment, real estate and satellite launching. It is believed it used to sell 83 percent of its industrial output to civilians, and an estimate suggests that commercial sales exceeded the official state defense budget of $9.7 billion.[131] It is widely regarded as being seriously involved in criminal activities, including smuggling. In July 1998, President Jiang Zemin ordered the PLA, as well as the police and judiciary, to close down all their commercial enterprises.[132] He apparently believed the temptations of commerce to be incompatible with honest dealing in their more normal military functions.

Any opposition to the authority of the CCP is resisted strongly. The Falung Gong sect is a group of religious believers, numbering tens of millions in China and has other members abroad. They engage in a meditation-exercise-breathing system but the sect is accused by the government of being a dangerous cult, involved in the supernatural and having harmful effects on it followers. In reality the CCP really seems to fear its secrecy and ability to organize gatherings and demonstrations without its intentions coming to the notice of the secret police. The leader of the sect is Li Hongzhi who lives in New York, and he and the group maintain that they are simply a peaceful body, aimed at improving health. The central authorities have declared the Falung Gong to be illegal and its members are prosecuted.

International politics

Since 1978, China's policies at the international level have been to move China back into the world and increase the number of friendly nations, while developing foreign trade and promoting foreign investment in China. In the longer term, the intention is to make China a great nation in global terms. Precise goals have included reducing tension with Vietnam, removing the wide political gap between China and South Korea, and moving closer towards Taiwan. These international aims have been achieved. The collapse of the Soviet Union fortuitously removed an enemy for China - previous border disputes, as well as major ideological differences, had put them seriously at odds with one another.

South Korea is now a major trading partner of China, standing in fourth place as a supplier of imports in 1998, and is an important source of foreign investment. Taiwan and China now talk openly as well as engage in trade. Taiwanese firms invest in China and *de facto* there are two political states, although both insist there is only one government of China, and the concept of "two Chinas" is a prickly one that neither China nor Taiwan will accept. China never refers to Taiwan as a "country" and Taiwan will not accept the concept of "one country, two systems" in case it might help to lead to reunification under a communist leadership.

The colonies of Hong Kong and Macao have both returned to China: Hong Kong at midnight on June 30 1997 and Macao on December 20 1999. They are run as Special Administrative Regions of China. With an eye on Taiwan, which China hopes to gather back into the fold at a later date, it was important that the process of transition of these two areas should be as smooth as possible. This is a major reason why in December 1993 China strongly objected to the introduction of a degree of Western-style democracy in the then colony of Hong Kong. China saw the issue as a blatant attempt to limit its future sovereignty and an exercise in cynical political maneuvering by Britain. China pointed out that democracy in Hong Kong was a feature that Britain was more than happy to do without, as long as it had sole responsibility for the territory. Britain saw the issue as a way of increasing the guarantee that China would abide by the agreement on Hong Kong, and in particular keep the promise to avoid any major changes for fifty years. Since Hong Kong reverted to China, it is clearly being run without the heavy-handed interference that some feared, at least so far.

Other strands of China's international political efforts include developing and increasing international respect for China, maintaining political independence, and preventing any interference in China's domestic affairs. The issue of civil rights for Chinese citizens, including the minority areas such as Tibet and Xinjiang, falls in this area. The aims of international respect and political independence have been successfully met, but civil rights, especially in Tibet, remain an issue for which China is regularly criticized, particularly in the USA. In May 2000, Congress finally voted to extend m.f.n. treatment to China although this still has to go through the Senate, and permanent normal trade relations (NTR) have not yet been granted. Prior to this vote, various American critics of China took advantage of the annual discussion to publicize the issue of human rights. The Chinese, who are a proud people with a long recorded history and culture, do not take kindly to this process of foreign criticism, which is resented as being an open interference in the internal affairs of China.

In 1986, China notified GATT, now the World Trade Organization, that it wished to resume its status as a member. It did this in December 2001, after lengthy discussions about the conditions for entry. Agreement was not easy, for although China's economy has been greatly reformed, it is still far from being a free one, and many market restrictions continue. These include subsidies to SOEs, quotas and licenses, tariffs (some of which are high), considerable arbitrary interference by officials, and the apparent continuation of secret, unpublished regulations, particularly at lower levels of government. None of these is compatible with WTO membership. On the issue of Taiwan, China agreed to allow it to join the WTO, but it must sit as a separate Customs territory of China, not as a country. Taiwan joined in January 2002.

The Economic Scene

Between Liberation in 1949 and the late 1970s, China put in place a ramshackle planned economy. Although total planning of the economy was sought, this was never achieved. The task was too immense in such a vast country, with its problems of communications and transport, shortage of skills, and record of regular political interference. During the Cultural Revolution (1966-76), radical political rectitude replaced economic progress as the goal. At the death of Chairman Mao (1976), the economy was in a parlous state. As a result of political extremism, the people had learned that it was dangerous to be seen to succeed or raise their personal living standard. An attitude such as this was clearly inimical to economic growth. The statistical reporting system was in tatters, so that no one knew much about the real situation in the nation. Resources had been grossly misallocated for years, and agriculture in particular had been starved of financial investment, so that no modernization had occurred. This meant that labor intensive methods were still used by hundreds of millions of peasants, organized in communes, production brigades and production teams, with low levels of productivity. In industry, workers had been demoralized and the once proud work ethic of the Chinese had been eroded or in many cases removed. Such economic change as had occurred had been uncontrolled, with the result that good agricultural land had been lost to cultivation, while pollution of air and water had become a serious issue. The state firms are still the worst offenders: in June 2000, a top environmental official ordered companies to work harder on reducing pollution and revealed that 65 per cent of it comes from 18,000 companies, most of them large SOEs.[133]

After Mao's death, the problem of the economy had to be tackled, especially as the population had increased considerably. By 1976, it was 73 percent above the level of 1949, but despite well-publicized land reclamation, the amount of arable land available had barely altered, which reduced the per capita availability. The land loss was caused by industrialization, urbanization, and road building.

On the social side, by the time of Mao's death, the Chinese people were ready for a change: they had suffered too much. They were tired of the political terror, the all-pervading influence of radical politics on every detail of ordinary life, and they wanted peace. A return to normality was clearly indicated, but it was not clear who could supply this, or indeed what normality meant. For many, it meant a return to Soviet-style communism, with five year and annual plans within a regime of a command economy, and the reinstitution of a rather grey, dull, bureaucratic but predictable situation. Such a group, under Hua Guofeng, seized the reins of power 1976-78, but soon lost them to Deng Xiaoping and his followers, who had a very different answer to the problems of the lackluster economy.

Starting in 1978, Deng began to allow relaxation of the commitment to central planning and permitted some, if minimal, use of the market. This policy was engineered from above, although it rapidly got out of hand and gained a momentum of its own as grassroot enthusiasm pushed ahead of central caution. The process began on a limited scale in agriculture but before long it led to the disbanding of communes and the introduction of private farming on what is still nominally state-owned land. Early efforts to introduce private methods in state run industry were not particularly successful, but shares in some state-owned enterprises were sold. A primitive capital market was established, and limited stock markets were set up in Shanghai and Shenzhen SEZ, on which selected companies could be listed. Currently, these number about seventy. Other large state firms have been broken up and their monopoly positions removed. The state airline, China Administration of Civil Aviation (CAAC) suffered this fate. In industry generally, privately run firms are now encouraged and the number has grown sharply in recent years.

Distribution

Until recently, wholesale markets did not exist, as there was no need for them under central planning. Several markets were established in the early 1990s, covering commodities such as timber, building materials, farm machinery, coal, petroleum and metals. In 1993, the Shanghai Metals Exchange became the third largest in the world, after London and Chicago. The previous ludicrously low prices for capital goods and basic raw materials have begun to increase and are slowly moving towards international levels. China hoped to have an efficient market distribution system for all such types of goods by the end of the last century but this proved impossible to achieve. Meanwhile, a foreign company can sometimes set up its own informal distribution system. PepsiCo managed this with a Sino-Taiwan joint venture called Wang Wang, which distributes Cheetos and some other PepsiCo products. In exchange, PepsiCo produces Wang Wang's *Lonely God* potato twists.[134]

Labor

A few steps along the way to establishing a labor market have been taken. No longer are the children of peasants doomed to labor in the fields for life,[135] nor are the offspring of urban workers allocated to jobs on a rather ad hoc and inefficient basis by the state. Youngsters are not now forced to "wait for employment", a euphemism which prevented them from being counted as "unemployed" and so artificially kept the figures low. Peasants are still in theory tied to their local area by the *hukou,* or household registration system. In practice, they now have the freedom to move and many have migrated to urban areas where they are called as "the floating population". The number is unknown but perhaps exceeds 100 million people. When they get to the city their situation is uncertain and unhappy: they are without a job, they have no legal right to remain, they lack access to official services, and they can be sent back without warning to their place of registration.

Within cities, workers can now apply for jobs rather than being forced to wait until one is allocated. They are also permitted to move to a new area to seek work, more or less legally. They can even set up their own firm if they wish, providing they have the capital necessary. Some government employees are now allowed to moonlight and accept second jobs, and many more do so without permission. Part-time and casual work proliferated during the 1990s. Local personnel exchanges have been established in major cities, allowing workers to register for transfers to new organizations or areas. Such transfers were previously almost impossible to achieve. Wages, once stuck in a rigid 8-grade system, have become flexible: local areas now set a minimum wage level and enterprises can fix the wage they wish at or above it.

The Labor regulations that came into force on January 1 1995 were an attempt to lay the foundations of a labor market, suitable for a modern economy based on the price mechanism. It aimed to bring the moribund state-run sector up to the standards of the enterprises operating with a degree of foreign investment. It made provision for a minimum wage, social insurance, workers' rights and an absence of discrimination in hiring. Previously, different labor rules applied to SOEs and to enterprises with foreign capital; this law aims to achieve unification by moving the SOEs up to the standards achieved by the best enterprises. It required the SOEs to end the provision of cradle-to-grave welfare coverage, including housing and sickness benefits, and "the iron rice bowl" had to be eliminated. This picturesque phrase meant that one's job (which provides or fills the rice bowl) was totally secure for life (a rice bowl breaks if dropped, but an iron one does not). Prior to this, without fear of dismissal, many of those employed in SOEs put in little effort and, partly as a result, overstaffing was general. In many SOEs, perhaps up to a third of the workers had no real work to do. To combat this, labor contracts, rather than jobs for life, are to be extended in the State-run sector until they became the norm. In 2000, it was again announced that the SOEs were to end the iron rice bowl system, showing that the effort continues but total success has not yet been achieved.[136]

To celebrate the 50th Anniversary of the founding of the PRC, in 1999 the government announced increases in pay, pensions and welfare for up to 84 million people. It was also intended to boost consumer demand, which has lagged for some years and resulted in underused capacity and slower growth.

A serious effort is being made to improve work habits, including merging some SOEs and dismissing surplus workers. Some of the worst SOEs have been allowed to go bankrupt. The number of SOEs losing money rose 49 percent between November 1995 and October 1996, indicating that there was much to be done.[137] The government stepped up the pace and in 1996, some 6,232 firms went bankrupt. In 1998 the serious effort to tackle the SOE problem was intensified, resulting in more closures and mergers. As a result, 7.1 million workers were officially laid off.[138]

Another strain on employment provision has come from the forced closure of many small, illegal and highly dangerous coal mines. A reduction in the size of the PLA was announced by Jiang Zemin in 1997[139] and one hundred thousand were released in September 1998 alone. It is thought that there is a target for downsizing of half a million for the year 2000. The ex-military men find it difficult to secure work and some have drifted into the more violent end of crime.

The unemployment position will be worsened again if the government fulfills its intention of dismissing millions of bureaucrats by abolishing some Ministries and halving the total number of government employees. This serious effort to improve efficiency looks to be an act of conspicuous political bravery, under the circumstances.

Official statistics claim an unemployment rate of around 3.1 percent in 1999 but this only measures those registering at Reemployment Centers. Few bother to do this, either because they know there is no work on offer and have given up, or else they mistrust the centers as exploitative, rip-off organizations. The many workers not formally dismissed from SOEs, but merely "sent home to wait", are also not included in the unemployment figures. In 1997, 11.51 million workers were laid off, of whom 7.87 million were from SOEs; 4.8 million of these did not find work, but are not counted as unemployed.[140] There is much uncertainty, but putting together those unemployed from previous years with the number laid off and still with no job, there could be 12 million unemployed.[141] Including those missing from the figures, a reasonable guess at the true level of urban unemployment might fall in the range of 25-30 percent although I have heard higher guesses. In late 1998, China admitted that that the unemployment rate would hit 9 percent in 1999. This figure is still too low and the authorities continue to mislead themselves and others. There are also about 160 million unemployed in rural areas who are not counted in the figures in any way.[142]

Starting in 1998, a social welfare scheme began to be introduced to help those laid off, retired or disabled. It was hoped that by the end of that year it would be in place in all large cities, and in about half of the townships. It provides payments of between 70 and 250 *yuan* (approximately $8-$30) a month to those who qualify.[143] Previously, the small number of workers able to receive benefits were paid by their work unit, rather than a state office. Many of those laid off have languished unemployed; some have tried to scratch a living working as a street trader or running a small food stall. Farmers, who make up two-thirds of the population, are excluded from the new scheme. This new welfare scheme placed heavy demands on budget revenue and by the end of the decade the funds available for pensions had run out. It seems that the government originally hoped that the savings in subsidies from merging or closing the loss-making SOEs would be sufficient to cover the new benefit payments to workers but were wrong. In the year 2000, the government is determined to institute a new tax in order to finance the rising social security needs and overdue pension payments.

In view of possible financial strain and the probability of tension that could culminate in serious social unrest, the government might be forced to stop closing loss-making enterprises. Rather than allow many SOEs to perish, it could choose to coerce them into conglomerates, rather like South Korea's *chaebols,* which are admired at high levels. This would be a movement away from the pursuit of microeconomic reform. China treads a delicate tightrope, balancing the need for reform against the problems that it causes.

Prices and the financial sector

In the consumer market, many prices have been freed from the straightjacket of administrative price fixing and perhaps 90-95 percent of prices now reflect supply and demand. Every effort to move a group of items onto the market has meant an immediate price rise, because for decades prices were held artificially low. Increasing prices hurts urban dwellers in particular, and the government tries to cushion the effect by providing a subsidy. This is too small to offset the price rise totally, but from the recipient's viewpoint, it is better than nothing. It does however add to the chronic problem in the central government budget of maintaining large subsidies on the expenditure side, while revenues languish.

The financial sector is generally weak while the banking system is poor and backward. For years, it was merely there to offer an outlet for savings and to supply SOEs with the funds they needed to meet the plan. The banks are as yet unable to function efficiently in the manner needed to run a market economy. There is no automated payments system; bad bank loans are endemic; and it is almost certain that if ever forced into adopting proper accounting, the entire system would be bankrupt. In 1997, the People's Bank of China conceded that bad loans were 5-6 percent of total loans, three times higher than previously admitted.[144] Another report claimed that the People's Bank of China admitted that 13-14 percent of outstanding loans were nonperforming, i.e., there was no payment of interest or repayment of capital. The same report pointed out that foreign analysts feared that as much as 40 percent of loans could be nonperforming.[145]

The *yuan* is not yet fully convertible, although China earlier stated that it would move to this, as part of its intention to join the WTO, by the year 2000. The process began in January 1 1994, when China discarded the fixed exchange rate system and abandoned Foreign Exchange Certificates (FECs), a special currency issued only to foreigners. These had discriminated against the foreigners, who were forced to buy FECs at a poor rate of exchange. The several different rates of exchange that once existed are now unified, and it is anticipated that the *yuan* will ultimately be allowed to float, although this will be a "dirty" or managed float, rather than a fully free one. The *yuan* is freely convertible at designated banks, but only for foreign trade purposes and by those enterprises with the necessary trade documents (i.e. there is current account convertibility). The free movement of currency across the border (capital account convertibility) is not yet allowed.[146]

Foreign investment and foreign trade

Foreign investment is strongly sought by China which, after a slow and shaky start in the early 1980s, has managed to attract a considerable amount. Despite economic fluctuations, caused by both domestic and foreign events, the flow of foreign investment has sharply increased. Between 1979 and 1998, total foreign funds invested in China amounted to some $395.9 billion. It is believed that four-fifths of total foreign investment comes from Overseas Chinese, often based on provincial ties and family relationships. In 1998, over half (59%) of the foreign investment came from Hong Kong and Macao alone but the data are skewed because some individuals and companies in China send capital to Hong Kong, then repatriate it as "foreign investment", in order to gain benefits. The USA was in second place with 12 percent followed by Japan with 10 percent.

Geographically, the Overseas Chinese investment tends to scatter more widely than non-Chinese foreign investment, which tends to concentrate on SEZs and the open cities.

The policy on foreign investment is to try to focus it on the areas of basic infrastructure and high technology. Only gradually is it being permitted in service areas, such as banking and insurance, where its role is still strictly limited.

Five Special Economic Zones have been established, which offer concessions and supply many necessary services. In 1992, the SEZs were responsible for supplying thirty percent of all China's exports. In addition to the SEZs, fourteen coastal cities have been opened to foreign investment. A myriad of tiny development zones have been established, with relaxed rules, but often with no location advantages, in both coastal and interior China. Many of these were closed in and after 1993, in an effort to reimpose central control and to prevent competitive wastes. Thirty-two national "Economic and Technological Development Zones" now exist. The provincial capitals of all coastal provinces are now accepting, and in almost all cases rather desperately seeking, foreign investment.

Since 1990, China has begun to move towards establishing free ports. Thirteen free trade zones have been set up around coastal harbors as a first step towards establishing free ports proper. At present, they are in embryonic stage, and look very similar to SEZs. Foreign currency circulates within the free trade zones, and bonded warehouses reduce the number of bureaucratic restrictions.

The efforts to attract foreign capital came under pressure in 1998 when the Guangdong International Trust and Investment Company (GITIC) collapsed with huge debts. Lenders had previously assumed that the government stood behind such trusts but were suddenly disillusioned.

As part of the transition to a market economy, the level of tariffs has been reduced, notably in 1995-96, when duty on about 4,000 goods was lowered. This brought down the simple average tariff level from 36 percent in 1995 to 23 percent in 1996, and a further cut in October 1997 brought the average to 17 percent, a sizeable fall, but still above the 15 percent that most developed countries strive to maintain.[147] Nontariff barriers loom large, and include special licensing requirements, certification requirements, and import quotas. Other problems include *guanxi*, whereby a Chinese firm with the right connections may be able to avoid duties; local rules at variance with national ones; and local officials, who have the power to make decisions in the many grey areas, determining which rules apply, and thereby altering the duty payable. Customs officers may treat the same goods differently, depending on the country of origin, the location of any intermediate manufacturing site, and the final destination market.

By 1998, surplus capacity had emerged in many industries. This was the result of years of high foreign investment and a rapid increase in the numbers of foreign-owned enterprises. Over five hundred goods were being produced at less than 60 percent capacity and competition was fierce. The government's response was to encourage companies in these areas to transfer factories overseas, to the Middle East, South America, Africa and Central Asia.[148]

Capital outflow, much of it illegal, is an ongoing problem. At times when it is feared that the *yuan* might be devalued, the outflow increases.

Since the modernization movement began in 1978, foreign trade has expanded sharply. Firstly, the success of the program of economic reform and moving back into world markets has pulled in imports and opened new export markets. Secondly, China has strongly promoted trade and offers a good market for many products. Thirdly, the efforts of the many foreign investors in China have boosted the capacity to both export and import. As a proportion of national income, foreign trade rose from 10.3 percent in 1977, on the eve of reform, to an average of 35.7 percent 1990-98.

The southern province of Guangdong is an area of particularly high growth, especially in the Shenzhen SEZ and around the Pearl River delta, including Guangzhou (Canton City). The British colony of Hong Kong returned to China in 1997 and has added considerable economic muscle and weight to southern China, although this is currently concealed by the effects of the Asian financial crisis that emerged in 1997. Other major Chinese cities try hard and offer special concessions to foreign investment. Notable among them are Shanghai, Dalian, and Tianjin, but many smaller cities are prepared to deal and offer extra help. The central government occasionally clamps down on such projects, because either in its view, a locally designated development area seems unlikely to succeed, or else the city or province is felt to be offering unreasonably large concessions.

The macro economy

China is undergoing a major economic change that amounts to a small revolution. The economic reforms have begun to introduce market elements into what was a planned economy, so that there is a mixture of State-run and private firms in both production and distribution. The process has been accompanied by confusion between the two systems, especially as the border between the two continues to change, and leakages occur across the boundaries. Control by the planners has been drastically reduced, corruption flourishes and grows, but on the plus side, much dynamism has been injected into the economy.

The reform program has been a success and China is now the third largest economy in the world. It proved immune to the world recessions of the 1980s and early 1990s, and even the major Asian financial crisis that emerged in 1997 had less effect on China than on most developing nations in Asia. With only a partially convertible currency, China did not face a serious problem of "hot money" and a rapid withdrawal of foreign funds.

The original long-term government target of an average growth rate of 6 percent until the year 2000 quickly seemed conservative and it was eventually increased to 8-9 percent. Economic growth slowed in 1998 to 7.8 percent and (for China) remained low in 1999 at 7.1 percent. Consumer spending was responsible for most of the growth. Until the Asian crisis, the only problem that China faced in the area of growth was trying to moderate it without causing a major slump. The tools of fiscal and monetary policy, once nonexistent, are still primitive and blunt, so that the process of controlling economic growth in China has been likened to slowing down a motorcar by running it into a brick wall!

The boom and bust cycle has often produced inflationary pressures. Complementary reasons include the inability of the center to raise enough revenue to cover expenditures; money supply blow outs; slack credit control by banks especially at the provincial levels (where local officials often force the banks to lend to local schemes); local government investment sprees; expanding use of trade credit among the rapidly increasing number of firms; and speculative property booms.

Since 1998 China has had the reverse problem of falling prices. Although beneficial to consumers on fixed incomes, it has caused difficulties for producers who find their profit margins squeezed. Adding to their problems has been a fall in exports, the result of the Asian crisis, accompanied by a consumer go-slow; together these have resulted in the emergence of surplus capacity in many industries. The response of the government has been to retreat towards administrative control by forbidding price reductions and encouraging the creation of cartels. In the medium term, these are likely to have deleterious effects on China's productivity levels. To tackle the issue of slow growth, the government has also engaged in monetary and fiscal pump priming and it is expected that the government budget deficit for the year 2000 will reduce from the record level of 180.3 billion yuan of 1999.[149]

In most countries, the balance of payments suffers when growth is rapid and deficits emerge. These are the result of economic expansion sucking in imports, often accompanied by domestic price rises that make it harder to export. China has done well in avoiding serious balance of payments difficulties, despite the high long-term growth rates recorded (average 9.7% p.a. over 1980-99).

Quota and licensing controls over imports have steadily been lowered, but have not yet been eliminated. The ability to apply administrative import controls still exists, and these are imposed without warning if the balance of trade deteriorates too much. When such controls are applied, they tend to be relaxed as soon as the economic situation improves.

Along with the adoption of freer market policies, the amount of central control has sharply diminished, as the provincial and large city governments have gained more power. This has meant a fall in tax revenues, which are gathered at local levels but are often not fully handed over to the center. The taxation system is being reformed, which essentially involves the introduction of tax farming. Provincial governments negotiate how much they will hand over to the center each year, and then can keep any surplus that they manage to raise. This favors the rich coastal and southern provinces, which can negotiate a deal that allows them to keep more.

There is no possibility of the central government replacing this lost tax revenue by profits from its own direct run industry. First, many state run firms have been privatized, while new ones are not being created. Second, previous tax reforms have increased taxation on the SOEs and reduced profits. Third, growing competition from the collective and new private industry continues to make life difficult for the SOEs. Finally, about one third of state firms lose money and admit it, while another third probably do so but manage to conceal it, so the profits are simply not there to be taken. The loss makers survive only because the banks are instructed to keep extending loans to them, which of course adds to inflationary pressures by increasing the money supply.

The brave attempt to reform the economy and use market mechanisms to improve economic efficiency that had been in force since the end of 1978 have begun to appear harder since 1998. The reasons include:

- The easiest things have been done; the harder ones, like reforming the SOEs, are proving to be more difficult.
- Social problems, like the increasing unemployment, are becoming a matter for serious concern.
- The Asian financial crisis has slowed the Chinese economy which adds to the difficulties. Problem fixing is always easier when it occurs within a growth framework.

In the year 2000, the economic outlook began to improve, as exports and growth started to pick up.

The Social Scene

China already had a large population for hundreds of years before it became a problem elsewhere in the world. Because of the large concentration of people in cities and the dangers of social unrest that this posed, effective methods of social control had to be developed. This included holding the entire family responsible for the actions any of its individual members and punishing them all for transgressions, even on occasion by death. There was also a crude neighborhood watch system, where one family was responsible for reporting any antisocial behavior by ten other families. This continues in today's urban street committees, which are currently (year 2000) being strengthened. Over the centuries, people learned to get along with each other as there was no real alternative. The social system, with its emphasis on family, has altered in detail, but has proved long-lived, backed as it is by Confucian values. This contrasts sharply with the Western rule of law, which with its emphasis on responsibility for individual actions has never been characteristic of China.

Social policies

Rather than taking center place in their own right, since 1978 social policies have mainly tended to be spin-offs from economic and political changes. The social policies have included the following.

- To encourage people to become rich; this compares with the pre 1976 period, when this was fiercely discouraged.
- To release latent entrepreneurial efforts in order to kick start the moribund economy and modernize quickly.
- To try to contain corruption and reduce it, or at the very least prevent it from continually increasing.
- To tackle crime in general and lower its level. China is still a safe country, especially for foreigners although there is no denying that the level of crime has increased substantially along with the enlarged freedoms and the breakdown of tight Communist Party control.
  To try to slow the rate of growth of population and aim for a long term fall. "The one child family" policy has been implemented widely, but with different degrees of severity, depending on locality. Exceptions have been made for a few groups, such as minorities and

some who have a female child the first time. Forced abortions, even late term, are common in those areas which impose the strictest control, yet are unknown in slacker areas where two children may be allowed. By 1993, the family planning program was showing signs of failure, and a baby boom was underway. Chinese statisticians pointed out that the targets for future population sizes would not be met. The key reasons were rapid economic growth and reduced control; these are expected to continue, which casts pessimism over the likely success of family planning policy.

- To allow private schools and education to cater for the needs and aspirations of the newly rich families. The state educational sector is under heavy pressure: teachers are poorly paid, inadequate in quality, and many have left to earn more money in other sectors.
- To allow private hospitals and medical care to cater for the *nouveau riche.*

Social change

Since the early 1980s, China has undergone rapid social change: freedom has been greater and incomes have increased. Workers in private industry, including the self-employed, are now numerous, and, once denigrated for political reasons, are better regarded in society. Until quite recently, a self-employed person was regarded as something of a failure, i.e., someone unable to get a proper job; now even some university graduates are opting opt to work for themselves rather than to join a state firm. A job in a foreign firm or joint venture is considered highly desirable, as it means more money and enjoys high social status.

The increased freedom is genuine but has occurred within defined limits, although what these are at any particular time is often unclear as the lines keep being redrawn. It is still not permissible to oppose the CCP, support the Kuomintang, set up a political party, or ask for Western style democracy. People are however freer to move. This was forbidden until recently, unless one was transferred (often forcibly) by one's work unit.

In the effort to increase living standards and promote economic growth, private entrepreneurs have emerged and are doing well. Some have become very rich, and there is a claim that there are now a million millionaires, even in terms of US dollars. Overall, the majority of the Chinese are unarguably materially better off than they were a decade ago, some of them considerably so.

However, not all have benefited as much as others, and income differtials have widened. In 1996, the ratio of incomes of urban and rural dwellers was 2.5:1; this is officially expected to widen to 2.7:1 by the year 2020[150] but the outcome looks more likely to prove wider than that. A survey in 1994 found a Gini Coefficient of 0.434, compared to only 0.20 in 1978 on the eve of reform, and 0.385 in 1984 after the early reforms had begun.[151] The ability of some to pull well ahead of others causes resentment amongst those left behind.

Private industry and trade are encouraged in this socialist country because of the belief in the efficacy of market systems and the constant population pressure requires the steady provision of large numbers of jobs. There are far more peasants than are required in agriculture, and after 1978 people were encouraged to move out of agricultural work. As they did so, the rate of growth of agricultural output roughly doubled, reflecting the pre-existing low marginal productivity of labor, as well as the newly released enthusiasm of those remaining. Most of China's peasants are now better off and a tiny proportion has become wealthy.

The standard of living of the Chinese people has improved immensely because of the reform policies. The measurement of "well-off-ness" using the traditional national income per head is misleading when applied to China, as it severely understates the ability of people to buy things. Estimates by the World Bank of GNP per capita in 1994 show it at $530 in current international prices; but using the "purchasing power parity" (ppp) approach, to take account of local prices being much lower than abroad, GNP per capita reached $2,510.[152] By 1997, again on a ppp basis, GDP per head was estimated at $3,130.

The higher living standard is not only the result of increased wages: an official survey involving 15,600 urban households drawn from 30 provinces, municipalities and autonomous regions, revealed that almost one in three urban workers were engaged in a second job. In 1996, this increased their earnings by 35 percent.[153] Moonlighting is common, especially for those in the public sector, where fixed wages have not kept pace with economic growth.

Along with freedom and growth has come increased corruption. Differential prices between the controlled and free market area once offered great opportunities for arbitrage and illegal movement of goods from the cheap planned sector to the higher priced market one. These price differentials have diminished as the market expanded and the prices of raw materials and goods to and from state operated enterprises have been increased. However, the rapid development and extension of the market sector has brought new problems into existence. Dishonest behavior is particularly prevalent in real estate, the securities industry, and future markets.[154] China lacks a full set of laws and the existing ones are often ill framed and unclear. The law is weak on property rights, there are few means of ensuring that those involved in corruption are exposed, and the Party has often seemed to lack the will to deal with problems of corruption where it involved high-level people. In 2000, the UNDP representative in China reported that the biggest obstacle to eradicating poverty in China was corruption.[155]

In order to demonstrate that it takes the problem of corruption seriously and is determined to stamp it out, the authorities took the unusual step of charging Chen Xitong, a member of the politburo, leader of the Beijing Communist Party and a former Mayor of Beijing, with corruption. He was placed under house arrest in April 1995 but it was not until July 1998 that he was tried in court and found guilty of misappropriating public funds and illegally accepting gifts valued at some 39.2 million yuan ($4.7 million dollars). He was sentenced to 16 years in jail. As a leading Party figure, he is thought to have been involved in a series of scams amounting to a further $2.2 billion.[155] Ordinary people routinely receive the death penalty for embezzling tiny sums, but Chen Xitong was let off lightly. It is believed that he knows much about the financial and sexual peccadilloes of numerous other high officials, and many in Beijing believe that he did a deal, his silence in exchange for no death penalty. Greed and corruption seem to have been a family interest: in mid 1997 his son, Chen Xiaotong received a 12 year jail sentence for embezzlement and accepting bribes.

In 1998, state grain purchases were revealed to be a major area of corrupt activity. A team of auditors discovered that loans to buy grain over a six year period amounted to $65.6 billion, but the total stock in grain depots was worth only $39.8 billion. Some thirty-seven percent of the missing money had been diverted to purchasing shares, cars and mobile phones, and the rest went on buying grain at high prices and selling below cost, or simple bribery.[156]

To help combat the growing corruption, some 3,600 watchdog offices have been set up since 1988, but so far they have not managed to put a dent in it, let alone demonstrate that they have the ability to eliminate it. The Party is antagonistic towards other possible centers of power and wishes to keep all anticorruption efforts firmly under its control. In October 1998, the leader of Corruption Watch, an unofficial group with members in fourteen provinces, was questioned for seven hours before being released and he was warned to stop his activities.[157]

In April 2000, the high-level Vice-Chairman of the National People's Congress, Cheng Kejie, was expelled from the Party and dismissed from his position for taking $4 million in bribes and executed in September 2000, the highest official to be put to death for graft since Liberation in 1949. In that month, major trials dealing with a huge smuggling racket in Fujian Province began under relatively secret conditions. Around two hundred local authority officials, police and Customs personnel were apparently involved but details are not yet available. The wife of Jia Qinglin, a member of the Politburo and ally of Jiang Zemin, is widely thought to be implicated in the case. The problem of corruption continues but the publicity attending such events demonstrates that serious efforts are being made.

Since 1978, the deluge of migrant workers into cities has caused social problems and placed pressure on urban infrastructure, but it was not until 1992 that the tide reached a flood. It has proved impossible to provide housing for them, so that they are often forced to sleep rough, in railway stations, building sites or anywhere they can. The public transport has been placed under strain and beggars have proliferated. Hundreds of migrants hang about seeking employment, often exhibiting a tool of their craft if they have one in the hope of attracting an employer. Local regulations often prohibit them from working in the better jobs: Shanghai has declared that illegal residents (all of whom are migrants) cannot work in management or financial services, run taxis, or become shopkeepers, telephone operators or security guards. They are restricted to those jobs that are avoided by the local residents, which are usually dirty, hard and badly paid.[158] Yet a peasant can still earn considerably more than back in the fields – if he can find work. The vast majority of the floating population is male.

Members of this "floating population" are unpopular with urban residents, and as a despised group are automatic suspects for any crime that occurs in the vicinity. Beginning in 1995, many cities attempted to tighten up on their migrant populations but the problem of what to do about them remains.

The increased incomes both in and outside agriculture have led to changes in the patterns of consumption. In rural areas, the peasants have spent much of their surplus building new houses. There is a tendency to invest shrewdly and if a family moves into its new house, the old one may be used for animal shelter or rented out. Local governments have also gone on construction spending sprees, sometimes for new buildings, often for roads, and occasionally for economic development zones.

In urban China, washing machines were effectively unknown before 1980 but have since become ubiquitous. Most families now own a radio, tape recorder, washing machine, stove or cooking range, a steam iron, bicycles and one or more electric fans. The ownership of other desirable consumer goods was low in 1998: personal pagers (15% of urban households), motorcycles (14%), VCRs (12%) air conditioners (6%) and mobile telephones (4%).[159] Mobile phones have become a major status symbol for those with power, influence and money. One in four urban families own both a telephone and a refrigerator.

Newly married couples have always had a set of "four items", which are considered highly desirable. A few short years ago it was a basic list, consisting of watches, bicycles, sewing machines and clothing. With rising living standards and aspirations, the list of four has changed to refrigerators, TV sets, washing machines and video players. Urban single children, many of whom are widely and accurately regarded in China as spoilt, are often referred to as "Little Emperors". They tend to have things like electric toys and computer games lavished upon them so that any company dealing in these high demand goods tends to do well.

The Chinese have traditionally eaten a lot of vegetables, but from the necessity of poverty rather than choice. With the rise in incomes, chicken and pork have become reasonably common in the diet, as have eggs and milk. Until recently, milk was restricted to invalids and the families of high Party officials. Western fast food has made an appearance in the major cities in the past decade or so, and despite being expensive by local standards, has proved remarkably successful. Domestic tourism is on the rise, and even visits to foreign countries are now possible. In short, China is in the process of doing a lot of catching up with the consumer preferences and habits of the outside world, from which it was deliberately excluded by its leaders for several decades.

The rapid economic development has begun to put pressure on existing values. The threat of social unrest, although small, is increasing. The growing unemployment, which is expected to worsen as policies on SOEs begin to bite harder, is already a matter for concern. Worker protests, strikes, sit-ins or demonstrations have occurred in major cities like Beijing, Xian, Shenyang, Wuhan, Changsha, and Anhui, where employees protest the increasing level of unemployment and unpaid wages. In May 2000, workers of an SOE in Liaoyang besieged the city hall, complaining of unpaid wages stretching back for two years and discovered that some of the officials themselves had not been paid for a year! This was merely one of a series of similar incidents over the years in the northeast of China[160]. Reducing wages in an effort to maintain employment levels has led to turmoil in Wuhan.[161]

Even the peasants have demonstrated about issues such as not being paid for crops delivered to the state; land requisitioning by the government; and illegal local taxation or the imposition of other unauthorized charges. Some used the classic method of shaming the authorities for wrong-doing: in Hunan province, hundreds of villagers knelt facing the government buildings for two hours in an attempt to persuade the officials to compensate for land requisitioned for building purposes. After some violence, the peasants won and the provincial government agreed to pay, but less than had been originally promised and without a settlement date.[162]

Ironically, at the same time as the introduction of new ideas, there has been a noticeable resurgence of more traditional values. The Maoist vision attacked and reduced the level of feudal attitudes, but the economic growth and development of newer views have eroded the communist ethos built up between 1949 and 1976. The new freedoms have allowed more traditional values to resurface. These include Confucian family-centered thinking, which the communists had never managed to eradicate, and Buddhism, together with a variety of feudal superstitions and practices, including belief in magic, witchcraft and shamans.

The Long View

In an historical perspective, China is still seeking a solution to the questions first asked after the ignominious defeat at the hands of the British in the First and Second Opium Wars, 1839-42 and 1856-60. These questions included what were the best ways of dealing with these technologically advanced if barbaric foreigners, and how to modernize China without losing Chinese social and cultural ways. These are universally regarded in China as superior to Western values. Whether China will eventually find a solution, and what this might be, is still unclear.

The biggest question, still to be answered, is whether or not it is possible to run a country successfully with a communist government in charge of a market economy. To many Westerners, it seems an obvious contradiction and they believe the attempt must fail. This school of thought sees successful economic growth as inevitably increasing the pressure on a dictatorial regime, until ultimately personal freedom must be allowed to increase, and the result will be something approaching a Western democratic system. Such observers feel that the main historical question, about what sort of China will be chosen, has now in fact been answered. It will be a Western-style democracy, and this, in the words of the developers of computer vaporware,[163] will appear "real soon now".

A small minority of observers feel that market socialism does not present a problem and certainly the theoretical demonstration of its viability appeared over sixty years ago.

Some commentators think that the view of the inevitability of Western-style democracy merely reflects our cultural and political bias. They suspect that the China, and perhaps some other Asian nations, might follow a different path. Rather than resembling a Western democracy, such countries might favor a kind of benevolent dictatorship within an Asian or modern Confucian system. In this scenario there would be no real place for an opposition party, except perhaps a nominal one with little power as a sop to the disaffected and the intellectuals. This view, once persuasive to some, has become unfashionable since the 1997 Asian financial crisis and the events in Indonesia that culminated in the fall of President Suharto.

Kevin B. Bucknall, London

A

accepting invitations · 153
accommodation · 36, 40, 58, 155, 172, 179, 186-7, 188, 202, 206, 218, 221, 233, 245, 265
Airbus Industrie · 151
alcohol · 10-1, 35, 43, 75, 139, 158, 160-3, 190, 198, 209
American · 25, 40, 40, 45, 67-8, 77, 89, 96, 109-10, 112, 119, 121-3, 126, 140, 150, 181, 195, 203-4, 212, 216-7, 230, 259-64
American Motors · 96, 126, 137, 173, 187
American United Autoworkers, · 110
Americans · 25, 217
Amway Corp · 77
Andersen Consulting · 151, 263
anger and rudeness · 17, 32, 45, 47-8, 64, 84, 102, 104-5, 126, 159, 184
Anhui · 246
Asia Electronic Holdings, · 123
attitude towards foreigners · 20-4
Australian · 20, 26, 45, 67, 117, 122, 150, 209, 263
avoid jargon · 92
avoid slang · 95
Avon Products · 77, 259

B

bad attitudes · 67
balance of payments · 239-40
banquets · 30, 75, 109,137,146, 150, 156-60, 162-3, 166-7, 170-1, 196, 206
Beatrice Companies, Inc · 203
beckoning · 50
Beijing · 16, 18, 27-28, 46, 51, 54-5, 57-8, 60, 62, 67, 96, 112, 119, 122, 126, 133, 141, 151, 161, 173, 182, 185, 187-8, 193, 195, 200, 207, 211, 218, 244, 246, 259-64

Beijing Jeep · 96, 126, 187, 195, 259-64
bicycles · 54, 147, 171, 179-80, 246
Bilho · 181
board of management · 84, 96, 193
boasting · 43, 46-7
body language · 33, 47, 70, 73, 94, 102, 131-2, 136
bragging · 43
British · 25, 38, 183, 209, 238, 247
Buddhism · 23, 165, 247
bureaucracy · 15, 65, 72, 86, 105, 116, 126, 135, 150, 188-9, 198-200
bureaucratic · 17, 22, 125, 128, 135, 144, 180, 189, 201, 212, 215, 231, 234, 237
buses · 55
business cards · 15, 35, 74-5, 81, 168
buying machinery · 68, 89

C

CAAC · 10, 232
Cantonese · 18, 27-8, 35, 43, 48, 76, 163, 195
CCP · 10, 224-9, 242
CCPIT · 10, 62, 71, 73, 192
Celestial Yacht Ltd · 150, 204, 214
centrally-planned · 36-7, 71, 194, 202, 204, 232
CEO · 10, 13, 43-4, 88, 92, 123-4, 169, 199, 208
chaebols · 10, 235
changing money · 42
Changsha · 246
Chengdu · 19-20, 161
Cherokee Jeeps · 207
China Intellectech · 214
China International Travel Service. · 126
China Star · 214
China's history · 223
Chinese food · 27, 46, 52, 155, 157-9, 162, 164-6, 171-2, 181
Chinese language · 17, 46, 51, 55, 63, 69-70, 73, 75, 82, 93, 114, 130-1, 167-8, 174, 176, 179, 185, 190, 195, 216

Chinese stereotype · 6, 26-8, 67-8
choosing a good name · 72-3, 259
chopsticks · 158-9, 164-5, 170
Christmas · 34
Chrysler Corporation · 195
cigarettes · 33, 139, 198
clapping · 51
clothing · 5, 27, 40, 57-60, 154, 182,
     197, 246
Coca Cola · 73, 79, 152, 160, 209
COFTEC · 10, 90
colors · 18-9, 38, 59-60, 65-7, 138-9
Combustion Engineering, · 104
Communist Party · 10, 35, 100, 105,
     177, 223-9, 241-2, 244, 261, 265
Compaq Computers · 28, 258
compensation trade · 62
competition · 31, 55, 101, 104, 142,
     193, 203, 209-11, 238, 240
composition of team · 68
computers · 23, 27, 215, 244, 260
concessions · 54, 97, 101-2, 104, 109,
     122, 132, 136-7, 142-4, 146, 149-
     50, 210, 237-8
condescending · 47, 49, 124
Confucian · 13-6, 19, 23, 31, 56, 120,
     158, 170, 200, 203, 241, 247-8
Confucius · 12-3, 15, 67, 224
contacts · 10, 16, 54, 62, 73-4, 144,
     147, 191, 195 201
contracts · 28, 62, 77, 96-7, 101, 104,
     107, 111, 113-9, 124, 126, 128,
     134, 140, 145, 149, 191, 203, 205-
     6, 228, 233 260
cooperation · 29, 31, 83, 86, 106, 127,
     134, 144, 148, 159, 168, 192, 202,
     211, 217
coping with the conditions · 66, 75, 97,
     102, 109, 126, 160, 164, 168, 174,
     179, 189-90, 194
copying machines · 63
Copyright Protection Center · 121
corruption · 140, 227, 239, 241, 243-5,
     266
costs · 107-8, 111, 133, 136, 171, 175,
     191-2, 203, 205-6, 213
Credit Suisse First Boston Company ·
     16
crime · 12, 37, 39-40, 42, 140, 234,
     241, 245

criticism · 14-5, 29, 31, 33, 42, 49, 52-
     4, 96, 104, 106, 159, 185, 196, 198,
     217-9, 223, 228, 230
culture shock · 34, 50, 99, 145, 175-6,
     190
Cummins Engine Company · 119
customs · 5, 32, 140
Customs · 198, 211, 228, 230, 237,
     245, 263

D

Daihatsu · 210-1
dangerous words · 52-3
death · 17-9, 40, 54, 61, 130, 139, 165,
     180, 224-5, 231, 241, 244-5, 261
delays · 17, 39, 43, 54, 63, 65, 69, 87,
     89, 107, 116, 125-6, 143, 145, 153,
     160, 198-206, 258, 261, 265-6
Deng Xiaoping · 36, 225, 231
details · 63-5, 68, 77, 84, 87-8, 93, 96-
     7, 102, 107, 109, 113-6, 118-9, 124,
     131, 133, 136-7, 149, 154, 168,
     174, 198, 201
discos · 22, 163, 182
discounting enthusiasm · 100
Disneyland · 141
distribution · 23, 77, 112, 114, 191,
     193, 203, 232, 238
doing favors · 16, 42, 52, 99, 128, 135,
     137, 146, 158, 169, 199
doorway behavior · 27, 44, 79-80, 91,
     155, 158,167, 201
Dresden · 197
drinking the water · 41, 161, 189
Dupont · 62

E

early meetings · 26, 39, 79-85, 88, 96,
     102, 107, 142-3
economic scene, the · 71, 130-41
Economist Intelligence Unit · 151, 213,
     263
education · 14-5, 20-1, 149, 175, 177,
     186, 216, 218, 242
egalitarianism · 15, 150, 177, 196

employment · 14, 39, 107, 110, 193, 202, 218, 232, 234, 245, 247, 265
engineers · 68-9, 92, 100, 109, 111, 171, 188, 205, 215, 259, 261
entrepreneurs · 7, 23-4, 147, 241-2
environment · 29, 36, 40, 92, 207, 231, 265
E-S Pacific Development Company · 126
establishing the ground rules · 174
expatriates · 30, 43, 56, 71, 144, 174-8, 180, 186, 189, 206, 213, 215, 218-9, 261, 264
eye contact · 33

foreigners · 5, 17, 20, 24-6, 28, 32-3, 37, 41, 43-6, 48, 50, 55, 57, 60-1, 67, 73, 77, 79-82, 85, 87, 96, 100, 102, 104, 106, 112, 115, 117-9, 127, 129, 134, 136, 140, 142, 146-8, 163-5, 168, 179, 209, 217, 236, 241, 247
France · 52, 162, 215
French · 27, 151, 181, 203, 205, 216
frustrations · 29, 31, 76, 125-6, 185, 188, 190
Fujian Oak Tree · 113-4, 203, 207, 217-8
Future Cola · 209

F

"face" · 17, 20, 28-30, 33, 35, 44, 51, 55, 70, 74-5, 80, 82, 84, 88, 91-2, 94-6, 103-6, 110, 114, 130, 132, 146, 156, 167-9, 196, 200, 206, 217-8, 220-1
factions · 14, 31, 36-7, 110, 192, 225
Falung Gong · 228-9
family · 12-4, 16, 22, 26, 31, 45, 51, 54, 70, 138, 147,153, 156, 169, 175-7, 179-80, 182, 185-6, 190, 196, 199, 219, 236, 241-2, 244-5, 247
fax · 52, 72, 74, 76, 87, 176
feasibility studies · 90, 107, 133, 151, 206
FEC · 9, 236
feeling guilty · 91, 93, 103
FESCO · 10, 214
financial crisis · 39, 187, 228, 238-40, 248
financial sector, the · 235-6
first meeting · 51, 82, 84, 124
fiscal · 212, 239
food · 17, 27, 46, 52, 79, 155, 157-9, 162, 164-6, 171-2, 181, 189, 196, 203, 206, 235, 246, 265
foreign exchange · 10, 42, 100, 113, 115, 203, 212, 228, 236
foreign investment · 29, 91, 107, 182, 210, 212, 224, 228-9, 233, 236-8
foreign trade · 10, 62, 71, 90, 99, 229, 236, 238

G

ganbei · 10, 160
GATT · 10-1, 121, 230
German · 181, 192, 216
Germany · 194, 216
getting about · 54, 180
gifts · 19, 30, 51, 70, 137-40, 149, 155-6, 198, 244
Giordano · 197
given name · 45
gloating · 127
Great Wall Hotel · 126-7, 260
group, the · 12-4, 22, 26-31, 36-7, 44, 51, 53, 55, 66, 69, 75, 120, 125, 134, 137-8, 140-1, 146, 154, 157, 163, 170, 172, 184-6, 188, 217, 224, 228-9, 231, 242, 244-5
growth · 7, 36, 39, 46, 152, 181, 228, 231, 234, 238-43, 247
Guangdong · 27-8, 54, 58, 211, 237-8, 263
Guangzhou · 60, 77, 106, 150-1, 193, 205, 215, 218, 238, 261-2, 264
Guangzhou Automotive Manufacturing Company · 215
Guangzhou Peugeot Automobile Corporation · 205, 262-2, 264
guanxi · 10, 15-6, 31, 52-3, 62, 86, 90, 109, 135, 146, 195, 215, 237

H

Hainan · 77
handshake · 48, 79-81
Harbin · 57
hard skills · 216
harmony · 12, 14, 16-7, 22, 27, 70, 88, 103, 127, 129, 162
health · 13, 33-4, 40, 149, 160, 184, 206, 218, 229
hierarchy · 14-5, 22, 30-1, 35, 44, 52, 66, 78, 80, 135, 160, 168, 170, 200, 215, 217
Hong Kong · 28, 34, 39, 42, 44, 57, 59, 61, 67, 74, 78, 111-2, 121, 138, 140, 170, 181-2, 184-5, 187, 204, 211, 221, 224, 229-30, 236, 238
host · 55, 78-80, 82-3, 86, 89, 91, 99, 125, 150, 155-62, 164, 166-7, 169-71, 178
housing · 36, 40, 58, 155, 172, 175, 179, 186-8, 202, 206, 218, 221, 233, 245, 265
HQ, your · 52, 65, 84, 87, 131-2, 137, 174-6, 183, 189, 193, 216-7
Hualu Electronics Corporation · 211
Hukou · 10, 232, 265
human rights · 40, 52, 227, 230
humor · 14, 44
Hungry Ghost Festival · 17

I

IBM · 31, 73, 81, 149, 179
income · 23, 39, 177, 238-9, 242-3, 245-6, 266
indirectness · 45, 49, 70, 74, 88, 94, 102, 119, 129, 132, 217, 223
Indonesia · 179, 195, 248
inflation · 23, 212-3, 227, 239-40
informal suggestions · 88
information · 6-7, 33, 37, 47, 53, 63, 65, 68, 72, 74, 76-7, 85, 97, 99, 102, 104, 111, 115, 125, 129-30, 133, 135, 141-3, 146-7, 153, 183, 210
initial contact · 6, 62, 147
innovative thinking · 37, 198, 217
insider · 15, 30-1, 37, 55, 64, 72, 86, 126, 129, 146, 178, 191, 200
intellectual property rights · 111-2, 121, 244, 260

international politics · 52, 103, 229-30
interpreter · 30, 45, 67-9, 73, 80, 92-6, 100, 125, 129-30, 138, 146, 167, 179, 216
interruptions · 29, 84, 95, 127-8
introductions · 32-3, 62, 76, 79-83, 87-9, 116, 124, 131, 157, 178, 185, 191, 200-1
introductory speech · 83, 87-9, 116, 124, 132
inventories · 202
Italian · 27, 49, 151, 162, 181, 264
ITT · 73, 126
ITT-Sheraton · 126

J

Japan · 15, 19, 21, 25-6, 66, 177, 188, 210, 214, 236
Japanese · 10, 18, 25-6, 38, 44, 96, 106, 110-1, 181, 188, 190, 211, 216, 223, 262
Japanese Toyota · 96
jet lag · 41, 176
Jia Qinglin · 245
Jiang Zemin · 36, 144, 211, 228, 234, 245, 265
Jilin · 57
joint ventures · 38, 54, 62, 65, 70, 84, 107-8, 113-4, 117-9, 122, 126, 133-4, 137, 150-1, 173, 177, 187, 191-3, 195, 199, 201-3, 205-11, 213-5, 217-20, 232, 242, 261, 263
jokes · 14, 18, 34, 42, 44-5, 52, 73, 163, 165

K

Kaiser Engineers · 111, 140, 259, 261
karaoke · 22, 164, 182
keeping notes · 68, 93, 100-1, 115-6, 135, 142
KFC · 181
Korea · 10, 15, 19, 25, 229, 235
Kuomintang · 223, 242
Kuraray Company Ltd · 188

L

labor · 26, 40, 107-8, 115, 133, 193, 195, 201, 214-8, 221, 224, 231-3, 243
laughter · 32, 35, 45, 76, 109, 162
law · 34, 43, 55, 77, 87, 107, 117-23, 140, 185, 200, 211, 225, 230, 233, 241, 244, 260
law and politics · 120
lawyers · 68, 100, 121, 123
leader · 30, 64, 66-9, 75, 79, 83-4, 88, 92, 95, 100, 125, 127-8, 130, 137, 140-1, 148, 154, 158-9, 163, 168-9, 173, 229, 244, 266
Levi-Strauss · 40
Li Peng · 151, 197
liaison officer · 30, 62, 71, 73-4, 100, 107, 132, 146, 156, 166-9, 191, 218, 220
Liaoyang · 246, 266
list · 15, 53, 63-4, 66, 73-4, 76, 80, 83, 94, 133, 135, 141, 159, 166-7, 174, 187, 246
long term relationship · 26, 66, 115, 128
Lotus hypermarket · 144
loud behavior · 24-5, 48
lunch · 34-5, 85, 102, 106, 153, 168, 206

M

Macao · 122, 229, 236
macro economy, the · 238-41
making a speech · 82-4, 88-9, 116, 124, 132, 162-3,
making changes · 117-8, 133, 197, 230
management · 21, 77, 84, 92, 96, 115, 123, 126, 138, 177, 191, 193-6, 209, 216, 245, 262, 264
Manchu · 194, 223
manners · 5, 21, 24, 28, 33, 46-9, 51-2, 76, 80, 106, 127, 156-7, 162, 164-6
Mao Zedong · 24, 33, 52, 145, 147, 163, 223-5
Maoism · 29, 60, 226
Maoist · 15, 25, 37, 106, 120, 188, 226, 228, 247

Maotai · 10-1, 160, 163
market exaggeration · 38-9, 90, 100, 258, 262
market mechanism · 21, 23, 32, 36-7, 71, 133, 182, 204, 209-12, 225-7, 232-3, 235-8, 240, 243-4, 247-8
marketing · 152, 191, 195
Mary Kay Cosmetics · 77
Matsushita · 38, 210-1
McDonalds · 119, 181, 203, 207, 260
meetings · 6, 8, 23, 49-50, 64, 70, 79, 82-5, 86, 88-91, 99-100, 102, 124-5, 143, 145, 148, 171, 196, 215
memorandum of understanding · 96, 121, 124, 260
Mexico · 133, 228
Microsoft · 112, 260
MOFTEC · 10, 90-1, 116
monetary · 103, 212, 239
motivation · 219-20
motor vehicles ·16, 18, 36, 54-5, 151, 171, 180, 192, 205-6, 210-1, 215, 239, 246
Motorola · 149

N

names · 12, 15, 22, 24, 35, 45, 60, 64, 66, 72-4, 80-1, 93, 114, 138, 154, 167-9, 181, 259
NASDAQ · 123
nationalities · 6, 24-5
negotiating · 6-7, 17, 33, 38, 41-2, 50, 53-5, 57, 61-2, 66, 69, 74, 86, 88, 93-5, 97, 100, 104-5, 107-10, 113-4, 118-24, 126, 132, 133-4, 136, 141-3, 145, 149-51
negotiations · 8, 17-8, 28, 39, 41, 43, 51-2, 54, 64-5, 69-70, 74, 76, 79, 83, 86, 88, 90, 92, 94, 96-7, 99-100, 103-4, 107-8, 115-7, 119, 121, 124, 128-30, 132, 134-5, 137, 143-6, 148-50, 154, 156, 161, 173, 179, 206
New York · 51, 94, 181, 187, 197, 229
Nike · 121, 134, 149, 204, 261-2
NPC · 10, 225
numbers · 18-9, 71-2, 74, 95, 100, 158, 194

O

Oak Tree Packaging Corp · 113-4, 203, 207, 217-8
OECD · 10, 140
officials · 12. 15, 18, 26, 28, 31-2, 39, 50, 55, 73, 90, 100-1, 105, 107, 122-3, 126, 135, 137, 140, 142, 144, 147-8, 150-1, 169, 172, 178, 188, 191-2, 196-9, 206-7, 214-5, 219, 221, 230-1, 237, 239, 244, 245-7, 261, 263
Oil of Ulan · 209
old friends · 32, 69, 111, 128
opening speech · 83-4, 116, 124
Opium War · 223, 247
outsider · 15, 30-1, 37, 45, 55, 72, 86, 111, 121, 126, 129, 170, 200
Overseas Chinese · 15, 39, 53, 69-70, 92, 94, 134, 139, 168, 195-6, 236-7

P

packaging · 114, 203-4, 218, 260, 262, 264
paintings · 19, 89
parallel imports · 209-10
parallel negotiations · 54, 143-4
partner · 43, 50, 64, 71, 90, 98, 107, 109, 111, 113-4, 116-9, 122, 172, 191-2, 195, 208-9
patience · 39, 41, 54, 75, 87, 109, 126-7, 174, 198, 201
patriotism · 23, 47
peasants · 22, 60, 202, 227, 231-2, 243, 245, 247, 265
People's Liberation Army · 10, 16, 22, 37, 226, 228, 234, 265
Pepsi Cola · 152
PepsiCo · 209, 232
perks · 30, 196, 200
perseverance · 144
persistence · 97, 105-6, 126, 130, 135, 140, 144, 156, 207
personal space · 50
Peugeot · 151, 192, 205, 215, 261-2, 264
Philippines · 179. 195

photographs · 43, 153-4, 168-9, 176, 220
physical appearance · 18, 27, 67-8
Pilkington · 209
piracy practices · 112, 121, 260
Pizza Hut · 181
'planes · 56, 208
poaching labor · 217-9
pointing · 49, 60, 116, 166
political policy · 14, 29, 36, 47, 54, 107, 110, 114, 118, 148, 202, 225-7, 232, 237,242
political scene, the · 224-9
political system, the · 12, 224-5
politics · 14, 40, 45, 52, 67, 103-5, 120, 123, 188, 223-4, 227, 229, 231
population · 39, 120, 152, 166, 194, 231, 233, 235, 241-3, 245
posture · 47-8
practicing English · 41
prices · 44, 84, 112-4, 116, 129, 133-4, 141, 146, 149, 171, 182, 203-4, 207-11, 232, 235, 239-40, 243-4, 263
privacy · 43, 48-9, 188
Procter & Gamble · 208
profits · 6-7, 38, 62, 84, 95, 97, 107, 113-4, 133, 151, 174, 177, 192, 203, 208-10, 212, 239-40, 263
punctuality · 91, 157

Q

quality · 16, 22, 26, 56, 59-60, 63-4, 71, 89, 100, 113, 139, 150, 154, 171, 179, 181-2, 185, 187, 189, 192-5, 202-5, 209, 213-4, 220, 242
quality control · 204, 214
questions · 5, 43, 46-7, 51, 64, 66, 68, 83, 87-8, 95, 102, 109, 111, 131-2, 141, 153-4, 247
quotas · 230, 237, 240

R

racist attitudes · 26, 38, 47, 67
radio · 34, 183, 189, 246

rank · 12, 14-6, 18, 24, 28, 46, 63, 75, 78, 135, 168, 170, 199, 266
reassurance about career paths · 174, 218
redundancy · 219, 234-5, 265
Reebok International · 40
regional differences · 27-8, 39, 122, 144
representative office · 54, 62, 259
retailing · 77, 181, 203, 209, 259
Rockwell International Overseas Corporation · 208
Rolligon Corporation · 68

S

safe topics · 20, 51, 162
San Francisco · 181, 207
Sarah Lee Corp., · 77
saying no · 29, 46, 64, 81, 89, 102, 105, 130-2, 147
seat of honor · 30, 80, 91, 158
seating · 30, 55-6, 80, 91-2, 158, 167, 171
secrecy · 37, 43, 72, 111, 121-2, 124, 129-30, 135, 142, 144, 189, 200, 229-30, 245
SETC · 11, 91, 116
SEZs · 10, 71, 193, 215, 232, 237-8
shame · 56, 103-4
Shanghai · 9, 27-8, 54, 57-8, 60, 62, 77, 91, 117, 123, 144, 181, 183-4, 187, 192-4, 199, 207, 209-13, 216-9, 232, 238, 245, 259, 261
Shanghai Jusco · 181
Shanghai No. 2 Textile Machinery Company · 212
Shaoxing · 11, 160
Shell Oil · 54
Shenyang · 57, 246
Shenzhen · 28, 181, 209, 232, 238
shopping · 42, 44, 99, 111-2, 181-2
showing affection · 43
silence · 102, 128, 131, 160, 170, 217, 244
Singer Company · 210
skills · 7, 15, 26, 68, 108, 141, 174, 177, 195-6, 199, 205-7, 214-9
smiling · 17, 32, 51, 55, 75, 79, 81-2, 109, 114, 136, 140, 156, 158, 163-4

smoking · 33-4, 139
smuggling · 40, 42, 44, 60-1, 211, 228, 245, 259, 263
social change · 7, 242
social policies · 23, 241
social scene · 179-84, 189-90, 241
socialist · 36, 225, 243
SOEs · 11, 39, 177, 208, 218, 230-1, 233-6, 240, 246
soft skills · 216
software · 112, 121, 266
South Korea · 10, 15, 119, 229, 235
spare parts · 89, 113, 192, 195, 202-3, 205
speak slowly · 94, 163
Special Economic Zones · 10, 71, 193, 215, 232, 237-8
spitting · 37, 189
standard of living · 5, 155, 172, 176, 187, 206, 231, 242-3, 246, 266
staring · 33, 44, 60, 184
state operated enterprises · 11, 39, 125, 177, 208, 218, 230-1, 233-6, 240, 246
status · 15-6, 57, 67, 70, 78, 86, 91-2, 116, 121, 135, 137, 147, 150, 157, 195, 203, 217, 224, 242, 246, 265
stereotype · 6, 26-8, 67
Steven Spielberg · 207
superstitions · 17-8, 21, 43, 49, 65, 78, 139, 164, 166, 247
surprises · 29, 34-6, 38, 41, 44, 50, 58-60, 84, 93, 101, 103-5, 110, 112, 117, 124, 129, 131, 145, 148, 150, 155, 165, 179, 184, 189, 199, 206-7, 214
symbolism · 9, 19-21, 67, 72, 81, 89, 139, 161, 164-5, 206, 246

T

tactical approaches · 8, 17, 41, 69, 76, 88, 90, 99, 101, 104-5, 107, 109, 124-5, 129, 136
Taiwan · 15, 39, 52-3, 63, 121, 138, 160, 193, 210, 223-5, 229, 232, 264
tariffs · 60, 115, 230, 237, 265
tax · 101, 107-8, 115, 196, 206-7, 210, 212-3, 228, 235, 240, 247, 262
taxis · 16, 55, 180, 211, 245

team · 19, 31, 35, 39, 45, 64, 66-70, 73-4, 79-80, 83-4, 88, 92, 94-5, 97, 99-102, 104, 109, 111-3, 124-9, 133, 136-8, 141, 144, 146, 153-4, 157, 159-60, 162-3, 166-7, 169, 171-3, 231

technicians · 68, 100, 109, 171, 187-8, 205, 262

technology · 16, 23-4, 26, 32, 46, 49, 53, 62-3, 65, 68, 88-9, 97, 99-100, 110-1, 113, 115, 124-5, 142, 197, 205, 224, 237, 260

telephones · 22, 35, 71-2, 74, 76, 113, 134, 176, 206-7, 245-6

Thailand · 179

things to do in China · 62-3, 91, 135, 178, 182

Tiananmen · 36, 226-8

Tianjin · 57, 60, 161, 210, 238, 263

Timberland · 40

time not seen as money · 108

tipping · 51

tiredness · 35, 41, 50, 83, 99, 145, 231

titles · 15, 30, 35, 64, 74

Toho Titanium Company Ltd · 188

Tokyo · 185, 187

Tops department store· 181

Total SA · 151

tourism · 77, 134, 228, 246

Toyota Motor Corp · 96, 211, 263

tradition · 12-3, 97, 157, 177

traditional · 7, 9, 12, 15, 17-23, 26, 28, 33, 35, 38, 45, 48, 66-7, 73, 77, 79-81, 88, 103-5, 120-1, 126, 139, 145, 155-6, 158-61, 171, 182, 217, 220, 226, 243, 246-7

training · 20, 48, 65, 97, 99, 111, 121, 127, 133, 136, 141-2, 149, 170-1, 175-8, 185, 188, 194-5, 198, 201, 204-7, 214, 221, 228

trains · 34, 55-6, 67, 208

transition · 21, 229, 237

transport · 54-5, 147, 156, 169, 171, 191, 193, 197, 203-4, 214, 228, 231, 245

triangular debt · 208

truth in China · 105-7, 110, 120, 132, 146, 195

Tsar Nicolai, · 207

TV · 77, 149, 164, 169, 189-90, 198, 204, 209, 218, 246

two set of books · 107, 194, 212

U

ultimatum · 129

unemployment · 13, 110, 221, 232, 234-5, 240, 246, 265

unsafe topics · 52, 162

USA · 7, 9, 62, 104, 112-4, 123, 140, 149, 187, 204, 210, 212-4, 216, 218, 230, 236, 243, 260

US-China Business Council · 114, 210, 212

use of the foot · 49-50

V

Venezuela · 133

video · 38, 112, 121,176, 178, 182-3, 190, 211, 218, 246

Vietnam · 229

Volkswagen · 192, 194, 216, 219

W

wages · 40, 108, 206, 220, 233, 243, 246-7, 266

Wahaha · 209

waiting · 49, 53, 55, 65, 76-7, 79-80, 91, 102, 116, 124-5, 135, 142, 156, 158, 164, 167, 183, 208, 217, 232, 233-4

Wal-Mart · 181

Westerners · 19, 22, 39, 49, 84, 97, 102-3, 108, 128, 149, 160, 181, 184, 223, 247

wife · 13, 155, 158, 163, 176, 184, 186, 224, 245

wives · 43, 158

women · 19, 27, 29, 35, 38, 55, 57-8, 66, 73, 158, 160, 177, 180, 189, 200, 261

Woodcock, Leonard · 110

work group · 13, 31

work incentives · 219-20

worker discipline · 220

workers · 15, 22, 39, 60, 108, 176-7,
192-4, 196, 198-9, 201-2, 204-7,
214, 221, 226-7, 231-5, 242-3, 245-
6, 265-6
World Bank · 243, 266
World Trade Organization · 10-1, 121-
2, 134, 181, 200, 230, 236, 241
Wuhan · 200, 246-7

Yaohan · 18, 181
yin yang · 11, 139
you are being watched · 43, 82, 102
youth · 5, 7, 13, 20-1, 23-4, 28, 43, 55,
60, 67, 94, 109, 139, 185, 200, 216,
221, 224, 232
yuan · 18, 39, 42, 90, 112, 205, 235-6,
238-9, 244, 258

X

Xerox Corporation · 54, 90, 117, 149,
203, 205
Xian · 57, 123, 246

Z

Zhengzhou · 57
Zhonghua Company · 16
Zhu Rongji · 16, 36, 144, 211

Y

ENDNOTES

: 258 :

[1] Alexandra A. Seno and Shimizu Zazuhiko, "Stuck in the Slow Lane", *Asiaweek*, Nov. 14, 1997, p.57.

[2] Stephen Vines, "HK Firms Kowtow to New Masters", *Sunday Times*, London, August 30th 1998, Business, p.6.

[3] "China's Growing Market is a Temptation, but a Troubling One", PR Central, http://www.prcentral.com/rmjf95china.htm, 1995.

[4] Dong Liu, Yin De An, "Internet Users Rise to 13 Million in China: Survey" *China News Digest Global*, 3 July 2000.

[5] "Compaq Burned in China Market", *Newsbyte Pacific Headlines*, 5 Feb. 1996.

[6] Wei Ling, "Survey Shows Joint Stock Firms Most Reliable", *The China Daily Business Weekly*, June 1-7, 1997, p1.

[7] See Jake Stratton, "The Straight and Narrow", *The China Business Review*, Jan.-Feb. 1998, pp.24-9.

[8] Helen Ho, "Buying a Piece of PRC Industry", *The China Business Review*, Jan-Feb 1996, pp. 34-37.

[9] Yuan Guanhua, Deputy Division Chief of the Foreign Financial Institutions Department of the People's Bank of China, *China Daily's Business Weekly*, Dec. 14-20, 1997, p.3.

[10] *China News Digest (Global)*, 27 July 1998; and *The Indian Express*, Bombay, July 26 1998, "China diverts money from pension fund, delays payment: report".

[11] Dong Liu, Wu Yiyi, "Three Gorges Construction Fund Free of Big Embezzlement: Official", *China News Digest*, September 11, 2000.

[12] See Jake Stratton, "The Straight and Narrow", *The China Business Review*, Jan.-Feb. 1998, pp.24-9 for a recent discussion.

[13] Todd Martin, "Safe Car Benefits from China Trade", *West Texas News and Sports*, Feb.2nd 1997.

[14] Amnesty International, London, 9 September 1998.

[15] Speech, Washington DC, January 17 1925.

[16] The difference between *renminbi* and *yuan* is similar to that of Britain, with its *Sterling* and *Pounds*: an item may cost "two yuan", but *renminbi* is the name of the currency.

[17] Kelly Nelson, "A High-Tech Success", *The China Business Review*, Jan-Feb 1992, pp.36-8.

[18] Dutch mission to China, *Mission China: Progress Report 1998*, http:www.cargweb.nl/Specials/China/newsbytes.htm

[19] Liu Wenhai, "Private Buyers Dominate China's Market", *TCFA Update, (A Newsletter of the Chinese Finance Association)*, Vol. 2, No. 15, Jan 29 1996.

[20] "China begins executing smugglers after contraband crack down", newsgroup clari.world.asia.china, 8 October 1998.

[21] Su Dongwei, "Foreign Representative Offices Face Closure Orders in Shanghai", *TCFA Update, (A Newsletter of the Chinese Finance Association)*, Vol. 3, No. 25, Mar. 25, 1997.

[22] "Spares Take a Little Longer", *The China Business Review*, Nov-Dec. 1977, pp. 3-4.

[23] Thomas N. Thompson, "How Not to do Business with China", *The China Business Review*, Jan.-Feb. 1985, pp.10-12.

[24] Geng Cui, "The Name Game", *The China Business Review*, Nov-Dec 1997, pp. 40-3.

[25] Scott D. Seligman, "Translating Your Trademark into Chinese", *The China Business Review*, Nov-Dec. 1986, pp.14-16.

[26] Steven Shi and Anne Stevenson-Yang, "Retail Roundabout", *The China Business Review"*, Jan.-Feb. 1998, pp.43-9.

[27] AFP, Beijing, 22 September 1998; "Avon begins retail business in China", clari.biz.industry.retail, 22 September 1998.

[28] Yuan Guanhua, "Foreign Financial Institutions Appraised", *The China Daily's Business Weekly*, Nov.9-15 1997.

[29] "China to test fire cruise missiles", *The Independence Morning Post*, Taipei, 1 October 1998.

[30] Thomas N. Thompson, "How Not to do Business with China", *The China Business Review*, Jan.-Feb. 1985, pp.10-12.

[31] Kelly Nelson, "A High-Tech Success", *The China Business Review*, Jan-Feb 1992, pp.36-8.

[32] Nicholas C. Hawson, "When the Center Doesn't Hold", *The China Business Review*, Jan.-Feb. 1995, pp.8-12.

[33] Jim Mann, *Beijing Jeep: the Short, Unhappy Romance of American Business in China*, Simon & Schuster, New York, 1989 and 1997, pp.61.

[34] Min Chen and Ying Wangjiang, "Beware the Fisherman", *The China Business Review*, pp.26-7.

[35] Min Chen, "Tricks of the China Trade", *The China Business Review*, Mar-April 1993, quoting Otto Schnepp, *United States-China Technology Transfer.*.

[36] Min Chen and Ying Wangjiang, "Beware the Fisherman", *The China Business Review*, pp.26-7.

[37] Jim Mann, *Beijing Jeep: the Short, Unhappy Romance of American Business*

in China, Simon & Schuster, New York, 1989 and 1997, pp.214-5.

[38] "How Kaiser Engineers Found a Formula in China", *The China Business Review"*, Nov-Dec 1979, pp.4-7.

[39] Estimate by the Business Software Alliance, reported in the Asian edition of *Microsoft Magazine*, Singapore, and at http://www.actrix.gen.nz/news/china/msmag.htm

[40] Michael White, "Computer Software Piracy Flourishes", AP, clari.world.asia+oceania, August 31 1998.

[41] Su Dongwei, "Microsoft (China) Fined for Theft of Ad Design", *TCFA Update, (A Newsletter of the Chinese Finance Association)*, Vol. 3, No. 25, March 25, 1997.

[42] Daniel Martin, "A Tale of Two Tech Transfers", *The China Business Review*, Mar.-April 1995, p.14.

[43] John W. Wichterman, "A Packaging Pioneer", *The China Business Review*, May-June 1996, pp.36-38.

[44] Daniel Martin, "Signing on the Dotted Line", *The China Business Review*, May-June 1995, pp. 26-31.

[45] "Legislature Reviews a New Contract Law to Curb Fraud", *China News Digest*, August 21st 1998.

[46] Hu Jian, "McDonald to Shut its Flagship China Store in Beijing", *TCFA Update, (A Newsletter of the Chinese Finance Association)*, Vol. 3, No. 11, Dec. 9, 1996.

[47] Min Chen, "Tricks of the China Trade", *The China Business Review*, Mar-April 1993, pp.12-16, quoting Otto Schnepp, *United States-China Technology Transfer.*

[48] "Memorandum of Understanding between the Government of USA and the Government of PRC on the Protection of Intellectual Property (1992)"; and the "Memorandum of Understanding between the Government of USA and the Government of PRC on the Protection of Copyrights (1995)".

[49] *TCFA Update, (A Newsletter of the Chinese Finance Association)*, Vol. 6, No. 21, "MNFs lobby government to get tough on pirates", Mar. 6, 2000.

[50] Jake Stratton, "The Straight and Narrow", *The China Business Review*, Jan-Feb. 1998, pp.24-9.

[51] Jake Stratton, "The Straight and Narrow", *The China Business Review*, Jan-Feb. 1998, pp.24-9.

[52] John Pomfret, Washington Post Foreign Service, *Washington Post*, July 24 1998.

[53] Jim Mann, *Beijing Jeep: the Short, Unhappy Romance of American Business in China*, Simon & Schuster, New York, 1989 and 1997, p. 68.

[54] Robert Borstin, "The Great Wall Story", *The China Business Review*, Sep-Oct 1982,pp.7-9.

[55] Jim Mann, *Beijing Jeep: the Short, Unhappy Romance of American Business in China*, Simon & Schuster, New York, 1989 and 1997, pp.80.

[56] Scott D.Seligman, "Nike's Running Start", *The China Business Review*, Jan-Feb 1982,pp.42-4.

[57] Jim Mann, *Beijing Jeep: the Short, Unhappy Romance of American Business in China*, Simon & Schuster, New York, 1989 and 1997, pp.137.

[58] Norman Givant, "The Sword that Shields", The China Business Review, *May-June 1994, pp. 29-31.*

[59] "How Kaiser Engineers Found a Formula in China", *The China Business Review"*, Nov-Dec 1979, pp.4-7.

[60] Julian Gearing, "All Out in China", *Asiaweek*, Aug. 29, 19997, pp.42-5.

[61] Scott D.Seligman, "Nike's Running Start", *The China Business Review*, Jan-Feb 1982, pp.42-4.

[62] Jim Mann, *Beijing Jeep: the Short, Unhappy Romance of American Business in China*, Simon & Schuster, New York, 1989 and 1997, pp.238-41.

[63] Jim Mann, *Beijing Jeep: the Short, Unhappy Romance of American Business in China*, Simon & Schuster, New York, 1989 and 1997, p.242.

[64] Eric Harwit, "Guangzhou Peugeot: Portrait of a Commercial Divorce", *The China Business Review*, Nov-Dec 1997, pp. 10-11.

[65] Wayne W.J. Xing, "Changing Gears", *The China Business Review*, Nov-Dec 1997, pp.8-9, 12-18.

[66] *Moving China Ventures Out of the Red and into the Black*, quoted by Allen T. Cheng, "Mainland Myths: Watch Out – a Few Bad Ideas Can Ruin Your China Venture", Asia Inc, 1996.

[67] Wu Fang and Liu Jian, "Joint Venture Refinery Delayed Again for Technical Problems", *China News Digest (Global)*, July 24, 1995.

[68] Jim Mann, *Beijing Jeep: the Short, Unhappy Romance of American Business in China*, Simon & Schuster, New York, 1989 and 1997, p.82-3.

[69] Shetla Melvin and Kirsten Sylvester, "Shipping Out", *The China Business Review*, May-June 1997, pp. 30-4.

[70] Li Wenfang, "Expatriate Staffers Expensive", *China Daily Business Weekly*, Sept 28-Oct. 4, 1997, p.2.

[71] AFP, Beijing, September 11 1998. "Chinese women must back Communist Party to get greater liberation", clari.world.asia.china

[72] AFP, Beijing, July 21 1998. "Chinese brewery official gets death sentence for drunk-driving killing", clari.world.asia.china

[73] AFP, Shanghai, September 4 1998. "Chain stores expanding fast in China", clari.world.asia.china.biz

[74] China uses the PAL video/TV system, but the USA uses the NTSC one. Many Chinese video players will play either system, but if yours does not, you may need a converter in China to play American videos or buy a newer player.
American TVs and video players will usually not work in China. For DVDs, China is region 6, but the USA is region 1; again some modern players can handle both.
[75] Teresa Poole, "China bans sale of blood", *The Independent*, London, 10 October 1998, p.14.
[76] Jim Mann, *Beijing Jeep: the Short, Unhappy Romance of American Business in China*, Simon & Schuster, New York, 1989 and 1997, p.132.
[77] Alistair Wrightman, "Foreign Technicians in China" the Japanese Experience, "*US China Business Review*", Nov-Dec 1976, pp. 28-32.
[78] "Merging Management Methods", *The China Business Review*, Sept-Oct. 1992, p.13.
[79] Leigh Stelzer, Ma Chungguang and Joanna Banthin, "Gauging Investor Satisfaction", *The China Business Review*, Nov-Dec 1992, pp.54-6.
[80] "Merging Management Methods", *The China Business Review*, Sept.-Oct. 1992, p.13.
[81] "China's Growing Market is a Temptation, but a Troubling One", PR Central, http://www.prcentral.com/rmjf95china.htm, 1995.
[82] Stephen Vines, "HK Firms Kowtow to New Masters", *Sunday Times*, London, August 30th 1998, Business, p.6.
[83] Jim Mann, *Beijing Jeep: the Short, Unhappy Romance of American Business in China*, Simon & Schuster, New York, 1989 and 1997, p.242.
[84] Jim Mann, *Beijing Jeep: the Short, Unhappy Romance of American Business in China*, Simon & Schuster, New York, 1989 and 1997, p.236.
[85] Anne Stevenson-Yang, "Making Your China Investment Work", *The China Business Review*, May-June 1995, pp. 34-8.
[86] Kelly Nelson, "A High-Tech Success", *The China Business Review*, Jan-Feb 1992.
[87] Jim Mann, *Beijing Jeep: the Short, Unhappy Romance of American Business in China*, Simon & Schuster, New York, 1989 and 1997, p.243.
[88] Scott D.Seligman, "Nike's Running Start", *The China Business Review*, Jan-Feb 1982,pp.42-4.
[89] Thomas N. Thompson, "How Not to do Business with China", *The China Business Review*, Jan.-Feb. 1985, pp.10-12.
[90] Daniel Martin, "A Tale of Two Tech Transfers", *The China Business Review*, Mar.-April 1995, p.14.
[91] Eric Harwit, "Guangzhou Peugeot: Portrait of a Commercial Divorce",

The China Business Review, Nov-Dec 1997, pp. 10-11.
[92] Kelly Nelson, "A High-Tech Success", *The China Business Review*, Jan-Feb 1992.
[93] John W. Wichterman, "A Packaging Pioneer", *The China Business Review*, May-June 1996, pp.36-38.
[94] Jim Mann, *Beijing Jeep: the Short, Unhappy Romance of American Business in China*, Simon & Schuster, New York, 1989 and 1997, p.267.
[95] "The Straight and Narrow", *The China Business Review*, Jan.-Feb. 1998, pp.24-9.
[96] AFP, 22 September 1998, "China cancels 20,000 illegal levies but tax rates still extortionate", clari.world.asia.china.biz
[97] *International Herald Tribune*, June 10th 1986, quoted by Jim Mann, *Beijing Jeep: the Short, Unhappy Romance of American Business in China*, Simon & Schuster, New York, 1989 and 1997, p.193.
[98] Allen T. Cheng, "Making China Pay", *Asia Inc*, May 1966.
[99] Tom Engle, "Making Money in China", *The China Business Review*, Nov.-Dec. 1985, pp.31-5.
[100] *The China Daily Business Weekly*, 26 July 1998.
[101] AFP, "Australia's Foster's says profits up, China breweries to go", clari.world.asia.china.biz, August 24 1998.
[102] Tong Yao, "Investments: the Three Year Performance Hurdle", *TCFA Update (A Newsletter of the Chinese Finance Association)*, Vol. 3, No. 24, March 17, 1997.
[103] Jane Greaves, "The Right Price", *The China Business Review"*, Sep.-Oct. 1995, pp. 30-3.
[104] Leigh Stelzer, Ma Chungguang and Joanna Banthin, "Gauging Investor Satisfaction", *The China Business Review*, Nov-Dec 1992, pp.54-6.
[105] Andersen Consulting and The Economist Intelligence Unit, *Moving China Ventures Out of the Red and into the Black*, 1997.
[106] "Feeling Upbeat", *The China Business Review*, May-June 1995, pp. 39-44.
[107] "The China Syndrome", *The Economist*, June 21 1997, pp.67-8.
[108] Toyota joint venture energizes Tianjin's car sector", *China News Digest (Global)*, June 7, 1996.
[109] Wayne W.J. Xing, "Shifting Gears", *The China Business Review*, Nov.-Dec. 1997, pp.8-18.
[110] Helen Ho, "Buying a Piece of PRC Industry", *The China Business Review*, Jan-Feb 1996, pp. 34-37.
[111] "Guangdong customs officials caught in billion-dollar smuggling scam", newsgroup, clari.world.asia.china, 12 Nov. 1998.

[112] *China News Digest (Global)*, July 17 1998.

[113] *China Daily*, editorial, 16 July 1998.

[114] Tong Yao, "Investments: the Three Year Performance Hurdle", *TCFA Update (A Newsletter of the Chinese Finance Association)*, Vol. 3, No. 24, March 17, 1997.

[115] "The China Syndrome", *The Economist*, June 21 1997, pp.67-8.

[116] Jim Mann, *Beijing Jeep: the Short, Unhappy Romance of American Business in China*, Simon & Schuster, New York, 1989 and 1997, p.243.

[117] Julia S. Sensenbrenner and John Sensenbrenner, "Personnel Priorities", *The China Business Review*, Nov.-Dec. 1994, pp.40-5.

[118] Eric Harwit, "Guangzhou Peugeot: Portrait of a Commercial Divorce", *The China Business Review*, Nov-Dec 1997, pp. 10-11.

[119] Li Wenfang, "Expatriate Staffers Expensive", *China Daily Business Weekly*, Sept 28-Oct. 4, 1997, p.2.

[120] Daniel Martin, "A Tale of Two Tech Transfers", *The China Business Review*, Mar.-April 1995, p.14.

[121] "Merging Management Methods", *The China Business Review*, Sept-Oct. 1992, p.13.

[122] John W. Wichterman, "A Packaging Pioneer", *The China Business Review*, May-June 1996, pp.36-38.

[123] Julia S. Sensenbrenner and John Sensenbrenner, "Personnel Priorities", *The China Business Review*, Nov.-Dec. 1994, pp.40-5.

[124] John W. Wichterman, "A Packaging Pioneer", *The China Business Review*, May-June 1996, pp.36-38.

[125] "Merging Management Methods", *The China Business Review*, Sept-Oct. 1992, p.13.

[126] Julian Gearing, "All Out in China", *Asiaweek*, Aug. 29, 19997, pp.42-5.

[127] *Time*, June 2nd 1986, quoted by Jim Mann, *Beijing Jeep: the Short, Unhappy Romance of American Business in China*, Simon & Schuster, New York, 1989 and 1997, p.193.

[128] Also in the running are Egypt, Greece and Italy, but the current inhabitants of those lands seem to me to be cut off from their ancient culture to an extent that is untrue of China. In Egypt, the language altered to Coptic, then Arabic, and the imposed cultures were not those of the pharaohs. Greece was taken over by Rome, then by a variety of people including Serbs, Byzantine Emperors, the Franks and the Ottomans. Rome might have a better claim to continuity, although its empire was ravaged by barbarians, and taken by Lombards, Franks, Spaniards and Austro-Hungarians, to name but some.

[129] Tamara Perkins and WU Yiyi, "Taiwan-Mainland Economic Links

May Ensure Peace", *China News Digest (Global)*, May 5, 2000.

[130] For a variety of explanations of this, see the author's "Why China Has Done Better than Russia Since 1989", Essays in Honor of Clement Allan Tisdell, Part III, *The International Journal of Social Economics*, Vol. 24, Nos. 7/8/9, 1997, pp.1023-37.

[131] AFP, "Scrapping of Chinese army's business empire impossible, analysts say", Beijing, 23 July 1998, clari.world.asia.china

[132] "Beijing Vows to Close Down Military-run Businesses", *China News Digest (Global)*, July 31 1998.

[133] Liu Weiming, Wu Yiyi, "Tougher Enforcement of Environmental Standards Expected", *China News Digest, Global*, June 2, 2000.

[134] Richard Bowles, "Food for Thought", *The China Business Review*, July-Aug. 1997, pp.8-11.

[135] Although legally they remain peasants, even if they gain employment as a worker in a city. Everyone in China is registered in the *hukou* system and this determines one's designation and class status for life. One way out for a peasant is to get into the People's Liberation Army and be redesignated a soldier, but relatively few can achieve this.

[136] "State-Run Institutions to End Lifelong Employment", *China News Digest (Global)*,16 August 2000.

[137] "The Chinese Economy", Chin@zone, http://www.chinapoint.com/news/business/asia/china/economy.htm

[138] *China News Digest (Global)*, 27 July 1998; and *The Indian Express*, Bombay, July 26 1998 "China diverts money from pension fund, delays payment: report".

[139] Party General Secretary Jiang Zemin, at the Chinese Communist Party's Fifteenth Congress, September 1997.

[140] "The Chinese Economy", Chin@zone http://www.chinapoint.com/news/business/asia/china/economy.htm

[141] "China: No Job, No House, No Welfare", *The Economist*, May 30 1998, pp.26-7.

[142] AFP, Beijing, 14 October 1998, "Chinese unemployment set to rise steadily: economist"; clari.news.labor

[143] "New Welfare System in Place for Massive Lay-offs", *China News Digest (Global)*, August 14 1998.

[144] "East Asia's Whirlwind Hits the Middle Kingdom", *The Economist*, Feb. 14 1998, pp.29-31.

145 Jonathan Sprague and David Hsieh, "Low in the Water: China's Banks Float – For Now", *Asiaweek*, Dec.5 1997.

146 Wen Kehong and Yan Hong, "China Takes a Step Towards Full Currency Convertibility", *TCFA Update(A Newsletter of the Chinese Finance Association)*, Vol. 2, No. 17, Feb. 12 1996.

147 Meredith Gavin and Kirsten A. Sylvester, "Tumbling Tariffs", *The China Business Review"*, May-June 1996, pp.44-48.

148 AFP, Beijing, October 11 1998, "China urges firms to shift plants abroad", clari.world.asia.china.

149 "Pump-priming to continue" *TCFA Update(A Newsletter of the Chinese Finance Association)*, Volume 6, No. 18, Friday, January 28, 2000.

150 Wang Lihong, "Income Disparities to Widen", *The China Daily's Business Weekly*, Dec. 14-20 1997, p.3.

151 Wu Jinglian, "China in the Great Transformation Part II: The Dark Side of the Picture and its Roots", *TCFA Update, (A Newsletter of the Chinese Finance Association)*, Vol. 3, No.7, Nov.11 1996. The Gini Coefficient measures income differentials: 0.0 means perfect equality and 1.0 indicates perfect inequality.

152 World Bank, *World Development Report 1996*, Oxford University Press, pp.188-9.

153 Da Shan, "Urban Incomes, Living Standards Rise Significantly", *China Daily's Business Weekly*, Sept. 14-20, 1997, p.8.

154 Wu Jinglian, "China in the Great Transformation Part II: The Dark Side of the Picture and its Roots", *TCFA Update, (A Newsletter of the Chinese Finance Association)*, Vol. 3, No.7, Nov.11 1996.

155 Xu Ming Yang, Wu Yiyi "Corruption Obstacle to Poverty Eradication: UN Representative", *China News Digest*, 10 April, 2000.

156 Patrick Baert, AFP Beijing, "Former Beijing mayor gets off lightly, protected by his rank", 31 July 1998.

157 AFP, 14 October 1998, "Chinese auditors track 25 billion dollars of missing grain purchase", Newsgroup clari.world.asia.china.biz

158 AFP, Beijing, 15 October 1998, "Chinese police detain corruption-watch leader", clari.world.asia.china

159 "China's 'Live Volcano'", Asiaweek, May 5 1995, pp.17-18.

160 Han Yongquing, "Rising Income Promotes Purchase of All Mod Cons", *China Daily Business Weekly*, Dec.7-13 1997, p8, quoting a survey by the Gallup Company.

161 Zhao Hua, Wu Yiyi, "Unpaid Workers Stage Protest Surrounding Liaoyang City Hall", *China News Digest, Global*, 19 May, 2000.

162 AFP, Beijing, October 14 1998, "200 workers stage protest in central

China over wage cut"; clari.world.asia.china

[163] AFP, Beijing, 1 October 1998, "Chinese villagers protest brutal treatment in land acquisition", clari.world.asia.china

[164] Vaporware is computer software that is promised by the producer, the release of which keeps being delayed; frequently it never seems to materialize at all!

NOTES

Printed in the United States
70613LV00003B/184-186

9 780917 990441